Christmas 99,

I & [barcode: D0567352] might
enjoy this. You have
taught me to appreciate
books like this. I
also take vitamins
everyday. Thanks so
much for being my
friend. I love you,

Angela

Quiet Moments

FOR THE HEART
AND SOUL

Quiet Moments

FOR THE HEART AND SOUL

Two Bestselling Works
Complete in One Volume

EMILIE BARNES

INSPIRATIONAL PRESS

NEW YORK

Previously published in two separate volumes:

15 MINUTES ALONE WITH GOD
Copyright © 1994 by Harvest House Publishers.

Unless noted otherwise, Scripture quotations are from the *Holy Bible, New International Version®*. Copyright © 1973, 1978, 1984 by the International Bible Society. Used by permission of Zondervan Publishing House. The "NIV" and "New International Version" trademarks are registered in the United States Patent and Trademark Office by International Bible Society.

15 MINUTES OF PEACE WITH GOD
Copyright © 1997 by Harvest House Publishers.

Except where otherwise indicated, all Scripture quotations in this book are taken from the New American Standard Bible, © 1960, 1962, 1963, 1968, 1971, 1972, 1973, 1975, 1977 by The Lockman Foundation.

Verses marked tev are taken from *The Bible in Today's English Version* (*Good News Bible*), © American Bible Society 1966, 1971, 1976. Used by permission.

Verses marked TLB are taken from *The Living Bible*, Copyright © 1971 owned by assignment by Illinois Regional Bank N.A. (as trustee). Used by permission of Tyndale House Publishers, Inc., Wheaton, Illinois 60189. All rights reserved.

All rights reserved. No part of this work may be reproduced or transmitted in any form or by any means, electronic or mechanical, including photocopying, recording, or any information storage and retrieval system, without permission in writing from Harvest House Publishers, 1075 Arrowsmith, Eugene, OR 97402.

First Inspirational Press edition published in 1999.

Inspirational Press
A division of BBS Publishing Corporation
386 Park Avenue South
New York, NY 10016

Inspirational Press is a registered trademark of BBS Publishing Corporation.

Published by arrangement with Harvest House Publishers.

Library of Congress Catalog Card Number: 99-71882

ISBN: 0-88486-252-6

Printed in the United States of America.

CONTENTS

15 Minutes ALONE WITH GOD

Emilie Barnes

Our grandchildren are a source of love and joy to me—

I dedicate this book to Christine, Chad, Bevan, Bradley Joe II, and those yet to come.

"Father God, thank You for all You do for our grandchildren. I pray that they will grow up to love You, serve You, honor and devour Your Word. I pray that they will be filled with knowledge, spiritual understanding, and wisdom, and that they might live a life worthy of You, Lord, and may please You from the top of their beautiful heads to the tip of their fingers to the bottom of their feet. May they walk in Your steps. In the name of Jesus, Amen."

Hugs,

Grammy Eve

Fifteen Minutes Alone with God

Traveling across America twenty-plus times a year speaking to women has given me a real heart for their hurting hearts. "No time, no time," they cry. "I have no time left for family, friends, housework, meals—let alone time to spend a quiet moment with God."

I've written this devotional book for every busy woman who wants to get in touch with her Lord and her life. Each quiet time is designed to take 15 minutes or less. That's not a huge commitment, but it's an important one. You'll spend some time in God's Word, and you'll find helps and direction for your everyday life.

Another unique feature is that you don't have to start at the beginning and go chapter by chapter. You can skip around if you would like. In the upper right-hand corner of each devotion, you will see three boxes. Put a checkmark in one of the boxes each time you read it. In this way, you can keep track of those devotions which have been read previously.

The 15-minute concept works! You just have to be willing to give it a try. Fifteen minutes a day for 21 days and you are on your way to devotions every day.

Allow God to hold your hand and lead you today to many quiet times with Him.

The only hope to the busy woman's cry is God Almighty Himself!

God the Father
God the Son
and
God the Holy Spirit

I love you all. May the Lord touch each quiet time with Him.

—Emilie

Power of Prayer

I got up early one morning and rushed into the day;
I had so much to accomplish that I didn't have time to
* pray.*

Problems just tumbled about me, and heavier came
* each task.*
"Why doesn't God help me?" I wondered. He
* answered, "You didn't ask."*

I wanted to see joy and beauty, but the day toiled on,
* gray and bleak;*
I wondered why God didn't show me. He said, "But
* you didn't seek."*

I tried to come into God's presence; I used all my
* keys at the lock.*
God gently and lovingly chided, "My child, you
* didn't knock."*

I woke up early this morning, and paused before
* entering the day;*
I had so much to accomplish that I had to take time to
* pray.*

—Author Unknown

Stand by Your God

Scripture Reading: Psalm 116:1-2

Key Verse: Psalm 116:2b
I will call on him as long as I live.

───── ❧ ─────

Consider the fruit that comes from spending time with your heavenly Father. In Galatians 5, Paul writes that "the fruit of the Spirit is love, joy, peace, patience, kindness, goodness, faithfulness, gentleness, self-control" (verses 22-23). Think about each item in that list. Which of us doesn't need a touch of God's love, patience, kindness, goodness, gentleness, and self-control in our life? Those are the things—as well as guidance, wisdom, hope, and a deeper knowledge of Him—that He wants to give to us as His children.

"But," you say, "who has time? My 'To Do' list is always longer than my day. I run from the time the alarm goes off in the morning until I fall into bed at night. How can I possibly find time to do one more thing? When could I find even a few minutes to read the Bible or pray?"

I answer your questions with a question: Are you doing what's *important* in your day—or only what is *urgent*?

People do what they want to do. All of us make choices, and when we don't make time for God in our day, when we don't make time for the most important relationship in our life, we are probably not making the best choices.

God greatly desires to spend time alone with you. After all, you are His child (John 1:12; Galatians 3:26). He created you,

He loves you, and He gave His only Son for your salvation. Your heavenly Father wants to know you, and He wants you to know Him. The Creator of the universe wants to meet with you alone daily. How can you say no to such an opportunity?

So make it your priority to spend time with God daily. There's not a single right time or one correct place. The only requirement for a right time with God is your willing heart. Your meeting time with God will vary according to the season of your life and the schedules you are juggling. Jesus often slipped away to be alone in prayer (Luke 5:16), but even His prayer times varied. He prayed in the morning and late at night, on a hill and in the upper room (Mark 1:35; Luke 22:41-45; Matthew 14:23; John 17).

I know people who spend hours commuting on the California freeways who use that time to be with God. I used to get up earlier than the rest of the family for a quiet time of reading the Scripture and praying. Now that the children are raised and the home is quiet, I find morning is still best for me, before the telephone starts to ring or I get involved in the day's schedule. And maybe I'm one of the oddballs, but I love getting to church early and having 10 or 15 minutes to open my Bible and think upon God's thoughts. Despite the distracting talk that is often going on around me, I use this block of time to prepare my heart for worship. (In fact, I believe if more members of the congregation devoted time to reading Scripture and praying for the service before the service, church would be more meaningful for every worshiper.)

Again, the times and places where we meet God will vary, but the fact that we meet alone with God each day should be a constant in our life. After all, God has made it clear that He is interested in us who are His children (1 Peter 5:7).

What should you do in your time alone with God? After you've read and meditated on God's Word for a while, spend some time with Him in prayer. Talk to Him as you would to your earthly parent or a special friend who loves you, desires the best for you, and wants to help you in every way possible.

Are you wondering what to talk to God about when you pray? Here are a few suggestions:

- *Praise* God for who He is, the Creator and Sustainer of the whole universe who is interested in each of us who are in His family (Psalm 150; Matthew 10:30).

- *Thank* God for all He has done for you . . . for all He is doing for you . . . and for all that He will do for you in the future (Philippians 4:6).

- *Confess* your sins. Tell God about the things you have done and said and thought for which you are sorry. He tells us in 1 John 1:9 that He is "faithful and righteous to forgive us our sins."

- *Pray* for your family . . . and for friends or neighbors who have needs, physical or spiritual. Ask God to work in the heart of someone you hope will come to know Jesus as Savior. Pray for our government officials, for your minister and church officers, for missionaries and other Christian servants (Philippians 2:4).

- *Pray*, too, for yourself. Ask for guidance for the day ahead. Ask God to help you do His will . . . and ask Him to arrange opportunities to serve Him throughout the day (Philippians 4:6).

Time with your heavenly Father is never wasted. If you spend time alone with God in the morning, you'll start your day refreshed and ready for whatever comes your way. If you spend time alone with Him in the evening, you'll go to sleep relaxed, resting in His care and ready for a new day to serve Him.

Remember, too, that you can talk to Him anytime, anywhere—in school, at work, on the freeway, at home—about anything. You don't have to make an appointment to ask Him for something you need or to thank Him for something you have received from Him. God is interested in everything that happens to you.

> *Father God, may I never forget to call on You in*
> *every situation. I want to call on You every day of my*
> *life and bring before You my adoration, confession,*
> *thanksgiving, and supplication. Thank You for*
> *being within the sound of my voice and only a*
> *thought's distance away. Amen.*

Thoughts for Action

❦ If you are not already spending time with God each day, decide today that you will give it a try for one month.

❦ Tell someone of your commitment and ask him or her to hold you accountable for that discipline.

Additional Scripture Reading

1 Peter 5:7
Matthew 6:6-13
1 Thessalonians 5:16-18

A Prayer for All Seasons

Scripture Reading: Colossians 1:9-12

Key Verse: Colossians 1:9

Since the day we heard about you, we have not stopped praying for you and asking God to fill you with the knowledge of his will through all spiritual wisdom and understanding.

Time has a way of defining true friends. I have discovered that passing years and growing distance are ineffective obstacles to the mutual love between my friends and me. Perhaps it is because of our common walk with the Lord that we can just pick up where we left off whenever we are together. And these are the dear ones I will spend eternity loving!

Of course, prayer is an important part of continuing that bond. Colossians 1:3-14 is an eloquent description of a Christian's prayer for her friends. Even though Paul had not even visited the Christians at Colosse (Colossians 1:7), his love for them through Christ was strong and ardent. (Taken from *The Women's Devotional Bible.* Copyright © 1990 by The Zondervan Corporation. Used by permission of Zondervan Publishing House.)

As we spend time with God, we open ourselves to His work in our hearts and in our lives. Then, as we see Him working, we will want to know Him even more. We will want our prayer life to be all that it can be. What does that mean? How should we be praying?

In the Scripture, we find many models of prayer, and probably foremost is the Lord's Prayer (Matthew 6:9-13). This wonderful example of a prayer includes important elements of prayer We find words of adoration, of submission to God's will, of petition, and in closing, of praise. We can learn much from the model our Lord gave when His disciples said, "Teach us to pray" (Luke 11:1).

As meaningful as the Lord's Prayer is to me, I have also found Colossians 1:9-12 to be a powerful guide in my prayer life. If you aren't in the habit of praying or if you want to renew your time with God, I challenge you to read this passage of Scripture every day for 30 days. Look at it in small pieces, dwell on its message each day, take action upon what it says, and you'll become a new person.

Read today's Scripture passage again and think about what a wonderful prayer it is for you to pray for your friend. Knowing that a friend is praying for me is a real source of encouragement and support. If you aren't praying for your friends daily, let me suggest that Colossians 1:9-12 be your model. Look at what you'll be asking God:

- That your friend will have the spiritual wisdom and understanding she needs to know God's will.

- That she will "walk in a manner worthy of the Lord, to please him, in all respects" (verse 10).

- That your friend will be bearing "fruit in all good work and increasing in the knowledge of God" (verse 10).

- That she will be "strengthened with all power . . . for the attaining of all steadfastness and patience" (verse 11).

You would then end your prayer by joyously giving thanks to God for all that He has given you—your friend being one of those gifts (verse 12).

Did you hear those words? What an armor of protection and growth you can give your friend with a prayer like that! With these powerful words and the Lord at her side, your friend will be able to deal with the challenges she faces. I also encourage you to tell your friend that you are praying for her each day, and if she is receptive, tell her the specifics of your prayers for her. Let me assure you that it is a real comfort to have a friend praying for me, asking God to give me wisdom and understanding, to enable me to honor Him in all I do, to help me bear fruit for His kingdom, and to grant me strength, steadfastness, and patience.

Know, too, that these verses from Colossians are a good model for your prayers for your husband, other members of your family, your neighbors, and yourself. After all, all of God's people need to know His will, honor Him in everything they do, grow in the knowledge of the Lord, and be strong, steadfast, and patient as we serve Him.

Thoughts for Action

- ❦ In your journal, write down the names of one to three friends that you want to pray for each day. Under each name list several specific areas which you want to pray for them.

- ❦ Read Colossians 1:9-12 for 30 straight days. Think specifically of the friends you listed in your journal.

Additional Scripture Reading

Ephesians 3:14-19   Philemon 4-7

Prayer pushes the light and hope
into little dark corners of your life.

I Didn't Believe It

Scripture Reading: John 6:35-40

Key Verse: John 6:40

> *For my Father's will is that everyone who looks to the Son and believes in him shall have eternal life, and I will raise him up at the last day.*

Bob and I arrived to our hotel late after flying from California to Hartford, Connecticut. It was our first holiday seminar for the season, and the church put us up at a beautiful Ramada Inn. We were anxious to see the turning of the leaves for the first time, and they were at their peak in early October.

We registered at the hotel, went directly to our room, took a hot bath, and crawled into bed. It felt so good after the waits, plane layovers, airport terminal delays, crowded cramped seating, and heavy luggage. We both fell into a much-needed sleep about 9:30 P.M.

Two and a half hours later we were wakened by what we thought was a smoke alarm. My Bob rolled to the phone to call the front desk while I peeked out the peephole in the door. I couldn't see any smoke, but Bob was not getting an answer from the front desk. He let the phone ring and ring as the alarm got stronger and louder. I peeked out the peephole again, only to see a man running down the hall pulling his pants and jacket on. "Bob, it's a fire!" I yelled. "People are evacuating the building."

Bob quickly hung up, and we put some clothes on—not much and I'm not sure what. We grabbed our briefcases and swiftly left the room. By now many other guests were doing the same. The alarm was still blasting, and we heard the sirens of the fire trucks headed for the hotel. As we walked toward the stairs to hurry down six flights, we ran into people pushing through to get ahead. One lady kept yelling, "Hurry, Ruth! Hurry, Ruth!" as she passed us. Poor Ruth! Her legs just couldn't move as fast as the others. We finally made it out into the very chilly, 34° midnight air. The whole hotel had been evacuated onto the street, and firefighters were all over—only to find it was a false alarm. People calmly headed back to their rooms.

As we got off the elevator on our floor, a little lady peeped out her door in her nighty and asked, "Was it a fire?"

"False alarm," we answered.

"Well, I didn't believe it anyway."

Crawling back into bed Bob and I both thought how that woman's words echoed the sentiment of so many at Jesus' first coming. "I didn't believe it anyway." How many had heard the message, saw the messenger Jesus, saw His miracles—and still didn't believe?

Today the message is clear: Jesus is here. The Bible tells us the truth, the life, the love, and the message of salvation. Today's Scripture reading tells us to believe and we will receive eternal life. However, it's as true today as it was 2,000 years ago—many say, "I didn't believe it." One day we will find that His Word is truth, and for some it will be too late.

Father God, never let me get to the point of unbelief. I have seen hardened hearts, and I don't want that to be me. I have found You to be believable in the past—and I know You will be in the future, too. Amen.

Thoughts for Action

❧ Share with a friend how you came to believe in Christ.

❧ Begin today to read the Bible, believing that it is God's inspired Word.

❧ I conclude my holiday seminar with this poem. As a thought for action, read it and expect a tear or two. Let your heart be touched.

'Twas the Night Before Jesus Came

'Twas the night before Jesus came and all through the
   house
Not a creature was praying, not one in the house.
Their Bibles were lain on the shelf without care
In hopes that Jesus would not come there.

The children were dressing to crawl into bed,
Not once ever kneeling or bowing a head.
And Mom in her rocker and baby on her lap
Was watching the Late Show while I took a nap.

When out of the East there arose such a clatter,
I sprang to my feet to see what was the matter.
Away to the window I flew like a flash
Tore open the shutters and threw up the sash!

When what to my wondering eyes should appear
But angels proclaiming that Jesus was here.
With a light like the sun sending forth a bright ray
I knew in a moment this must be THE DAY!

The light of His face made me cover my head.
It was Jesus! Returning just like He had said.
And though I possessed worldly wisdom and wealth,
I cried when I saw Him in spite of myself.

In the Book of Life which He held in His hand,
Was written the name of every saved man.
He spoke not a word as He searched for my name;
When He said, "It's not here," my head hung in shame.

The people whose names had been written with love
He gathered to take to His Father above.
With those who were ready He rose without a sound
While all the rest were left standing around.

I fell to my knees, but it was too late;
I had waited too long and thus sealed my fate.
I stood and I cried as they rose out of sight;
Oh, if only I had been ready tonight.

In the words of this poem the meaning is clear;
The coming of Jesus is drawing near.
There's only one life and when comes the last call
We'll find that the Bible was true after all![1]

Additional Scripture Reading

    2 Timothy 3:16   Acts 13:38-39

□ □ □

Be Content in Everything

Scripture Reading: 1 Timothy 6:1-10

Key Verse: 1 Timothy 6:6

But godliness with contentment is great gain.

One of the Barnes' famous sayings is, "If you're not happy with what you have, you'll never be satisfied with what you want." I meet so many people who are always looking to the future—the next paycheck, the next home, the next church, the next month, the next school, and, in some cases, the next marriage partner. We are a country characterized by discontent. Do you find yourself being drawn into this mindset?

Recently I was visiting our newest grandchild, Bradley Joe Barnes II. As I was holding him, rubbing my hands through his hair, tracing the shape of his toes and fingers, my mind went to thinking about what he was going to be as he grew to manhood. Was he going to have good grades and go to college? Would he be a fireman, a pastor, a teacher, a coach, a salesman? Suddenly I realized that I was thinking about *what* he could be rather than focusing my thoughts and prayers on *who* he would be.

In today's culture we are all drawn away from spiritual pursuits to putting our hope into wealth (1 Timothy 6:17) and to building our lives around ways to accomplish this ambition. As I sat there in Bradley Joe's room, I began praying that all of his extended family might teach him higher values than money, career, and fame. Not that these are evil, but the value we place on them can lead to our downfall (1 Timothy 6:9).

In today's passage Paul states, "Godliness with contentment is great gain" (1 Timothy 6:6). When we find ourselves looking to the future because we aren't content with today, may God give us a peace of mind that lets us rest where He has placed us. Be content in today!

> *Father God, You know that my heart's desire is to be content in whatever state I'm in. I want to be like Paul in that regard. You have given me so much and I want to graciously thank You for those blessings. Amen.*

Thoughts for Action

❧ Instead of being preoccupied with your station in life, start praising God for where you are.

❧ Pray to God asking Him to reveal to you what you are to learn in your present situation.

❧ Write a letter to God thanking Him for all your blessings. Name them individually.

Additional Scripture Reading

1 Timothy 6:11-21   Proverbs 22:1-2
Mark 10:17-25

□ □ □

What a Friend!

Scripture Reading: 2 Timothy 1:16-18

Key Verse: 2 Timothy 1:18b

> *You know very well in how many ways he helped me in Ephesus.*

Oh, how our heart yearns to have friends! In today's Scripture reading we find the ways in which Onesiphorus helped Paul: 1) He often refreshed him, 2) he was not ashamed of Paul's chains, and 3) he searched hard for Paul until he found him.

I'd like to share a story with you about another friendship:

Damon was sentenced to die on a certain day, and sought permission of Dionysius of Syracuse to visit his family in the interim. It was granted, on condition of securing a hostage for himself. Pythias heard of it, and volunteered to stand in his friend's place. The king visited him in prison, and conversed with him about the motive of his conduct; affirming his disbelief in the influence of friendship. Pythias expressed his wish to die that his friend's honor might be vindicated. He prayed the gods to delay the return of Damon till after his own execution in his stead.

The fatal day arrived. Dionysius sat on a moving throne, drawn by six white horses. Pythias mounted the scaffold, and calmly addressed the spectators: "My prayer is heard: the gods are propitious; for the winds have been contrary till yesterday. Damon could not come; he could not conquer impossibilities; he will be here tomorrow, and the blood which is shed today shall have ransomed the life of my friend. Oh! could I erase from your bosoms every mean suspicion of the honor of Damon, I should go to my death as I would to my bridal. My friend will be found noble, his truth unimpeachable; he will speedily prove it; he is now on his way, accusing himself, the adverse elements, and the gods: but I haste to prevent his speed. Executioner, do your office."

As he closed, a voice in the distance cried, "Stop the execution!" which was repeated by the whole assembly. A man rode up at full speed, mounted the scaffold, and embraced Pythias, crying, "You are safe, my beloved friend! I now have nothing but death to suffer, and am delivered from reproaches for having endangered a life so much dearer than my own."

Pythias replied, "Fatal haste, cruel impatience! What envious powers have wrought impossibilities in your favor? But I will not be wholly disappointed. Since I cannot die to save, I will not survive you."

The king heard, and was moved to tears. Ascending the scaffold he cried, "Live, live, ye incomparable pair! Ye have borne unquestionable testimony to the existence of virtue; and that virtue equally evinces the existence of a God to reward it. Live happy, live renowned, and oh! form me by your precepts, as ye have invited me by your example, to be worthy of the participation of so sacred a friendship."

If heathenism had such friendships, what may be expected of Christianity?[2]

If the world is to pay attention to us as Christians and to our lifestyle, we must reflect true friendship with those people we contact each day.

Father God, thank You for my many friends who stand beside me in all situations. They are always there when I need them to listen, laugh, and cry. They are so special to my life. May they realize what their friendship means to me. Amen.

Thoughts for Action

❦ Go out today and refreshen someone's life through a kind word or action.

❦ Ask the Lord to give you a heart that is not ashamed of another person's "chains"—those things that put him or her in a different status of life than your own.

❦ Seek out a friend you haven't seen for a while.

Additional Scripture Reading

Proverbs 18:24   Luke 10:33-34
Proverbs 27:17

One Day at a Time

Scripture Reading: Zechariah 4:1-7

Key Verse: Zechariah 4:6b

> *"Not by might nor by power, but by my Spirit," says the LORD Almighty.*

—————— ❧ ——————

Dear Mrs. Barnes:

I've just finished reading your book *Survival for Busy Women.* I feel that it helped me a good bit. It's very easy for me to get down because of my daily schedule. I know you're a very busy woman, but if you have a few minutes to look at my average daily schedule and offer any helpful ideas about how to organize my day better so I would have more time to spend with my husband and six-year-old son, I would greatly appreciate it.

5:45-6:50 A.M.	Get ready for work.
6:50-7:15	Fix a quick bite of breakfast for my little boy. Pack his snack and my lunch for the day.
7:20	Leave home to take my son to school. I go on to work.
8:00	Get to work. (At work I'm able to do all of my personal paperwork, read my Bible, etc.)

5:00 P.M.	Get off work.
5:20	Pick up my son.
5:35	Get home. (I get home at this time if I do nothing else but go straight home.)
5:35-6:30	Help my son with his homework. Do minor housework.
6:45-8:00	Load up my son's bike to go down to the track so I can walk for one hour.
8:00	Fix a bite of supper while my son takes his shower and gets ready for bed. Between 8 and 9 we eat.
9:00	Get my son into bed. I need to go to bed also, but I'm usually trying to wash or fold clothes or clean up the kitchen. Sometimes it's 11 before I go to bed.

I never do any "housecleaning" during the week, and I hardly vacuum the floors on the weekend. Most of the time I just can't stand doing major housecleaning on my only day off (besides Sunday, of course, but I'm not cleaning house on Sunday—that day is filled with church and family).

With a schedule like this, when do I have time to spend with my husband or my child?

This woman leads an active life! I imagine she often feels like a juggler in a circus. Sound familiar to you? Many of us are overwhelmed by the pressures and responsibilities we face, yet we still keep taking on more and more. We have not learned to say "No" to good things and save our "Yeses" for the best.

Are there some good things we are doing which we should say no to? We are not superwomen. The secular world has led us down the path of lies which says, "We can do it all. We can have it all." Very few of us are that capable. We must learn to major on the major issues of life and not get sidetracked on the minors that drain us of all the creativity, energy, and productivity God has given us.

A good way to major on the major issues is to learn to live one day at a time. Go to the Lord each day and seek His guidance and wisdom for today—not tomorrow, not next week, not next year, but today. There is great value in doing a "TO DO" list each day as well. On a pad of paper list only those things that need to be done today, not tomorrow or next week, but just today. After a few days of making lists, you will find yourself having to rank your activities by priority, certain things being more important than others. Concentrate on the most important activity first and let the least important items settle to the end of the day. (Some of these will even drop off the page, because of their low priority.) You will be amazed at how much you will accomplish when you do this one project— a TO DO list.

At night as you crawl into bed, look at your list, smile, and thank God for helping you stay on schedule. Utter a prayer of thanksgiving that expresses your appreciation for God giving you the power to say no to "minor" requests.

> *Father God, I pray for my schedules. I ask for wise discernment in order to gain control of my life. Give me the courage to say "no" to the time wasters and say "yes" to the things that have eternal value. Amen.*

Thoughts for Action

❧ Make tomorrow's TO DO list before you go to bed tonight.

❧ Share your list with the Lord and ask Him to help you honor this list.

❧ Check off (✔) each item as you complete your activity.

❧ Reward yourself at the end of the day. (However, no fat grams are allowed!)

❧ It takes 21 days to establish a new habit.

❧ Do it again tomorrow.

Additional Scripture Reading

Ecclesiastes 2:17-26   Philippians 3:12-14

Becoming as Gold

Scripture Reading: Job 23:1-12

Key Verse: Job 23:10

> But he knows the way that I take when he has tested
> me, I will come forth as gold.

When pain comes into our lives it's so easy to ask "Why, Lord?" Why, Lord, do the righteous suffer?

If there ever was a man who loved and obeyed God, it was Job. Yet his testing was very dramatic and ever so painful. Today all we have to do is pick up a newspaper in any part of the world and we can read of tragedy touching the just and the unjust.

Our friends Glen and Marilyn Heavilin have lost three sons prematurely: one to crib death, one twin, Ethan, to pneumonia as an infant, then the second twin, Nathan, was killed as a teenager by a drunk driver. Were Glen and Marilyn tested? You bet. Yet did they come forth as gold? You bet! Today they use their experiences to glorify the name of the Lord.

Marilyn has written five books. Her first, *Roses in December*,[3] tells the story of their great loss. Marilyn has had the opportunity to speak all over the country in high school auditoriums filled with teenagers. There she shares her story and has the platform to talk about life and death, chemical dependency, and God Himself.

Did God know what He was doing when He chose the Heavilins? You bet. They have come forth as gold fired in the heat of life and polished to shine for Him. Is their pain gone? Never. Can they go forth to minister? Absolutely. They have been very active in a group called "Compassionate Friends" which supports families who have experienced the death of a child. I thank God for Christians like the Heavilins. God knew the way they would take when tragedy came into their lives.

Everyone has experienced some kind of tragedy. How we handle these events when they happen is key. Today there are so many wonderful support groups available in churches and the local communities.

I grew up with a violent, alcoholic father. I had no place to go and no one to talk to, so I stuffed my pain. Now there are several groups to help people who find themselves in situations like mine.

A church in Southern California has a large group that meets weekly and has become like a church within a church for those who are chemically dependent and their families. Lives have changed as they pray for each other, support each other, and cry together. Many are coming forth as gold.

Bob and I visited a church in Memphis, Tennessee, which had a support group for homosexuals. Because of this church's outreach, many were coming out of the gay lifestyle and coming forth as gold.

Whatever your test is today, please know that others have experienced and are experiencing your pain. Don't go through the testing alone. Contact the local church and find another with whom you can share and cry. You, too, can and will come forth as gold.

Jesus knows and has also experienced our pain. He is always with us to help us get through the tough times in life. Trust Him now. It's all part of the coming forth as gold that Job talks about.

> *Father God, it is hard to desire testing in order to be more Christlike. However, I know from experience that we rarely grow in good times. It's the intense heat that makes us pure. May I be gold and not wood, hay, or stubble. Amen.*

Thoughts for Action

❦ Write down in your journal what pain and/or test you are experiencing today.

❦ Take a step to help yourself work toward becoming as gold.

❦ Write a letter to God about how you feel.

❦ Get involved in a support group.

Additional Scripture Reading

Psalm 66:10   2 Corinthians 4:7-9
Psalm 51:10

We must always
remember that God
has given to every soul
the responsibility of
deciding what its
character and destiny
shall be.

—Charles Jefferson

A Rat in a Maze

Scripture Reading: Galatians 5:7-10,13-15

Key Verse: Galatians 5:7

> *You were running a good race. Who cut in on you and kept you from obeying the truth?*

The timer clicked, the TV screen fluttered, and the speaker blared the morning news.

"Morning already?" groaned Larry. He rolled over and squeezed the pillow tightly over his ears, not seriously thinking he could muffle the announcement of another day in the rat race. Then the aroma of coffee from the timer-operated percolator lured him toward the kitchen.

Six hours of sleep may not have been the house rule growing up, but success at the end of the twentieth century demanded a premium from its active participants. A rising star like Larry couldn't squander time sleeping.

Curls of steam rose from the bowl of instant oatmeal; the microwave had produced predictably perfect results in perfect cadence with his thirty-five minute wake-up schedule.

Slouched in his chair, propped against his elbow, Larry noticed the computer screen staring back at him. Last night he balanced his checkbook after the eleven o'clock news, and, weary from the long day, he must have neglected to switch it off.

His wife, Carol, had welcomed a day off, so she slept in. Larry went through the rote motions of getting the kids off to school. After the two younger children had been dropped off at day-care, he was alone in the car with Julie. Twelve-year-old Julie seemed troubled lately. "Daddy, do you love mom anymore?" she asked. The question came out of the blue to Larry, but Julie had been building the courage to ask it for months. Their family life was changing, and Julie seemed to be the only member of the family diagnosing the changes. Larry reassured her he loved mom very much.

Carol didn't plan to go back to work when she first started on her MBA degree. Bored with her traditional, nonworking-housewife role, she just wanted more personal self-fulfillment. Her magazines conferred no dignity on the role of mother-tutor.

Although her family satisfied her self-esteem need for many years, other neighborhood women her same age seemed to lead glamorous lives in the business world. She couldn't help but question her traditional values.

"Maybe I'm too old-fashioned—out of step with the times," she thought to herself.

So, two nights each week for three and a half years she journeyed off to the local university, a big investment—not to mention the homework. By the time she walked across the stage to receive her diploma, Carol was convinced women had a right to professional fulfillment just as much as men.

Larry, a tenacious, carefree sales representative, advanced quickly in his company. Fifteen years of dream chasing rewarded him with a vice-president's title. The pay covered the essentials, but they both wanted more of the good life.

"I've been thinking about going back to work," Carol told him.

Larry didn't protest. She earned extra money as a bank teller at the beginning of their marriage, and the money helped furnish their honeymoon apartment. By mutual agreement, Carol stopped working when Julie was born, and ever since they had been hard-pressed to make ends meet.

Even though his own mother didn't work, Larry knew things were different for women. Still, he had mixed emotions about sending their two small children to a day-care center. But since money was always a problem, he just shrugged and kept silent when Carol announced she had started interviewing for a job.

Larry clearly understood the trade-off. More money, less family. More family, less money. Yet, they really wanted the good life.

Their neighbors bought a twenty-four-foot cabin cruiser. Larry was surprised to learn they could own one, too, for only $328 per month. By scrimping for five months they pulled together $1,000 which, when added to their savings, gave them enough for the $2,500 down payment.

Larry loved cars. His gentle dad had always loved cars. If a shiny two-door pulled up to him at a traffic light, Larry's heart always beat faster—he could just picture himself shifting through the gears of a fancy European import. By accident he discovered that for only $423 a month he could lease the car of his fantasies—a racy import! Leasing never occurred to him before.

Carol desperately wanted to vacation in Hawaii that year; her Tuesday tennis partner went last spring. But they couldn't do both.

"If you go along with me on this one, I'll make it up to you, Carol. I promise!" Larry told her, his infectious grin spreading across his face. She reminisced how that impish, little-boy smile had first attracted her to him. He had been good to her, she thought.

"Okay, go ahead," Carol told him.

His dad had always loved Chevys. Larry's tastes had evolved with the times.

Carol dreamed of living in a two-story home with a swimming pool, but, with the car and boat payments so high, it remained a dream for years. Larry slaved twelve- and fourteen-hour days—always thinking of ways to earn more money for Carol's dream house. When Carol went to work, they added up the numbers and were elated to see they could finally make the move.

The strain of keeping their household afloat discouraged them. There were bills to pay, kids to pick up from day-care, deadlines to meet, quotas to beat, but not much time to enjoy the possessions they had accumulated.

Words from a Simon and Garfunkel song haunted Larry's thoughts: "Like a rat in a maze, the path before me lies. And the pattern never alters, until the rat dies." He was trapped.

Carol pressured out—she just couldn't take it anymore. She believed Larry had let her down. He was supposed to be strong. He was supposed to know how to keep everything going. But Larry was just as confused about their situation as she was.

As the U-haul van pulled away from the house Larry couldn't quite believe she was actually doing it—Carol was moving out. She said she just needed some time and space to sort things out, that she was confused. The question Julie had asked a few months earlier burned in his mind, "Daddy, do you love mom anymore?" Yes . . . yes he loved her, but was it too late? How did things get so out of hand?[4]

My heart aches and breaks when I look around my city, my neighborhood, and yes, even my church, and see those who are caught in the heat of the "rat race." Who wins the rat race? No one!

Today, if you are caught up in this thing called Life, look introspectively and ask yourself the hard question, "Am I one of those trying to win the rat race?" If you are, you might want to make some dramatic changes before your children ask you one day, "Mommy, do you love Daddy?" And you can't say, "Yes."

Why do people like to run in races that have no winners?

> *Lord God, take away my confusion. Give me clarity in direction. Please unhinder all that gets me off-track. I want to be efficient in all that I do. Amen.*

Thoughts for Action

❧ Write the answer to these questions today in your journal:

1. Why am I here on planet earth?

2. Why do I do what I do?

3. How do I find importance in my life?

4. How did I get caught up in this race that doesn't produce winners?

5. What changes am I going to make today?

Additional Scripture Reading

1 Corinthians 6:12   Ecclesiastes 5:10
Romans 12:1-2   2 Corinthians 5:17

A House Divided

Scripture Reading: Mark 3:24-27

Key Verse: Mark 3:25

> If a house is divided against itself, that house cannot stand.

———— ❧ ————

"A house divided against itself cannot stand," Abraham Lincoln said in his acceptance speech of his nomination for the United States Senate. "Either the opponents of slavery will arrest the further spread of it and place it where the public mind shall rest in the belief that it is in the course of ultimate extinction, or its advocates will push it forward, till it shall become alike lawful in all the states, old as well as new—north as well as south."

Lincoln's pursuit of the equality of peoples eventually brought his defeat in the Senate election. Lincoln responded to his downfall philosophically: ". . . and though I now sink out of view and shall be forgotten, I believe I have made some marks which will tell for the cause of civil liberty long after I am gone." Lincoln certainly didn't "sink out of view"! He left marks not only upon our country but on the whole world. His gift to the United States was to heal those hurts that wanted to divide us, to bring together those who had been at war.

Many of our families are divided and need to be healed

and brought together. I had two aunts (they were sisters) who hadn't spoken to each other for 10 years because of some insignificant verbal disagreement. They behaved like little children with small hurts who could not let their souls confess their error. As I saw my aunts get older without sharing their later years in harmony, I decided that I was going to be the peacemaker, even though I was 30-plus years younger than they were. I was able to arrange a family gathering where both attended. After a short time together in this setting, they began to open up and talk to each other. By the end of the evening they had made amends. Because of this reuniting, they were able to enjoy the last 15 years of their lives together as sisters.

Maybe you have division in your family. As today's Scripture reading states, "If a kingdom is divided against itself, that kingdom cannot stand." If we stay divided we know what the outcome will be—collapse of the family unit. *You* become the healer of your divided home. It will take much prayer, patience, and conviction, but in the end you'll discover that a united house has many blessings.

> By wisdom a house is built, and through understanding it is established; through knowledge its rooms are filled with rare and beautiful treasures (Proverbs 24:3-4).

You be the one to restore your house with a rare and beautiful spirit.

> *Father God, may I be a healer in my family. May my spirit be one that unifies rather than divides. Show me any traits that I might have that need change. I thank You for being here when I need You. Thank You for Your continuing love and Your sweet spirit. Amen.*

Thoughts for Action

❦ Pray about and identify one person in your family who needs to be reunited with your family.

❦ Seek your spouse's support in this prayer need.

❦ Establish a plan on how to reunite this family member with the family.

❦ Step out and risk rejection.

Additional Scripture Reading

Matthew 12:25   Luke 11:17-22

Make Me a Blessing

Scripture Reading: Song of Solomon 2:8-13

Key Verse: Song of Solomon 2:12a

> *Flowers appear on the earth; the season of singing has come.*

———— ❦ ————

My Bob loves to drive from Riverside to San Diego each spring after it rains. Within a few days after these soft rains, the banks of the freeway are covered with the delicately waving state flower—the golden poppy. Truly the "Golden State" is golden. What a beautiful array of God's creation in flower form.

For a few years we had severe drought in California and the flowers were thinly populated. But now rain has returned and we are lavishly blessed with the golden poppy again. Our key verse for today states, "Flowers appear on the earth; the season of singing has come." All fall and winter the seeds lay dormant in the ground, and then the rains come and turn these seeds into a song.

Our lives are like that at times. We may lie sleeping—forgotten, we think. Then something happens that makes us come forward, take a look at the sun, and decide we are going to be a blessing to someone today. May today be that day when we reach out, near or far, and bless someone.

I watched the golden poppies spill
Like liquid gold across the hill
As petals wilted one by one
And faded with the summer sun.
The plants did not reseed themselves
To golden-glow the hillside shelves;
The rains that washed the mountain's face
Transplanted them some other place.
But when I walk their trail I find
My feet are light; my heart gold-lined—
Knowing, though they left no chart,
They gladden someone else's heart.[5]

Thoughts for Action

❧ Reach out and be a blessing to someone today.

❧ Telephone, write a letter, drop a note, send a gift—be that golden poppy in someone's life.

❧ Don't put any expectations on your actions. Act out of pure love.

❧ Record a blessing to someone on an audio cassette tape and mail it to them.

Additional Scripture Reading

Hebrews 10:24-25   Romans 15:29
Ephesians 5:1

In His Steps

Scripture Reading: 1 Peter 2:13-25

Key Verse: 1 Peter 2:21
> *To this you were called, because Christ suffered for you, leaving you an example, that you should follow in his steps.*

Many years ago I read a book entitled *In His Steps*. It was the story of a man who for a period of time attempted to walk in the steps of Jesus. Everything he said, everywhere he went, all decisions he made were done as if he were Jesus. As you can imagine, it was just about impossible. However, the experience changed this man's life forever.

We are not Jesus—nor will we ever be. Yet Jesus left us with His example of a godly life. As we walk through life on earth we will experience daily situations that will reveal our character. Jesus gives us the example of kindness and gentleness. He was full of sympathy and affection, and always loved with mercy.

Jesus said, "Beloved, I understand your pain, your grief, the tragedy of friends who betray you. I know you live in a world where others have sickness and sin you can do nothing about. I care, and I can help you. I can cleanse you and heal you today." As the Lord lives in you, He will form you into the beautiful, marvelous image of God according to your own uniqueness.

No we can't be Jesus. But we can develop a teachable spirit. We can love Him and desire Him in our hearts with all our soul, mind, and strength. We will then find ourselves transformed into a giving, loving spirit with the joy of Jesus in our hearts. Our character will then reveal the likeness of Jesus. Our spirits will help the helpless, pray for the sick, feed and clothe the homeless, and support those whom God lifts up to be missionaries where we can't go.

May we walk in His steps as we follow His call to us today.

Father God, oh You know how I want to be like You. The deepest part of my heart and soul aches for Your wisdom. May today be a special day for new revelation. Amen.

Thoughts for Action

❦ Ask yourself, "Are the qualities of Jesus evident in my life?"

❦ How can you follow in His steps today? List at least one way.

Additional Scripture Reading

Ephesians 2:6-7   John 15:12

The Minimum Daily Adult Requirement

Scripture Reading: Ephesians 2:4-9

Key Verse: Ephesians 2:8-9

> For it is by grace you have been saved, through faith—and this not from yourselves, it is the gift of God—not by works, so that no one can boast.

A couple of years ago I had a young college student ask me, "How much beer can I drink as a Christian?" Others have asked:

- How long should I read my Bible each day?
- How long should I pray each day?
- How much money do I have to give to the church?
- Do I have to sing in the choir to be a good Christian?
- How many times a week must I be in church?
- Do I have to _____, _____, _____?

On and on we go. We all want to know what the "minimum daily adult requirement" is for being a Christian. What do we *really* have to do, day-by-day, to get by?

43

Sue Gregg and I have written a lot of cookbooks dealing with God-given principles for a balanced lifestyle regarding food. The American consumer is very sophisticated when it comes to reading labels. Some even have small calculators with them as they stroll the aisle with shopping carts under tow. They can tell you unit costs, what kind of sugar is being used, what the derivative of the fat content is, how many calories, how much sodium, what is the nutritional information per serving, and yes, even the percentages of the minimum daily adult requirement.

If we want to know about the daily requirements in regard to our food, should we not also be concerned about this in our Christian walk? Of course! It only makes sense that we would definitely want to know how long Christians pray, how long they read their Bible, how much money they should put in the offering plate, how many church activities they participate in each week, etc.

Paul addresses these very basic questions in Ephesians. He very clearly states, "For it is by grace you have been saved, through faith—and this not from yourselves, it is the gift of God—not by works, so that no one can boast" (verses 8-9). Christ has freed us from this bondage of minimum daily adult requirements! It is not of works, but of grace.

You might ask, "Do I do nothing as a Christian? Aren't there some requirements?" The Scriptures challenge us to be like Christ. If I am to grow as unto the Lord, I need to study to see what He did and how He did it. For example,

- I find Him studying the law.
- I see Him meeting with other believers.
- I see Him praying regularly.
- I see Him serving others around Him in need.
- I see Him giving to those in need.

Christ did not do them because He was *told* to do them. He did them because He *wanted* to do them.

Seek from the Holy Spirit what your minimum daily adult requirement is. It is different for every one of us.

> *Father God, help me not to worry about how long or how often. Put a strong desire in my soul to spend time with You today in prayer and study. Let time stand still and let me forget all about my watch and schedule. Amen.*

Thoughts for Action

❧ List in your journal the things you are doing because you think they are required of you as a Christian.

❧ Cross off the things you don't want to do.

❧ Why are you still doing those things that are left? Cross some more off the list.

❧ Now list only those activities that you feel you want to do in order to grow unto the Lord. You may very well have the same list, but the items are listed because you want to do them rather than someone telling you to do them. Simply stated, this is grace and not law.

Additional Scripture Reading

1 Corinthians 1:4-8   Ephesians 6:5-8
2 Timothy 1:8-10

☐ ☐ ☐

The Whys of Life

Scripture Reading: Ecclesiastes 7:13-18

Key Verse: Ecclesiastes 7:16

> *Do not be overrighteous, neither be overwise—why destroy yourself?*

———— ❧ ————

You have to know that fame is fleeting, and I know—I always had my parents to refresh my memory.

No matter how important you think you are, they taught me, you're a mere nothing in the passage of time. Once you reach a certain level in a material way, what more can you do? You can't eat more than three meals a day; you'll kill yourself. You can't wear two suits, one over the other. You might now have three cars in your garage— but six! Oh, you can indulge yourself, but only to a point.

One way to make sure fame doesn't change you is to keep in mind that you're allotted only so much time on this earth—and neither money nor celebrity will buy you a couple of extra days. Although I do have a rich friend in New York who says, "What do you mean I can't take it with me? I've already made out traveler's checks and sent them ahead."

Life is so complicated that it's hard for anyone, especially kids, to figure out what their purpose is in life, and to whom they're accountable. Of course, we should all be accountable to God throughout our lives—and live our lives that way every day, not just on our deathbeds begging for forgiveness.

A lot of people don't believe in God because they can't see him. I'm not a Doubting Thomas, though. I truly believe. When we were kids, our Sunday School teachers used to address this question by telling us: "You can't see electricity either, but it's there. Just stick your hand in the socket now and then to remind yourself." I've never seen an ozone layer or carbon monoxide or an AIDS virus, but they're out there somewhere.[6]

Lee Iacocca has learned a very valuable lesson in life, and that is balance and proper prospective toward wealth and fame. The wise man will live life in obedience to God, recognizing that God will eventually judge all men.

In today's Scripture reading we see that God brings both prosperity and adversity into our lives for His sovereign purpose without always revealing His plan. Our minds do not have the horsepower to think as God does. By faith we must rely on His words to do what He says He will do. A long time ago Bob and I claimed 2 Timothy 3:16-17 as one of our important verses of Scripture:

> All Scripture is God-breathed and is useful
> for teaching, rebuking, correcting and training
> in righteousness. So that the man of God may be
> thoroughly equipped for every good work.

Are you being equipped to handle life: birth, death, fame, divorce, fortune, bankruptcy, health, sickness? When we're young we often think we know all the answers of life. But as we get older we begin to realize that we fit into a master plan that can't always be explained.

Have you ever asked the question, "Why?" Of course you have. We all have. That is the mystery question of life. Solomon realized that God has a sovereign purpose, and that He doesn't always reveal to us the key to His plan.

> *Father God, humble my spirit so that I might be open to new truths today that I might better understand the whys of life (the big and the small). You know that I want to expand my mind to be more like You! Amen.*

Thoughts for Action

🐦 In your journal list several of your "why" questions. Realize that you will not always know the answer to these whys.

🐦 Turn these questions over to God in prayer and give them up to Him. Someday you will realize how these whys fit into His sovereign plans.

🐦 Thank God, also, for all the questions you have answers for.

Additional Scripture Reading

Ecclesiastes 3:1-8	Ecclesiastes 3:14
Ecclesiastes 9:1	

Is Your Mate Looking Upward?

Scripture Reading: Genesis 2:18-23

Key Verse: Genesis 2:18

> *It is not good for the man to be alone. I will make a helper suitable for him.*

A pastor meeting an irreligious lady whose husband was trying to serve God addressed her thus: "Madam, I think your husband is looking upwards, making some effort to rise above the world towards God and heaven. You must not let him try alone. Whenever I see the husband struggling alone in such efforts, it makes me think of a dove endeavoring to fly upwards while it has one broken wing. It leaps and flutters, and perhaps rises a little way; and then it becomes wearied, and drops back again to the ground. If both wings cooperate, then it mounts easily."

This principle is one of the great principles of marriage. What a difference it would make if more women would uphold their husbands as they attempt to rise above the world towards God and heaven! In his letter to Titus, the apostle Paul gives some excellent exaltations to women. He writes:

> ... train the younger women to love their husbands and children, to be self-controlled and

pure, to be busy at home, to be kind, and to be subject to their husbands, so that no one will malign the word of God (Titus 2:4-5).

Oh, how we need to teach our women:

- to love their husbands and children.

- to be self-controlled.

- to be pure.

- to be busy at home.

- to be kind.

- to be subject to their husbands.

These traits are so contrary to what the world is attempting to teach you. Unfortunately the world's ways seem to be winning, so how about stepping forward and trying God's ways? I am not a strong supporter of "formulas that work," but these six characteristics will definitely help your husband reach up unto God.

Thoughts for Action

❦ Do something to lift your husband heavenward.

❦ Concentrate on one of the six principles from the Titus list.

❦ Tell your husband how much you love him.

Additional Scripture Reading

1 Peter 3:1-7   Ephesians 5:21-28

His Outstretched Hand

Scripture Reading: Isaiah 53:3-10

Key Verse: Isaiah 53:3a

> *He was despised and rejected by men, a man of sorrows and familiar with suffering.*

The pain of rejection can hurt so bad that you think you want to die. We all have experienced it from time to time, probably from someone we cared about very deeply—a parent, husband, child, friend, brother or sister, or possibly all the above.

What great pain this can cause, and yet we can overcome the pain of rejection. Yes, there is life after rejection.

Jesus Himself experienced rejection. If anyone knows this pain, it's Jesus. His own people who He came to save and teach were the very ones who nailed Him to the cross: "He came to that which was his own, but his own did not receive him" (John 1:11).

My Jewish family wanted me to marry within my own faith. Yet when I was 16, my Bob introduced me to Christ. Within a few months Bob and I were engaged, and eight months later we were married. My very own family, those I loved, rejected me for my stand with Jesus and my stand to marry the Christian young man I loved.

God honored my heart and my faithfulness to Him. My family grew to adore my Bob as I do, and our family was restored. It didn't happen all at once, but in His time, one by one, hearts were softened and attitudes changed. The pain in my heart was great, but little by little His mighty strength took over and peace filled my heart. I hung in and loved my family when it was difficult to love the attitudes and mockery thrown at me. I'm grateful today I trusted Jesus.

Isaiah prophesied that Messiah would be despised and rejected of men, yet this foreknowledge did not make the experience any less painful for Jesus. And to make it even worse, Jesus felt rejected by His own Father. When Jesus bore the sins of the world He felt deep, deep pain. He cried out, "My God, my God, why have you forsaken me?" (Matthew 27:46).

Yet in the middle of all this rejection, Jesus never abandoned the mission that God had given to Him. He never fought back against the ones who rejected Him. How did He respond? With love—love even for those who crucified Him.

Do you think the Lord knows how you feel? You bet! And the Lord Jesus offers you His strength. The Bible says that He sympathizes with our weakness and He offers His grace for our time of need. When Jesus suffered on the cross, He bore our penalty for us. He paid the price for our sins. Then He gave us a promise: "Never will I leave you; never will I forsake you" (Hebrews 13:5). No matter what happens, God will never reject you. You will never be alone again. You may be rejected by others, but remember God Almighty will always be there to comfort you. His hand is stretched out to you. All you need to do is place your hands in His. Allow His strength to empower you today.

> *Father God, You know rejection far better than I do. I ask You to touch me when I'm rejected (or when I feel rejected) and ease that pain. Please make me sensitive to the times when I reject people. You know that I don't want to hurt others' feelings. Protect my words, body language, and attitude, that they may heal and not reject. Amen.*

Thoughts for Action

❦ Don't dwell on your pain but place it in Jesus' hands today.

Additional Scripture Reading

Philippians 4:13	Hebrews 4:15-16
2 Corinthians 1:3	John 1:1-5

☐ ☐ ☐

Your True Motivation

Scripture Reading: Matthew 19:27–20:16

Key Verse: Matthew 19:29

> *And everyone who has left houses or brothers or sisters or father or mother or children or fields for my sake will receive a hundred times as much and will inherit eternal life.*

Throughout my life I have asked myself over and over, why do I serve? What is my motivation for speaking, writing, giving financially to the church, being a mother, giving freely to my husband and to my extended family?

In today's passage Peter asks Jesus, "What then will there be for us?" Have you ever caught yourself asking this very basic question? I know I have. When Bob was in business, he would share with me the reaction from different employees when he would tell them about a promotion they were going to receive. Most would ask:

- How much more money will I make?
- Any increase in health insurance, vacations, bonuses, retirement, etc?

In the verses you read, Jesus answers Peter's very basic question, giving us three important principles for our daily living:

- Whatever we give up we will receive a hundred times as much.
- We will inherit eternal life.
- Many who are first will be last, and many who are last will be first.

Many times in our religious life we think God will punish us if we don't serve Him rather than being truly motivated by a pure desire to serve Him.

My daily prayer is for God to reveal to me what my true motivation is in serving Him. In Psalm 139:1 David states, "O Lord, you have searched me and you know me." I truly yearn to know me as God knows me.

Can I accept from God the promises He has given me in today's beautiful reading? Do I honestly accept by faith what God has so graciously given to us, a hundredfold return for all we have given up *and* eternal life because of our acceptance of Jesus?

As I look around to see what God has so graciously given to me, I am amazed and blessed at His generosity. As the old church hymn says, "Count your blessings, name them one by one." Name a few:

- I know Jesus face-to-face
- salvation
- family
- a wonderful home
- a wonderful ministry
- good health
- a Bible-teaching church

The third principle, that the last shall be first, I found puzzling. But I was looking at it through man's eyes, rather than taking time to see what God was trying to teach me. We all want to be fair in our dealings with other people and in their dealings with us, yet this passage seemed unfair. Why would the farmer pay the late worker the same amount as the early worker who had been in the fields all day?

In Matthew 20:14 the owner of the farm says, "I want to give the man who was hired last the same as I gave you." To me this represents God's amazing grace and generosity that knows no bounds. What we as man might feel is right is irrelevant. God chooses to do what He chooses to do.

Are we willing to serve God? Our reward is eternal life—even if we come to the field at three o'clock in the afternoon and others have been there since early morning.

> *Father God, search my heart and test my motivation for what I do. Don't let any selfishness enter into my life. You know my intent. May my actions be done with a clear heart. Amen.*

Thoughts for Action

- Write down in your journal why you do what you do.
- Write down at least 10 of your blessings.
- Think of at least two more blessings and write them down too.
- Be willing to freely serve.

Additional Scripture Reading

Matthew 6:33   Mark 10:29-31

God Has a Master Plan

Scripture Reading: Jeremiah 18:2-6

Key Verse: Jeremiah 18:6

> O house of Israel, can I not do with you as this potter does?

When our son Brad was in elementary school one of his class projects was to shape clay into something. Brad made a reddish dinosaur-type thing. It's on my bookshelf today as a display of Brad's first work of art—molded and shaped with his small hands, brought home to me with pride.

In high school Brad enrolled in a ceramics class as one of his electives. His first pieces were crooked and misshaped, but as time went on he was able to fashion beautiful works of art. He made vases, pots, pitchers, a butter pot, and many other kinds of pottery. Many pieces of clay were thrown on the wheel to become beautiful but during the process they would take a different direction. Brad would then work and work to reshape them, and sometimes he would have to start all over, working and working again to make each piece just as he wanted it to be.

God has taken, so to speak, a handful of clay in each one of us. He is the Master Potter. We are the vessels in His house. Each one He knows intimately. Each one is different.

We might ask ourselves, "What kind of vessel am I?" Maybe the pot that holds a plant, its roots growing deep in the soil that produces the beauty above in a flowering bloom. Or a cup to hold the tea of friendship. Or a pitcher from which flows the words of wisdom, or a casserole dish with a tightly-sealed lid so nothing from inside will leak out.

Almighty God picks us up like a piece of ugly clay and begins to shape our lives. On the potter's wheel we begin to spin around. God says, "I want you to be strong and beautiful inside and out." The hands of God move up and down as the wheel spins, forming with one hand the inside and with the other the outer side. He says, "I'm with you. I am the Lord of your life, and I will build within you a strong foundation based upon the Word of God."

It feels so good to us as we grow in beauty. Then something happens in our life—a child dies, fire takes our home, we lose our job, our husband leaves, a child rebels. The world cries out to us, "Stop! Jump off the potter's wheel and come with me. I'll give you what you need to feel good." So we place the lid on our vessel and we escape inside ourselves to try to forget the hurt and pain we feel. The beauty God was shaping is put on the shelf only to get dusty and pushed to the back behind all the books and magazines. We feel so lost and far from God as time passes. We've become sidetracked, and yet God has not side-tracked us. He says, "I will never leave you nor forsake you."

I love the bumper sticker I saw, "If you feel far from God, guess who moved?" It wasn't God who placed you on the shelf. We are the ones who tighten the lids on our hearts, who put ourselves on the shelf. It's time to push off the lid and jump back on the potter's wheel. We need to become obedient to Almighty God, the Master Potter. He will take the time we were sidetracked and use it to help mold us into His master plan.

In pottery the true beauty of the clay comes out after the firing in the kiln. Allow the Lord to use the negatives in your life to become someone of beauty.

Father God, You truly are the potter and I am the clay. Mold me into the person You want me to be, not what I want to be. I know that is placing a lot of trust in You, but I know that You love me and are concerned about me. May my clay pottery reflect Your light like a fine porcelain vessel. Amen.

Thoughts for Action

❦ Write down in your journal the pain you're feeling today that caused you to place your vessel on the shelf and secure the lid.

❦ Picture yourself pushing off the lid and allowing the Lord to continue healing and reshaping your beautiful vessel.

Additional Scripture Reading

Psalm 73:26   Hebrews 12:7-11
Psalm 121:7

□ □ □

A Marriage Needs Refreshed Inhabitants

Scripture Reading: Proverbs 17:14-22

Key Verse: Proverbs 17:17

A friend loves at all times, and a brother is born for adversity.

——— ❧ ———

Ed and Carol Nevenschwander (a pastor and his wife) write:

Although the shell of a union may endure, the spirit of the marriage may disintegrate in time unless mates take periodic and shared reprieves from the pressures they live under.

The pressures we must often escape are not those we create for ourselves, but those brought into our lives from the outside. Nonetheless, they can wear our relationships thin.

The key to keeping a cherished friendship alive may be found in breaking away long enough and frequently enough to keep ourselves fresh and our love growing. And usually that involves childless weekends. Without such moments of focused attention, it's difficult to keep the kind

of updated knowledge of one another that keeps
two hearts in close proximity alive and growing
together. A growing marriage needs refreshed
inhabitants. [7]

We live in a very hectic world that cries out for stillness,
quietness, and aloneness. For the sake of our marriage and for
our own personal sanities, we must seek solitude.

For the last 12 years my Bob and I have made it a point to
get away from all the noises of life and just be by ourselves. We
sleep in and disregard clocks. We have no schedules and only
limited interruptions. We eat when and if we want. Our favorite time has been from December 27 to January 3. For you this
might not be a good time, so choose your own calendar. Get
away from everything. Rethink life. Write down some individual and family goals. Be in agreement that these things are a
high priority for you and your mate. Under each goal write
down what you are going to do to accomplish that desire along
with a date when you expect to have it accomplished.

When was the last time you had marital solitude? You've
got to make it happen; it just doesn't happen. You must plan to
have these special times with your mate. But you say, "We
don't have the money!" Don't let excuses sidetrack this desire.
Bob and I have found that people do what they want to do. You
can find extra money somewhere. If not, start using coupons
with your grocery shopping, Put your savings in a special
account just for that special time you will have with that
special friend—your mate.

*Father God, may I learn to be still and know
that You are God. I truly want to get off this hectic
merry-go-round and be serene and hear the precious
words that You give me each day. I want to be
refreshed for myself and all those around me. Amen.*

Thoughts for Action

❦ Plan a special day and time for your mate. Leave your troubles behind and get away for at least one night (two or three if you can).

❦ Set aside a fund for this adventure.

❦ Mail your mate a special letter of invitation.

❦ Keep a modest level of expectation for this time. Too many expectations lead to great disappointments. Try to keep it in perspective. Just let it happen.

Additional Scripture Reading

1 Corinthians 13:3-8   Song of Songs 2:10-13

Using Our Talents

Scripture Reading: Matthew 25:14-30

Key Verse: Matthew 25:21

> *Well done, good and faithful servant!*

This passage contains two important points:

- God's call for faithfulness in the use of our talents to Him.
- A warning for those who do not use their talents.

I am continually amazed as I talk to women across America that so many don't realize that God can use ordinary people to spread the gospel to those around them.

As a young child growing up behind my mother's dress store, I had no idea that God could use me for much. It wasn't until many years later that God challenged me to take small steps to venture out into this world called "risks" and to be faithful to this calling.

We often think that our talents are going to come out full-grown. However, it is only as we cultivate them that they become mature. As a young seventh-grade girl, I took up playing a beautiful string instrument—the cello. Only after several years of hard practice was I able to play second chair in the Long Beach All City Honors Orchestra.

As with any talent, we must be willing to be used. Yes, there is a risk, but it's worth the insecurity to find out how far God can take us if we are willing. In today's parable we see that the first two servants were willing to take that risk. Their stewardship gave them a blessing of 100-percent return for their efforts, plus their master said, "Well done, good and faithful servant! You have been faithful with a few things; I will put you in charge of many things. Come and share your master's happiness!"

If you want to be successful in God's eyes, you must first be faithful with a few things; then God will cheerfully put you in charge of many things. Is there a talent that people keep telling you you are good at, but you just shrug it off as not being good enough? No one could be blessed by my talent, you think. This passage tells you to take the risk. Don't limit God—He is not to be put into a box. How many of you have a poem to be written, a song to be sung, a book to be authored? Listen to God today as He calls you to a life of adventure. Life is not boring when you have a purpose.

A warning to those who don't use their talents. Even though today's passage talks about faithfulness to use our talents for God, we can't leave this Scripture without looking briefly at God's warning in verses 24-30. This third servant was afraid. He wasn't willing to take a risk with his one talent. He went and buried it in the ground. How many of us are fearful and bury our talents? The warning of these few verses is that God holds us responsible for our lives and what we do with them.

We want to stand before God one day and hear Him say, "Well done, good and faithful servant!"

> *Father God, at times I don't feel I have any talents, but I know You have given each of Your children special gifts. Today I'm asking for direction in using my talents for Your glory. Thank You for listening to my prayer. Amen.*

Thoughts for Action

❦ Ask God today to reveal to you those special gifts that He wants you to develop.

❦ Ask a friend to share with you her perception of your special gifts or talents.

❦ Develop a plan and a timetable to begin using these talents and gifts for the Lord.

❦ Be a risk-taker.

Additional Scripture Reading

Exodus 4:10-12   Ephesians 3:14-21

God's Gift

Scripture Reading: John 10:10-18

Key Verse: John 10:10

> *The thief comes only to steal and kill and destroy; I have come that they may have life, and have it to the full.*

When our son, Brad, and daughter-in-love, Maria, were expecting Bradley Joe II, their joy was so great. Maria took extra care of that little one inside her. She ate well, exercised properly, and got plenty of rest. It never occurred to me that Bradley Joe was not in the safest environment for those nine months before he was born.

One evening we attended a service at an Evangelical Free Church in Fullerton, California. Pastor Chuck Swindoll introduced the speaker for the evening, a man by the name of Ravi Zakaria. His opening statement was "The most dangerous place for a young child today is in his mother's womb." Tears filled my eyes and flooded down my cheeks. I wanted to sob. *Oh, God,* I thought, *what has happened in the world today?* Children are being thrown away as trash, right in our own cities. God says, "Behold children are a gift of the Lord" (Psalm 127:3). We aren't even waiting to unwrap the gift, or allowing the fruit of the womb to be God's reward.

When I held our new little grandson, Bradley Joe II, I saw the miracle of God—a child planted and formed by the Almighty. As I watch our children raise their children, God has impressed upon me the desire to teach women to love and care for children. What a blessing of trust that God would count us women worthy to care for one of His dear children!

Our niece, Becky, and her husband, George, adopted a son. They could never have a child from her womb due to cancer in her body at a very early age. God allowed a child to be born to another woman so Becky and George could be the parents they so desired. This child is sent from God, a gift of God. Thank You, Lord, that this child was not a throwaway, but a child who will contribute much to our society, adopted into a family who wanted a child.

That's exactly what God has for us. He wants to adopt us into His family. We are not God's throwaways. We are His reward. He said, "I have come to give you life" (John 10:10). God sent His Son Jesus as a sacrificed gift to us. He laid down His life for us. Jesus went to the cross so we will never have to suffer the punishment. He took the sins of the world upon Himself and died for you and me.

> *Thank You, Jesus, for Your love to me that while I was yet a sinner, You died for me. Thank You for the little children. Please protect them in their mother's womb, and may these children be an opened gift to parents. May we, as a country, rise up and defend our children in and out of the womb. Amen.*

Thoughts for Action

- Ask yourself, "Am I a child of God, adopted into His family?"

- If no, ask Jesus into your heart and life now.

- Read the whole book of John.

- Pray for the child in the mother's womb—for the gift to be opened at its fullness.

─────── 🍎 ───────

Additional Scripture Reading

1 John 1:9	Luke 9:23
Mark 9:37	John 1:12
1 Peter 3:18	

Overload

Scripture Reading: Proverbs 3:1-8

Key Verse: Proverbs 3:6

> *In all your ways acknowledge him, and he will make*
> *your paths straight.*

Do you have the type of home where nothing seems to get done? Where each room would take a bulldozer just to clean up the mess? You rush around all day never completing any one job, or if you do complete a task, there is a little one behind you, pulling and messing everything up again! There isn't one of us who *hasn't* experienced these feelings.

When I was 20 our baby daughter Jennifer was six months old. We then took in my brother's three children and within a few months I became pregnant. That gave Bob and me five children under five years old. My life was work, work, work— and yet I never seemed to get anywhere. I was running on a treadmill that never stopped and never moved ahead. I was always tired and never seemed to get enough done, let alone get enough sleep. I was fragmented, totally confused, and stressed.

Then one day during my rushed quiet time with the Lord I read Proverbs 3:6: "In all your ways acknowledge him, and he will make your paths straight." I fell to my knees and prayed, "Please, God, direct my path. I acknowledge You to help me, Lord. I'm going to allow You to lead me and not lead myself in my power. I want Your power and direction. Lord, I'm tired.

I'm on overload with husband, home, children, and meals. I have no time left over for me or anyone else. I can't even do any of us justice. Please help me to put it all together and make it work to glorify You and Your children. Amen."

The Lord not only heard my prayer that day, but He honored it as well. I began a program that changed my life. I committed 15 minutes (at least) per day to my quiet time with the Lord. With Brad in hand, I got up earlier each morning. The house was quiet, and my Lord and I talked as I read His Word and prayed.

Next I committed 15 minutes each day to the organization of our home, concentrating on things I never seemed to get done: the silverware drawer, refrigerator, hall closets, photos, bookshelves, piles of papers. I committed to this for 30 days and the pattern was set. God was directing my path. Our home changed dramatically. The cloud of homemaking stress lifted, and I had new direction. The Lord redeemed my time with Him. I had more time to plan meals, make new recipes, play with the children, take walks to the park, even catch a nap from time to time.

Looking back now as a grandparent, I can truly understand the meaning of acknowledging Him in all my ways. It's looking to God for help and comfort in *all* the ways of our life—our families, home, finances, commitments, and careers. God gives us a promise: "I will direct your path."

Father God, sometimes I feel my life is truly on overload. There are days I am confused, frustrated, and misdirected. I come to You on my knees, seeking Your undying patience and the hope You so graciously give. I ask for Your direction in my life. Make order out of disorder. Thank You! Amen.

Thoughts for Action
❦ Acknowledge Him today.

❦ Allow Him to direct your path.

❦ Commit to 15 minutes today to clean something up.

Additional Scripture Reading

Luke 10:40-42   Psalm 139:23-24
Philemon 1:14

□ □ □

Spread the Fragrance

Scripture Reading: 2 Corinthians 2:14-17

Key Verse: 2 Corinthians 2:14

> But thanks be to God who always leads us in triumphal procession in Christ and through us spreads everywhere the fragrance of the knowledge of Him.

The dictionary defines "fragrant" as a pleasant odor. The opposite of that would be the smell of a baby's dirty diaper! Yet how sweet the smell of a clean, freshly lotioned and powdered baby after his bath. Baby and mother are happy as the sweet smell permeates the nursery. One baby, two different smells. One you want to hand over to Mom as quickly as you can and the other you want to reach out and pick up from Mom's arms.

Today's Scripture reading says that as we grow in the knowledge of Jesus Christ we become a sweet odor to others. We become a fragrance others want to enjoy and hang around with.

In Riverside, California, where we live, the orange blossoms in the spring from our orange trees become so potent that the aroma permeates the entire area. The evenings are beautiful with the smell. We keep the bedroom French doors open just to enjoy the fragrance. After a while the blossoms die away and tiny green oranges appear. They slowly grow, and in the late fall those green oranges turn to orange. In December we begin to pick, eat, juice, and give away. But it isn't until late-January, mid-February, that the sugar content is at its height. That's when the fresh orange juice is oh-so-sweet and wonderful. But we never forget the fragrance of the first blooms. Does the fragrance die? Not at all. The smell of that sweet juice is just as wonderful as the blossom.

What is your fragrance? Are you one who others don't want to be around? Or are others wanting to smell the freshness of your sweet spirit because you are a blossom so strong with the fragrance of the spirit of Christ? It takes the knowledge of God's Word to develop that fragrance—learning about God's holy book and the principles taught chapter by chapter.

Where do we begin? We begin with the tiny bloom of time in God's Word, the Bible. A little now, a little later, step-by-step as the months go by we begin to mature just like the orange. We become so full of God's juices that others want to pick us up and squeeze His fragrance from us. The sweetness gets even sweeter as we share His Word with others, pouring out what we've filled our juice pitcher with. As His fragrance enters others' lives, they then begin the same process—a small blossom growing to full maturity. As the process continues from person to person, our orange tree will be full of blossoms, creating a fragrance that can eventually permeate the whole city and eventually the world.

Thoughts for Action

🐛 Start today to read God's Holy Bible one chapter per day.

🐛 Share with someone the sweet smell you learned.

🐛 Pray for God to lead you in triumphal procession to reach the fullness of the sweet fragrance.

Additional Scripture Reading

Galatians 5:22-23   Colossians 1:9-14

Godly Examples

Scripture Reading: Psalm 78:1-7

Key Verse: Psalm 78:4

> *We will not hide them [commandments] from their children; we will tell the next generation the praiseworthy deeds of the Lord, his power, and the wonders he has done.*

——— ❦ ———

A young father was having a talk with his young son as they were preparing to get ready for bed. The father was telling the lad what Christians should be like and how they should act. When Dad had finished describing the attributes of a Christian, the young boy asked a stunning question: "Daddy, have I ever seen a Christian?" The father was aghast. *What kind of an example am I?* he thought.

How would you feel if your child asked you the same question? In our reading today we are given some help to make sure this doesn't happen. This passage establishes some patterns for parenting, patterns we can use to help our children know the things of God and to realize that we are God's children. The writer of Psalm 78 states we can do this by:

- Telling the next generation the praises of the Lord (verse 4).

- Teaching our children the statutes and laws of God (verse 5).

Then our children will see by our words and examples that we are Christians.

In Deuteronomy 6:6-7 Moses said, "These commandments that I give you today are to be upon your hearts. Impress them on your children. Talk about them when you sit at home and when you walk along the road, when you lie down and when you get up."

As a parent we are to be a reflector of God to our children. As they look into our faces, our lives, they are to see a man or woman of godly desires and actions. In America today, we earnestly need more parents who will stand up and do the right thing. Christian growth is a daily process of taking off the old self of attitudes, beliefs, and behaviors which reflect the dark side of our nature (sin) and changing to those characteristics that reflect the presence of Christ in our lives. The only way we can grow and succeed in this continuous process is by being renewed in the spirit of our mind (Ephesians 4:22-24). It is a moment-to-moment decision.

By word and by personal example we must train and nurture our children. In this way they can know what a Christian is, because they have known you—the reflector of God's grace.

> Lord God, I thank You for the godly men and women You have put in my life. They have been a real inspiration to my Christian growth. Help me to continually seek out those godly people who will live the Christian walk in front of me. Amen.

Thoughts for Action

- Talk to your children today about spiritual things.
- Say a prayer today with your children thanking God for all your blessings.
- Choose today to do one thing that is spiritual (eternal) rather than something that is secular (temporal).

———— 🍎 ————

Additional Scripture Reading

Ephesians 6:4   Deuteronomy 6:6-7
Ephesians 4:22-24

Find Favor in God's Eyes

Scripture Reading: Genesis 6:8-22

Key Verse: Genesis 6:8,22

> *Noah found favor in the eyes of the Lord....Noah did everything just as God commanded him.*

Almost every day we can read newspaper articles dealing with people who are being honored by the world:

- government
- sports
- medicine
- education
- theater
- music

On and on we can go. Man finding favor with man. Have you ever thought how much richer it would be to have God find favor with you? I stand in awe when I think of God finding favor in me, but He does. Only through His marvelous grace are we able to come to Him face-to-face.

Noah lived in a world much like today, a world full of sin. Man hasn't changed much over the centuries—we just give sin a different name. Yet through all this wickedness, Noah was a person who lived a godly life. His life was pleasing to God even during those evil days.

Noah didn't find favor because of his individual goodness but through his personal faith in God. We are also judged according to the same standard—that of our personal faith and obedience. My daily prayer is that my family and I will be worthy of the goodness God so richly bestows upon us.

Even though Noah was upright and blameless before God, he wasn't perfect. God recognized that Noah's life reflected a *genuine* faith, not always a *perfect* faith. Do we sometimes feel all alone in our walk with God? Noah walked in greater deprivation than we, yet he still walked with God (verse 9). Noah found that it wasn't the surroundings of his life that kept him in close fellowship with God, but it was the heart of Noah that qualified him to find friendship with God.

How often do we try to find favor with man only to fall on our face in rejection? Noah only wanted to please God. Have you ever asked in that small voice of yours, "Do I find favor in the eyes of the Lord?" When we come to Him and admit we are sinners, we please God. At that time we find God's grace, and we are able to move into a relationship with Jesus Christ. Then we are able to find favor with God.

As we live in this very difficult time of world history, we might ask, "Do I find favor in God's sight?" God gives us grace to live victoriously: "He gives us more grace" (James 4:6).

Father God, oh may I find favor with You. What an honor for Noah to be favored by You, yet I realize that he was obedient to Your Word. Give me a hunger to fall in love with Your Word and put it to work in my life. You are worthy of praise. Amen.

Thoughts for Action

❦ Write down in your journal how you know that you find favor in God's eyes. If you can remember, jot down the exact date you gave your life to Christ.

❦ If you don't think your life finds favor with God, turn to Revelation 3:16. Be assured that by accepting Jesus Christ as your Savior you will find favor with God.

❦ Tell someone today of your new-found favor with God.

❦ Seek out a church if you don't already fellowship with other believers.

❦ Be obedient to God's Word.

Additional Scripture Reading

John 3:16   Philippians 2:12-15
Psalm 19:14

□ □ □

Be Imitators of Christ's Humility

Scripture Reading: Philippians 2:1-5

Key Verse: Philippians 2:5

> *Your attitude should be the same as that of Christ Jesus.*

We've all heard of the pastor who was given a badge for being the most humble person in the church. Of course, the badge was taken back when he wore it! We all struggle with the idea of humility. What is too much and what is too little?

Billy and Ruth Graham's daughter, Gigi, gives a very true-to-life experience that reflects how we are to have the mind, heart, and attitude of Christ.

I stood in the upstairs hallway, looking down over the bannister and waiting for the younger children to come in for their baths. My oldest daughter, taking a piano lesson, was in the living room directly below, and the repetitive melody she was playing echoed through my mind.

I noticed, however, that one of my young sons was trudging slowly up the stairs, his bowed, grubby hands covering his small, dirt-streaked face. When he reached the top, I asked him what was wrong.

"Aw, nothing," he replied.

"Then why are you holding your face in your hands?" I persisted.

"Oh, I was just praying."

Quite curious now, I asked what he was praying about.

"I can't tell you," he insisted, "because if I do, you'll be mad."

After much persuasion I convinced him that he could confide in me and that, whatever he told me, I would not get mad. So he explained that he was praying about a problem he had with his mind.

"A problem with your mind?" I asked, now more curious than ever, wondering what kind of problem a child of six could have with his mind. "What kind of problem?"

"Well," he said, "you see, every time I pass by the living room, I see my piano teacher, and my tongue sticks out."

Needless to say, it was hard to keep a straight face, but I took his problem seriously and assured him that God could, indeed, help him with it.

Later, on my knees beside the bathtub as I bathed this little fellow, I thought how I still struggle with the problem of controlling my mind and my tongue. That afternoon as I knelt to scrub that sturdy little body, the tub became my altar; the bathroom, my temple. I bowed my head, covered my face; and acknowledged that I, like my son, had a problem with my mind and tongue. I asked the Lord to forgive me and to give me more and more the mind and heart and attitude of Christ.[8]

In our world where the media bombards us with "self-esteem," we become confused with what is real humility. In verse 3 of today's passage we read: "Do nothing out of selfish ambition or vain conceit, but in humility consider others better than yourself."

As we study the life of Christ, we observe that His humility had its roots in confidence, strength, and security. He had a life that reflected a positive perspective of strength and self-worth. He knew the value He had to His Father. Knowing our value to God is the first step in learning true humility.

It's out of strength, not weakness, that we grow in humility. Dr. Bruce Narramore has summed up humility well. He states that humility has three elements:

- Recognizing your need for God.

- Realistically evaluating our capacities.

- Being willing to serve.[9]

That's healthy. That's humility.

Thoughts for Action

❧ Answer this question in your journal: "Do I recognize my need for God?" If yes, thank God for that awareness. If no, why not?

❧ Evaluate your abilities. Under each column write at least 10 strengths and weaknesses. What are you going to do with your strengths? What plan do you have for turning your weaknesses into strengths?

❧ List three areas where you would be willing to serve. Volunteer your services in one of these areas this week.

Additional Scripture Reading

Philippians 2:8-9   James 1:26-27
Psalm 39:1-13

Know the Bent of Your Child

Scripture Reading: Proverbs 22:1-16

Key Verse: Proverbs 22:6

> *Train a child in the way he should go, and when he is old he will not turn from it.*

As I think about our children, Brad and Jenny, and look into the various shades of color in the eyes of our grand-children, Christine, Chad, Bevan, and Bradley Joe II, I see six unique people. How am I ever going to understand the uniqueness of each of these children? I know that I have to attempt to understand each of them if I am going to have an impact upon molding a healthy, godly character in their lives. At the heart of each child is a cry, "Please take time to know me. I am different from anyone else. My sensitivity, my likes, dislikes, tenderness of heart are different from my brothers and sisters."

In raising our own children, we saw so many differences between Jenny and Brad. Even as adults they are still different. I, in God's wisdom, had to realize that my approach to motivating them had to be styled differently for each of them. Children want to be trained in a personal and tailor-made way.

In our key verse for today, we first see the word "train." In the Hebrew, this word originally referred to the palate (the roof of the mouth) and to the gums. In Bible times the midwife would stick her fingers into a sweet substance and place her fingers into the new child's mouth, creating a sucking desire in the child. The child would then be delicately given to the mother, whereby the child would start nursing. This was the earliest form of "training." The child mentioned in this text can fall between a newborn and a person that is of marrying age.

The second part of this verse is, "when he is old he will not turn from it." At first I thought this meant an older person who had become wayward yet finally returned to the Lord. Little did I know that this word "old" meant "bearded" or "chin." Solomon is talking about a young man who begins to grow a beard when he approaches maturity. For some it might be in junior high school and for others it might be college. The concept is that we as parents are charged to continue training our children as long as they are under our care.

Note that we are to train a child in *his* way—not our way, our plan, our idea. It's important to see that the verse is not a guarantee to parents that raising a child in God's way means he will return back again when he is old. I honestly don't believe this is the proper principle for us as parents. When we train our children according to "his way"—the child's way—we approach each child differently. We don't compare them one to another. Each child is uniquely made.

When I became a student of my two children, I began to design different approaches for each child. Jenny was not Brad, and Brad certainly wasn't Jenny. Each child has his or her own bent and is already established when God places them in our family. God has given you a unique child. Get to know him or her.

> *Father God, You know how much I want to know the bent of my children. Give me the godly wisdom to understand who they are and to be an encouragement to them. Help me to build them up to be all that You designed them to be. Amen.*

Thoughts for Action

❧ Write down in your journal the ways your children are different.

❧ Take into thought how you will train them based on these differences.

❧ Learn one new thing about each of your children today. Do something with that information.

❧ Praise your child today for being uniquely made.

Additional Scripture Reading

Psalm 139:13-16

□ □ □

Who's the Older Woman?

Scripture Reading: Titus 2:1-8

Key Verse: Titus 2:4

Then they can train the younger women to love their husbands and children.

When I was younger I wanted to cross Titus 2:4 out of the Bible. I thought, *I will never be an older woman!* Today I consider it a privilege to be an older woman. To have the opportunity to teach another woman is an honor. It doesn't matter how old we are; we will always be older to someone. I've overheard Chad at nine years old teaching his young brother Bevan to play a game, read a book, or count his money.

I've learned much from other women. My mother-in-law, Gertie Barnes, has been a beautiful example to me. I watched her love her husband, serve him with a soft spirit, nurse him during his last days, and never tire of the task even when her physical body was exhausted. I thank her today for raising such a fine son who has become my wonderful husband. Actually most of what I am today I learned from the older women in my life. It's now my joy to teach those very things to other women God puts before me.

I remember a young woman who came to speak with me after one of my seminar workshops. She said, "How do I treat my unsaved husband?" I looked into the beautiful young brown eyes, "Honey, you treat him as if he were saved." I then shared with her the great advice I heard at a luncheon when I was a younger bride. I'll never forget this advice and have used it all my married life: "Tell God the negative and tell your husband the positive." Ruth Graham Bell shared a real truth also. "Women," she said, "you will never change your husband. But God can." Yes, Almighty God can change husband, child, and most of all you.

It usually begins with me first. When I begin to change, the other person begins to change. We are the ones who set the thermostats of our homes. When our spirits are warm, loving, peaceful, and soft, others begin to take on the same feeling.

When my Bob would come home from a hot, busy, tiring summer day at the office, I wanted him to find peace and rest as he walked in the door. I worked hard to plan his first 30 minutes at home in the evening. I'd offer him a cold glass of tea or lemonade and allow him a few minutes to change into something comfy and cool. I'd keep the children somewhat settled until Dad could catch his breath and refocus.

Today's working woman can do the same if hubby arrives home before she does. Leave a soft note that says, "Your cold drink is waiting for you in the refrigerator and there are cookies in the jar."

I'm grateful that God has addressed the older woman, because we are the ones who will pass down much wisdom to future generations. I would not be writing books today had it not been for Florence Littauer who mentored me and encouraged me when I was younger to do something I never thought I could possibly do.

Father God, let me be an older woman to someone younger today. Oh, how I want to share the truths You have given me about marriage, children, friendship, church, and all the other areas of life. You are worthy of worship and I want to share that with others. Thank You! Amen.

Thoughts for Action

❧ Be an older woman to someone this week.

❧ Pray for your husband's needs.

❧ Tell your husband today one thing you love about him.

❧ Nurture a teachable spirit in you.

Additional Scripture Reading

Proverbs 31:26   1 Thessalonians 2:7-12

His Name Is Wonderful

Scripture Reading: Isaiah 9:6-7

Key Verse: Isaiah 9:6b

> *And he will be called Wonderful Counselor, Mighty God, Everlasting Father, Prince of Peace.*

His name is Wonderful, Jesus my Lord. His name is full of wonder, miracles, excitement, fulfillment, peace, and joy. There is something about that name! Our thoughts today must be positive—looking for the good and wonderfulness of the Lord. He is Almighty God who parted the Red Sea, raised Lazarus from the dead, and lives today in our hearts, wanting to be a miracle in our life.

As Isaiah wrote, "Of the increase of his government or peace there will be no end."

The peace of Jesus is in our hearts. God didn't promise joy, but He did say He would increase our peace.

To be sure, life will bring sorrow, broken hearts, health problems, financial difficulties, and much, much more. Our life in and with our Lord will bring dependence, maturity, refreshment, refuge, redemption, righteous judgment, and many rewards. Plus, He will restore your heart, mind, and soul.

Take your problems and worries of today, wrap them in a box, and close the lid very tightly. Then, my dear, put it into the wonderful hands of Jesus. Now walk away and don't take it back. Eighty percent of the things we worry about never happen anyway—so let Jesus take the remaining 20 percent. He will give back to you 100 percent of His life and peace. In fact, He has done it already for you as He hung on the cross of Calvary.

Let's sing His wonderful name: Jesus, Jesus, Jesus. There is just something about that name!

> *Father God, You have so many wonderful names. May I search out the Scripture and really get to know You by Your names. Each one has a special meaning and gives me deeper understanding to who You are. Reveal Your character to me today. Amen.*

Thoughts for Action

❦ In your journal, make a list of your worries today.

❦ Imagine putting them in a box—all of them.

❦ Now burn or throw the box away.

❦ Expect a miracle from our Wonderful God.

❦ List your blessings, naming them one by one.

❦ Use a page in your journal to write down all the various names of God as your read them in Scripture.

Additional Scripture Reading

Philippians 4:8   Psalm 23:6
Psalm 136:1

I'm Special Because

Scripture Reading: Psalm 139:13-17

Key Verse: Psalm 139:14

I praise you because I am fearfully and wonderfully made; your works are wonderful, I know that full well.

One evening our seven-year-old grandson, Chad, was helping me set the dinner table. Whenever the grandchildren come over, we have a tradition of honoring someone at the table with our red plate that says, "You Are Special Today" (even though it isn't a birthday, anniversary, or other special occasion). It was natural for me to ask Chad, "Who should we honor today with our special plate?" Chad said, "How about me?" "Yes, Chad, you are special," I replied. "It's your day."

He was so proud as we all sat around the table and said our blessing. Then Chad said, "I think it would be very nice if everyone around the table would tell me why they think I'm special." Bob and I got a chuckle out of that, but we thought it might be a good idea so we did it. After we were all through Chad said, "Now I want to tell you why I think I'm special. I'm special because I'm a child of God." Chad was so right on. Psalm 139:13-14 tells us that God knew us before we were born. He knit us together in our mother's womb and we are wonderfully made.

When I was seven, 10, or even 22, I could not have told anyone why I was special. I didn't even talk, I was so shy. My alcoholic father would go into a rage, swearing and throwing things. I was afraid I'd say the wrong thing, so I didn't talk. My self-image wasn't too good. But the day came when I read Psalm 139, and my heart came alive with the realization that I, too, am special because I am a child of God. And so are you. We were uniquely made as He knit us together in our mother's womb.

Verse 16 says, "All the days are ordained for me." It's not by accident you are reading this devotion today. Perhaps you, too, need to know how very special you are. We have all been given unique qualities, talents, and gifts. And you, my dear one, have been made by God. You are His child. He loves you more than any earthly father could possibly love you. Because He is your Heavenly Father Almighty God, He cares for you even when you don't care for yourself. You are His child even when you feel far from Him. It's never your Heavenly Father who moves away from you. It's you who moves away from Him.

Today is ordained by God for you to draw near to Him and allow Him to be near to you. Because today is your day, my friend, "You Are Special Today." A child of God, as Chad said.

> *Father God, thank You for making me so special, with a heart to love You more and more each day. Please today help me to draw near to You and to feel Your presence. Thank You for being my Heavenly Father. I know that I'm never alone. You are always with me. Amen.*

Thoughts for Action

❦ Tell someone why you are special today.

❦ Ask someone why he or she is special.

❦ Write a note in your journal to God and thank Him for who you are, His special child.

Additional Scripture Reading

Psalm 73:28   Ephesians 1:11
Ephesians 1:4   Proverbs 31:29

Children Are a Reward from God

Scripture Reading: Psalm 127:1-5

Key Verse: Psalm 127:3

Sons are a heritage from the Lord, children a reward from him.

———— ❧ ————

"Oh look, Daddy, I catched it!"

That's my boy. Now get ready; here comes another. Make me proud and catch this one too.

"Look, Daddy, I'm only eight years old and I can throw faster than anyone in the league!"

But your batting stinks, Tiger. Can't play in the big leagues if you can't hit.

"Look, Dad, I'm sixteen and already made the varsity team."

You better do a little less bragging and a little more practicing on your defense. Still need a lot of work.

"Look, Father, I'm thirty-five and the company has made me a vice president!"

Maybe someday you'll start your own business like your old man, then you'll really feel a sense of accomplishment.

"Look at me, Dad, I'm forty, successful, well-respected in the community. I have a wonderful wife and family—aren't you proud of me now, Dad?

"All my life it seems I've caught everything but that one prize I wanted most—your approval. Can't you say it, Dad? Is it too much to ask for? Just once I'd like to know that feeling every child should have of being loved unconditionally. I'd like for you to put your arm around my shoulders and, instead of telling me I'm not good enough, tell me that in your eyes I'm already a winner and always will be no matter what.

"Look at me, Daddy, I'm all grown up . . . but in my heart still lives a little boy who yearns for his father's love. Won't you pitch me the words I've waited for all my life?

"I'll catch them, Father, I promise."[10]

Our children are continually reaching out to see if Mom and Dad really love them. When are we going to learn to say, "I love you and I am very proud of you"? They long to hear those words, and they will continue to test us until they hear *and* believe those words from us.

- They yell and scream in the grocery store.

- They have temper tantrums in the restaurant.

- They wear strange clothes.

- They have funny haircuts in odd colors.

- They use vulgar language.

- They run away from home.

- They get bad grades in school.

- They run around with friends that you don't approve of.

In these unacceptable behaviors, they are indirectly asking, "Do you approve of me?" And they aren't hearing your response.

We had a good friend whose son was not into sports and athletics like his dad desired. He was into motorcross racing. The parents came to our pastor, and the dad asked the pastor what he should do. The pastor, not surprisingly, said, "Take up motorcrossing!" The dad predictably said, "I don't like . . .

- dirt
- grease
- motorcycles
- the crowd
- etc.!

The pastor replied, "How much do you love your son? Enough to get grease on your hands and clothes?" The next week Dad was off with his son to the local motorcross event. Soon after they were involved with dirt, grease, and different people. Through these actions Dad showed his son that he really loved him more than anything else, even if everything wasn't the way Dad would have liked.

We need to understand that our sons and daughters are a heritage from the Lord and that children are a reward from God. And we need to start living as though we believe it.

> *Father God, may You reveal to me today that my children are a reward from You. Sometimes I get so discouraged that I want to throw in the towel. I'm looking forward to some special encouragement from You today. Amen.*

Thoughts for Action

❦ Write your children a note letting them know how much you love them. Give a few specific traits you like about them. (Do it even if your children are young.)

❦ Make a point to spend quality one-on-one time with each of your children.

❦ Place a note on your calendar next month to do it again.

Additional Scripture Reading

Psalm 128:1-3   Genesis 33:5
Psalm 127:4-5

The Quiet Spirit

Scripture Reading: 1 Peter 3:1-9

Key Verse: 1 Peter 3:4

> *Instead, it should be that of your inner self, the unfading beauty of a gentle and quiet spirit, which is of great worth in God's sight.*

It's been a tough day. You were late getting off work, the children need picking up at day-care, you have no clue as to what to have for dinner, and the car needs gas. Stopping at the market to pick up some kind of food is a disaster—the check-out lines are long and the checkers are slow. Finally you get home, kick off the shoes from your aching feet, and throw the food on the stove, turning it up high to cook faster for starving and cranky children. The phone rings and the dog barks while the children cry for dinner. Are you supposed to have a quiet and gentle spirit? You probably don't even want one.

You know what I used to do on days like that? I would go into the bathroom, stick my head in the toilet, and cry to God, "If You only knew what it's like out there, You wouldn't let me be in this situation." Sometimes I would have to make two or three trips in and out of the bathroom until I could settle down enough to say, "Lord, help me!" I would then count to 10, take a deep breath, and attack.

You know how you can avoid days like this? By making a

plan for just those kind of days! Plan ahead by preparing make-ahead freezer meals, getting gas in the car before it reaches empty, and having on hand a quick, pre-dinner snack for the children—pretzels, popcorn, a few crackers and cheese, or a frozen smoothie.

It's not God who gives the confusion. It's our own mismanagement of time and organization.

The quiet spirit comes as we plan to eliminate the stress in our life. We must learn to slow down and refocus our goals and priorities.

There was a woman in my Bible study who had 10 children. Jeanette was worn out physically. She needed dental work and a good haircut. Her clothes didn't fit, and her shoes were worn over on the heels. Yet she came to the study every week by bus, and she was always prepared. She added great spiritual depth to the class. This busy, overworked mother had a beautiful inner spirit, and after our first study together, none of us saw the outside of Jeanette. We saw and felt her inner spirit, the gentle and quiet spirit that never complained or blamed God for a drug-dependent husband who wasn't working. She was absolutely beautiful. God honored her heart. Today Jeanette has victory in her life and so does her husband.

Thoughts for Action

❧ Praise God for a gentle and quiet spirit of a godly woman.

❧ Plan your meals for the week.

❧ Check the gas gauge.

❧ Think of several ways you can work toward a gentle and quiet spirit.

Additional Scripture Reading

Psalm 37:3-8   1 John 5:14-15

□ □ □

Offer Hospitality

Scripture Reading: 1 Peter 4:1-11

Key Verse: 1 Peter 4:9

Offer hospitality to one another without grumbling.

My mother, at 77, lived in a one-room efficiency apartment on the fifteenth floor of a senior citizen building. She continually shared hospitality with a cup of tea, a cookie, a piece of carrot cake or banana bread. Her guests always felt special sipping tea in a real china tea cup, eating cookies placed on a pretty plate with a paper doily, and enjoying a few flowers on the table with a lit candle.

Do you grumble at the thought of inviting guests into your home? Many of today's women seem to avoid hospitality due to the pressure of their busy lives.

It didn't take much for Mama to be hospitable. One cup of tea, one cookie. Hospitality is the act of caring for one another. We can entertain all we like, but not until we care does it become hospitality.

So many times we feel things have to be perfect—the right time, a clean house, the right food. Yet today's Scripture tells us to cheerfully share our homes. When was the last time you had guests over?

Our daughter Jenny has a hard-working dentist husband and a busy home to care for. Often, Dr. Craig will ask Jenny if the staff meeting or office party can be held at their home.

Jenny has every reason to grumble, yet she joyfully whips a buffet together, sometimes asking the guests to bring a dish—which they are happy to contribute. (By the way, Jenny gets a lot of great recipes from the potluck entertaining.)

Some people have a gift of serving others through hospitality, but I've found one thing to be true: Hospitality can be taught. Also, the more you entertain, the easier it becomes. Some of the best times in our home have been the simplest.

One very busy working mom discovered the way to fast, convenient hospitality. On her way home from work she picked up a bunch of flowers and frozen lasagna from the freezer department of the supermarket, which she threw in her own casserole dish. She tossed a prepared salad in her wooden bowl, bought a frozen cake for dessert, and lit a candle. Within moments she served a lovely dinner to guests who later helped clean up the kitchen, exclaiming, "This has been a delightfully delicious evening."

No one knew she didn't work hours preparing the meal. We can do whatever we want to do however we want to do it.

First Peter 4:11 says that if anyone serves he should do it with the strength God provides. God will provide the strength as we provide the desire. Jesus often fed people before He preached. Having friends in our home gives us the opportunity to let them see Jesus in us, to feel our spirits, to be touched by our love and caring. Many doors have been opened in the hearts of our friends when we've shared a meal together.

Father God, put a hunger in my heart to have people in my home. I want to learn to break bread with those around me, as Jesus did. You know I often don't feel confident in offering hospitality to others, but I ask You for courage to take a risk in this area of my life. Amen.

Thoughts for Action

❧ List those you can invite to your home.

❧ Call and invite someone on your list today.

❧ Don't panic—plan instead. Make it simple.

❧ Pray that God will use it as you serve Him through hospitality.

Additional Scripture Reading

Philippians 4:13   1 Timothy 5:9-10
Romans 12:13

Just as the
lovely flowers lend
their sweetness to
each day, may we
touch the lives
of those we meet
in a kind
and gentle way.

□ □ □

The Lord Is My Shepherd

Scripture Reading: Psalm 23:1-6

Key Verse: Psalm 23:4

> *Even though I walk through the valley of the shadow of death, I will fear no evil, for you are with me; your rod and your staff, they comfort me.*

It was a cool February evening in California. My 88-year-old Jewish Auntie's hospital room had its lights dimmed to gray. It had been a few days since I had seen her. We had had such a nice visit then. She was alert as we talked about family and how she missed Uncle Hy, who had passed away nine months earlier. Now she lay there so thin and frail. Her breathing was heavy and irregular.

As I sat by her bedside, holding her cool, clammy hand, I thought of the other times I had seen her in similar situations. Auntie had had surgery 25 years earlier, and because of complications, she almost died. A few years later she was a passenger in a car that rolled down a steep hill and hit a power pole. Her face had been smashed, her jaw and nose broken, and other complications set in. Again, she almost died. As life went on, illnesses came and went, but mostly came. The doctors had already told us three times in the past year that

Auntie wouldn't make it through the night. But she always did. Was this February night going to be any different? The doctor had been in to check on her and just shook his head. The rabbi arrived to look in for a visit with no response from Auntie. Would this be the night she would give up her fight for life?

On the other side of the curtain that was three-quarters drawn between us and the bed on the other half of the room there was a charming, late-middle-aged Jamaican woman who was almost blind and suffered from diabetes. She spoke eight languages and had a sweet sense of peace and joy about her in spite of her pain. We enjoyed talking with her and found out that she was a Christian believer who grew up learning to read from the Bible. Every night before she closed her eyes to sleep she would recite Psalm 23. On sleepless nights she would repeat it over and over again. As she talked, I felt our spirits meet, and she would tell me how Auntie's day had gone. In only a few hours with her I knew I loved that woman.

Bob and I were both tired as the clock read 11 P.M. that February night. We'd had a busy day in the office and had driven almost two hours through Los Angeles traffic to be with Auntie.

By now Auntie's breathing was very labored. I leaned over to pat her forehead and give her a last hug goodbye. My lips were by her ear when the Spirit of God began to speak from my lips, "The Lord is my Shepherd, I shall not want." Then the angel from "bed B" joined me: "He makes me lie down in green pastures." It was like the sound of a million voices surrounding the room. "Even though I walk through the valley of the shadow of death, I will fear no evil, for you are with me; your rod and your staff, they comfort me." That precious black woman and I dueted to the end of the psalm. "You prepare a table before me in the presence of my enemies. You anoint my head with oil; my cup overflows. Surely goodness and love will follow me all the days of my life, and I will dwell in the house of the Lord forever."

With a last kiss Bob and I walked out of the hospital room forever. Thirty minutes later Auntie died, with the words of the Twenty-third Psalm surrounding her room.

> *Father God, I do want to trust in You during all the various times of my life. Help me to realize in good health that You are my shepherd so that in bad times I can trust You to take care of me. You are such a wonderful guardian of all of my life. Amen.*

Thoughts for Action

- Memorize Psalm 23.

- Share it with a friend this week.

- Thank God for David, who wrote these beautiful words and truly knew the meaning of each verse.

- Call a friend who might need encouragement and tell her that you are thinking and praying for her today.

Additional Scripture Reading

Psalm 40:11   Revelation 7:17
Psalm 36:8

How Careless

Scripture Reading: Proverbs 16:16-28

Key Verse: Proverbs 16:18

> *Pride goes before destruction, a haughty spirit before a fall.*

Candi's dad gave her husband, Vinnie, a Rolex watch. But Vinnie had trouble wearing it because of the weight, size, and discomfort on his wrist. So during the day he would take it off and set it on his desk at work, planning to exchange the watch for something more to his liking as soon as he could. Would you believe that one day when he went to lunch the watch was stolen off his desk? Unfortunately, Vinnie was not able to claim insurance on it even close to its true value.

How mindless, Candi thought. *I can't believe he was so careless as to leave such an expensive watch laying around on his desk.* She was angry with him about the loss, thinking to herself, *I would never do anything like that.*

A few weeks later Candi was picking up her children at school. In a hurry and distracted by the errands, schedules, and church projects to be done, she mindlessly jumped out of her car, leaving the window down and her purse sitting on the front seat. After collecting her girls and jumping back into the car, away she went. She stopped at a drive-through window to buy a treat for the girls, and—you guessed it—her purse was gone, stolen out of her car in front of the school.

Angry and feeling frustrated with herself, she couldn't wait to get home and make the calls to credit card companies. She soon discovered the thief had already charged $500 worth of goods on her cards.

Candi began to realize how she had treated her husband so badly when she herself had done the same careless act. When Vinnie returned home, she didn't wait to apologize to him for her attitude—and she confessed her careless act as well.

What a great lesson for all of us—treating others as we want to be treated. That old motto has certainly proven to be true over our years, "What goes around comes around."

Thoughts for Action

❦ Does someone need an apology from you? If so, who? Do it today. Write a letter, make a phone call, whatever it takes.

❦ Take your time. It will avoid careless mistakes.

❦ Hug your husband today—just for a hug's sake.

❦ When someone makes a mistake, think of how you would like to be treated should you be in their shoes. Keep this in mind.

❦ Write love notes using a heart (♡) where the "o" in "love" goes.

Additional Scripture Reading

1 John 1:9   Psalm 51:10
1 Peter 5:6-7

A Heritage from the Lord

Scripture Reading: Psalm 127:1–128:4

Key Verse: Psalm 127:3

> *Sons are a heritage from the Lord, children a reward from him.*

———— ❧ ————

In a recent Bible study that I was in, the teacher asked us, "Did you feel loved by your parents when you were a child?" Many remarked:

- "They were too busy for me."
- "I spent too much time with the babysitters."
- "Dad took us on trips, but he played golf all the time we were away."
- "I got in their way. I wasn't important to them."
- "Mom was too involved at the country club to spend time with us."
- "Mom didn't have to work, but she did just so she wouldn't have to be home with us children."
- "A lot of pizzas came to our house on Friday nights when my parents went out for the evening."

I was amazed at how many grown women expressed ways they *didn't* feel loved in their homes growing up. What would your children's answers be if someone asked them the same question?

Today's Scripture reading gives an overview of what it takes to make and develop a close-knit and healthy family. We first look at the foundation of the home in verse 1: "Unless the Lord builds the house, its builders labor in vain. Unless the Lord watches over the city, the watchmen stand guard in vain."

The protective wall surrounding a city was the very first thing to be constructed when a new city was built. The men of the Old Testament knew they needed protection from the enemy, but they were also smart enough to know that walls could be climbed over, knocked down, or broken apart. Ultimately, the people knew that their real security was the Lord guarding the city.

Today we must return to that trust in the Lord, if we are going to be able to withstand the destruction of our "walls"—the family. As I drive the Southern California freeways, I see parents who are burning the candle at both ends to provide for all the material things they think will make their families happy. We rise early and retire late. In Psalm 127:2 we find this is futile. Our trust must be that the Lord has His hand over our families. The business of our hands are only futile efforts to satisfy those we love.

In verse 3 we see that, "Children are a reward [gift] from the Lord." In the Hebrew, "gift" means "property," "a possession." Truly, God has loaned us His property or possessions to care for and to enjoy for a certain period of time.

My Bob loves to grow vegetables in his "raised-bed" garden each summer. I am amazed at what it takes to get a good crop. He cultivates the soil, sows seeds, waters, fertilizes, weeds, and prunes. Raising children takes a lot of time, care, nurturing, and cultivating as well. We can't neglect these responsibilities if we are going to produce good fruit. Left to itself, the garden—and our children—will grow into weeds.

Bob always has a big smile on his face when he brings a big basket full of corn, tomatoes, cucumbers, and beans into the kitchen. As the harvest is Bob's reward, so children are parents' reward.

As we move on to Psalm 127:4-5, we see a picture of how to handle our children. They are compared to arrows in the hands of a warrior. Skill in handling an arrow is vital. Wise parents will know their children, understand them, examine them before they shoot them into the world. When I was in high school, I took an archery class and I soon learned that I wasn't Robin Hood. I found archery much more difficult than basketball, and it was more dangerous if not done properly. Shooting a straight arrow and hitting a target was a lot harder in real life than what I saw at the movies or on TV. Proper parenting takes a lot of skill. It's not a one-shot experience.

In our last section of this passage, Psalm 128:1-3, we dwell upon the importance of the Lord's presence in the home.

- The Lord is central to a home's happiness (verse 2).
- Through the Lord, wives will be a source of beauty and life to the home (verse 3a).
- Through the Lord, children will flourish like olive trees, which generously provide food, oil, and shelter for others (verse 3b).

Let your home reflect a place where its members come to be rejuvenated after a very busy time away from it. Say "no" when you are tempted to just become a harried taxi driver, delivering the family from one activity to the next. God has a better plan. He wants you to walk in His ways.

Father God, slow me down so I can spend
valuable time with my family. Help me to realize that

our children will only be with us for such a short time, and that what I do to and with them will affect their children's lives too. What an awesome responsibility! I can't wait to be with them today. Amen.

Thoughts for Action

❧ Reflect upon this statement: "Our attitude toward our children reveals our attitude toward God."

❧ Stop and take time to listen to your children, eye-to-eye.

❧ Be consistent in your training on what's right and what's wrong.

❧ Give your child a beautiful gift today—TIME!

Additional Scripture Reading

James 1:19-20   Proverbs 18:10
Matthew 18:5-6   Proverbs 16:24

A Wisdom Only God Can Provide

Scripture Reading: Proverbs 3:11-12; 13:24; 15:13; 17:22; 22:15; 29:15

Key Verse: Proverbs 15:13

> A happy heart makes the face cheerful, but heart-ache crushes the spirit.

With all the media attention given to child abuse, we as Christian parents become confused regarding the area of discipline. The book of Proverbs, fortunately, contains some specific verses which offer good biblical principles for raising our children.

We often feel we are in a tug-of-war between child and parent. The natural tendency is to throw in the towel and give up. Far too often we have seen parents who have given up this task to gently yet firmly shape their child's will, as would a trainer of a wild animal or as the potter would a piece of clay. Dr. James Dobson, in his book *The Strong-Willed Child*, gives some insight into this area:

> It is obvious that children are aware of the contest of wills between generations, and that is precisely why the parental response is so important. When a child behaves in ways that are

disrespectful or harmful to himself or others, his hidden purpose is often to verify the stability of the boundaries. This testing has much the same function as a policeman who turns doorknobs at places of business after dark. Though he tries to open doors, he hopes they are locked and secure. Likewise, a child who assaults the loving authority of his parents is greatly reassured when their leadership holds firm and confident. He finds his greatest security in a structured environment where the rights of other people (and his own) are protected by definite boundaries. [11]

It takes a special kind of person with godly wisdom to provide this kind of balance. How do we accomplish this? First, we must note there is a difference between *abuse* and *discipline*. Proverbs 13:24 tells us that if we truly love our children, we'll discipline them diligently. Abuse is unfair, extreme, and degrading. This action doesn't grow out of love, but from hate. Abuse leads to a soiled self-image that will often last a lifetime. Discipline, on the other hand, upholds the child's worth and is fair and fitting for the infraction.

Second, we must be sure the child understands the discipline he is to receive. When we disciplined Jenny and Brad, we spent a lot of time with them discussing what they did and making sure they understood what the infraction was. We realize that every child is different, so the way you approach them will be through your knowledge of that child. In our day, we didn't have "Time Out." However, we've found this to be a very good technique, and we use it with our grandchildren very effectively. There are times, though, when a sterner approach is necessary, and on occasions we did give spankings. They were firmly applied to the beefy part of the buttocks, and they did hurt.

In reality, this was very rarely done and never in anger—always in stern, tough love. After each such encounter we met with the child, reviewed why he was disciplined, and talked about how his actions might be altered in the future. One of our main purposes was to have the child remember that he is responsible for his actions and must be accountable for his behavior. After every time we disciplined our children, we ended in prayer and warm hugs and assuring words. This form of correction strengthens the child's self-image. It builds his spirits up when he knows his boundaries. Our love and concern for both our kids and their well-being created stronger motivation for them to behave according to our family's conduct and behavior standards.

Third, we want to shape and not crush our children's spirit. You can look into the eyes of children around you to see those who are being crushed and those being shaped.

> A happy heart makes the face [eyes] cheerful, but heartache crushes the spirit (Proverbs 15:13).

Our goal as a parent is to build up our children with solid direction and self-assurance that will see them throughout life. The child that is shaped will have a love for life, but a crushed spirit produces a child with no hope for the future.

Fourth, we must always keep balance in our lives. We don't want to be so rigid that we don't allow members in our family to make mistakes, or so loose that family members are bouncing off the walls trying to find their boundaries. Children must know where the boundaries are and what the consequences are if they choose to go beyond these limits.

In Scripture we read about physical discipline, such as using the rod. Naturally, none of us wants to risk being an abusive parent.

> Folly is bound up in the heart of a child; but the rod of discipline will drive it far from him (Proverbs 22:15).

Dr. Dobson underscores the importance of a child being able to associate wrongdoing with pain:

> If your child has ever bumped his arm against a hot stove, you can bet he'll never deliberately do that again. He does not become a more violent person because the stove burnt him; in fact, he learned a valuable lesson from the pain. Similarly, when he falls out of his high chair or smashes his finger in the door or is bitten by a grumpy dog, he learns about physical dangers in his world. These bumps and bruises throughout childhood are nature's way of teaching him what to fear. They do not damage his self-esteem. They do not make him vicious. They merely acquaint him with reality. In like manner, an appropriate spanking from a loving parent provides the same service. It tells him there are not only physical dangers to be avoided but he must steer clear of some social traps as well (selfishness, defiance, dishonesty, unprovoked aggression, etc.)[12]

Fifth, be consistent in your approach to guiding and directing your children. Several of these have already been discussed:

- Make sure there is a clear understanding of the rules.
- Discipline in private. If you're in a public setting, wait until you can be alone.
- Review the infraction and its consequences.
- Be firm in your discipline.
- Assure your child of your love and concern.

- Hold your child firmly after each discipline.

- End your session with a time of prayer. (Give your child an opportunity to pray too.)

As Bob and I look back over those training years, we made plenty of mistakes. But when we did, we were the first to admit them to our children. Even when you miss the mark occasionally, you still are moving in a proper direction. If you don't have a goal or direction in this area of your life, you will miss the mark totally. Be encouraged. Your children want to know their boundaries. There is self-assurance in knowing.

Thoughts for Action

❦ Do you have a clear direction in your life regarding your children's discipline? If not, spend some time today thinking about it and possibly write down some of your ideas in your journal.

❦ If you are married, you may want to review these ideas with your mate.

❦ Tell each member in your family today that you love them, and state why you do.

Additional Scripture Reading

Mark 12:28-31   1 Peter 5:5-6
Galatians 5:16   Colossians 3:17

❑ ❑ ❑

Choose to Be Thankful

Scripture Reading: Ephesians 5:15-20

Key Verse: Ephesians 5:20
> *. . . always giving thanks to God the Father for everything, in the name of our Lord Jesus Christ.*

I love to travel. In our ministry, I get the great opportunity to travel to various regions in America and Canada. While in the south and midwest, I love to have the children come up and address me, "Mrs. Emilie" and to offer a polite gesture of "thank you." It not only tells me a lot regarding the child and that region of our country, but also the teaching that the parent has given to that child.

I would do almost anything for a person who has **proper** manners and a thankful heart. And if I'm that way as a **human** being, how much more God must be overjoyed when one of His children responds with a thankful heart. There are two kinds of people in the world: the givers and the takers. It seems like today there are more takers than ever before. We drastically need people with thankful hearts.

In Galatians 5:22 we read a list of Christian characteristics that are universally known as the "fruit of the Spirit." They are: love, joy, peace, patience, kindness, goodness, faithfulness, gentleness, and self-control. Being thankful is not on this list. Evidently to be thankful comes about by choice. We *choose* to be thankful. Have you made that choice today?

We're encouraged to be "always giving thanks to God ... for everything" (Ephesians 5:20). That means everything from the littlest to the biggest. I have made thanksgiving a part of my lifestyle. In the morning upon waking, I thank God for another day, good health, and purpose for life. In the evening upon retiring, I thank God for watching over me, giving me a meaningful day, and providing safety, food, and shelter. The psalmist expresses it like this, "To proclaim your love in the morning and your faithfulness at night" (Psalm 92:2).

An example of a lady who understands the true meaning of having a thankful heart is reflected in this short excerpt:

> The room is clean, even airy; a bright little fire burns in the grate; and in a four-post bed you will see sitting up a woman of sixty-four years of age, with her hands folded and contracted, and her whole body crippled and curled together as the disease cramped it, and rheumatism has fixed it for eight and twenty years. For sixteen of these years, she has not moved from her bed, or looked out of the window, or even lifted her hand to her own face; and also is in constant pain, while she cannot move a limb. But listen! She is so thankful that God has left her that great blessing, the use of one thumb! Her left hand is clinched and stiff, and utterly useless; but she has a two-pronged fork fastened to a stick, with which she can take off her great old-fashioned spectacles, and put them on again, with amazing effort. By the same means, she can feed herself; and she can sip her tea through a tube, helping herself with this one thumb. And there is another thing she can accomplish with her fork; she can turn over the leaves of a large Bible when placed within her reach. A recent visitor addressed her with the remark, that she was all

alone. "Yes," she replied in a peculiarly sweet and cheerful voice, "I am alone, and yet not alone."—"How is that?"—"I feel that the Lord is constantly with me."—"How long have you lain here?"—"For sixteen years and four months; and for two years and four months I have not been lifted out of my bed to have it made: yet I have much to praise and bless the Lord for."—"What is the source of your happiness?"—"The thought that my sins are forgiven, and dwelling on the great love of Jesus my Savior. I am content to lie here so long as it shall please him that I should stay, and to go whenever he shall call me."

Here is a truly divine example of a woman with a thankful heart.

Start today if you aren't already—be thankful.

Father God, bring to my mind all that I need to be thankful for. I sometimes get so hurried and hassled that I don't still my heart and know that You are God. At this moment I say thank You, thank You. Amen.

Thoughts for Action

❧ Jot down in your journal 10 things for which you are thankful.

❧ Call someone today who means a lot to you and tell her how thankful you are for her friendship.

❧ Write a note of thanks to someone today: a friend, a family member, a pastor, an instructor.

❧ Tell God tonight before you go to bed how thankful you are for Him.

Additional Scripture Reading

Hebrews 13:15   1 Thessalonians 5:16-18
Colossians 3:17

*Our life is
like a garden,
and with God's
loving care
it blossoms
with the flowers
of His blessings
everywhere.*

Stop and Come

Scripture Reading: Genesis 22:1-18

Key Verse: Genesis 22:8
> *Abraham answered, "God himself will provide the lamb for the burnt offering, my son." And the two of them went on together.*

There were two words we were firm about teaching our children when they were growing up: "Stop" and "Come." If you think about it, you probably use these words often with your own children. Children who learn them will be obedient people. I can honestly say the one thing our children learned was obedience. It has and is paying off, even in their adult lives.

Abraham is a beautiful example of obedience to his Father God. God tested Abraham to the limit of obedience. God called his name, "Abraham." Abraham *stopped* and replied, "Here I am, Lord." Then God instructed Abraham to take his only son to Moriah. There Abraham was to sacrifice Isaac as a burnt offering on one of the mountains. I wonder what Abraham thought. He loved Isaac so much. Isaac was the son of Sarah, who had prayed for many years for a child. Sarah had been in her nineties when she gave birth. Isaac was a miracle child, so wanted and so loved. Abraham knew God intimately. He had experienced the mighty power of God when He gave them Isaac in their later years. Now God was telling Abraham to sacrifice Isaac.

Early in the morning after God spoke to Abraham, Abraham took Isaac, saddled up his donkey, and along with two servants headed up to the mountain in Moriah. After cutting enough wood for the burnt offering, they set out as God had told him. "On the third day Abraham looked up and saw the place in the distance. He said to his servants, 'Stay here with the donkey while I and the boy go over there. We will worship and then *we* will come back to you'" (Genesis 22:5, emphasis added).

"*We* will worship. *We* will come back." Abraham believed God. He trusted God, and he kept moving ahead in obedience to God. I'm sure the servants and Isaac were puzzled. Where was the sacrifice? The servants didn't ask. Isaac didn't ask.

"Abraham took the wood for the burnt offering and placed it on his son Isaac, and he himself carried the fire and the knife" (verse 6). Isaac obviously wasn't a small child—he was big enough to carry heavy wood up a mountain. So I would guess he was probably pre or early teens.

As father and son walked up the mountain, they probably talked together. "Isaac spoke up and said to his father Abraham, 'Father?' 'Yes my son,' Abraham replied. 'The fire and the wood are here,' Isaac said, 'but where is the lamb for the burnt offering?'" (verse 7). I'm sure Isaac was a bit puzzled. *We have everything but the lamb,* he may have thought. *Where will we ever find a lamb up here in the wilderness?*

I love Abraham's reply: "God himself will provide the lamb for the burnt offering, my son" (verse 8). And the two of them went on together. When they reached the place God had told Abraham about, he went to work, removing the wood from Isaac's back. He built an altar for worship and then arranged the wood on top. This was the ultimate of worshiping God—an altar built by hand and an offering of obedience.

Then Abraham said, "Come," to Isaac, and he placed him on top of the wood and bound him on the altar. Isaac was also obedient. He must have learned this from Abraham. Isaac came to his own father who he loved and trusted—his father who loved and trusted Father God. While the Bible doesn't say anything about Isaac's words or thoughts, I'm sure he was very frightened. But perhaps he knew, too, that God would provide. Maybe Isaac was willing to die for God. I don't know, but there was Isaac—bound on top of the wood he had carried himself.

Abraham had the knife. Everything was prepared and ready. "Then [Abraham] reached out his hand and took the knife to slay his son" (verse 10). When an animal is sacrificed as an offering to God, it is bound on the altar of wood and the knife is plunged into the throat and sliced down the middle through the stomach. Abraham's arm was lifted up, ready to plunge the knife into his only son's throat when "the angel of the LORD called out to him from heaven 'Abraham! Abraham!'" (verse 11). Abraham *stopped*. "'Do not lay a hand on the boy,' he said. 'Do not do anything to him. Now I know that you fear God, because you have not withheld from me your son, your only son. Abraham looked up and there in a thicket he saw a ram caught by its horns. He went and took the ram and sacrificed it as a burnt offering instead of his son" (verses 12-13). I'm sure Isaac must have thought, *That was a close call, Dad.*

Abraham named that place on top of the mountain "The Lord Will Provide." There was no doubt in Abraham's heart that God would provide. Can you imagine what the two servants must have thought when they saw Abraham and Isaac come back with no wood and a blood-stained knife? But then Abraham did say, "*We* will return." They did worship, and they did return. I know my worship today is stronger because of this passage. I'm sure Abraham and Isaac's was as well.

Isaac showed obedience when his father said, "*Come* with me to worship," and "*Come* get on the pile of wood." Abraham showed obedience, and he experienced in a truly deep and unique way that the Lord will provide. When the angel called his name, Abraham stopped to listen.

Perhaps our cup needs to be filled with an obedience like Abraham's. We say we trust God, but then we take matters into our own hands and try to move ahead in our own power, not allowing the Lord to provide. We miss seeing and experiencing the miracle hand of God.

What are you asking God to provide for you today? Job, children, husband, finances? Are you willing to trust Him and know He will provide? How obedient are we to God's call? Come! Come to His altar and lay the pain of your heart there. Stop and worship. And as you walk away from your worship with God, you will know with hope and trust that God says, "I will provide."

Thoughts for Action

❧ Make a worship center in your home—a chair where you pray, a corner of a room, a closet, a bathroom, under a tree, by the creek, at the kitchen table.

❧ Come and worship.

❧ Stop and listen.

❧ Trust God.

❧ Obey His Word.

Additional Scripture Reading

Galatians 4:28   Romans 9:7
Hebrews 11:17-19

How to Preserve a Husband

Scripture Reading: Titus 2:3-5

Key Verse: Titus 2:4

Then they can train the younger women to love their husbands and children.

The home, and more specifically the kitchen, is a great setting for what happens in a family. In this "laboratory" you and I have excellent opportunities for loving our husbands and children. In Scripture we see that many events occur around a meal and much is written about the preparation of food. Jesus must have known that people are more willing to listen when one of their basic needs is met, that of food.

Unfortunately, we have sold out to the idea of "fast foods." It's time to get back to the wonderful smells of the home. We can accomplish much when we love our family through our time and efforts at home.

Many years ago the Ball Jar Company issued a serving tray with the following words of wisdom:

How to Preserve a Husband

Be careful in your selection. Do not choose too young. When selected, give your entire thoughts to preparation for domestic use. Some wives insist upon keeping them in a pickle, others are constantly getting them into hot water. This may make them sour, hard, and sometimes bitter. Even poor varieties may be made sweet, tender, and good by garnishing them with patience, well sweetened with love and seasoned with kisses. Wrap them in a mantle of charity. Keep warm with a steady fire of domestic devotion and serve with peaches and cream. Thus prepared, they will keep for years.

Yes, this writer not only knew how to select and prepare good fruit and vegetables, but she also was wise enough to know how to preserve that husband. Oh, if we too could learn to manage our homes so beautifully.

Thoughts for Action

❧ Prepare a new recipe for dinner. Set the table with your finest dishes, light a candle, and dim the lights. Spruce yourself up with a dress, run a brush through your hair, dash on a little perfume, and freshen your makeup. Invite the children to go along with the evening and have them come to the table with their best manners.

❧ Write out in your journal a contract binding you to several actions that will make you a better wife and mother. Be sure to sign it.

❧ Buy one new cookbook that has recipes to fit your family's palate. Plan at least one new recipe each week. If it's good, use it again in the near future.

Additional Scripture Reading

1 Timothy 2:9-15   Proverbs 27:15-16
1 Timothy 3:11

A Treasure in Jars of Clay

Scripture Reading: 2 Corinthians 4:7; 6:3-10

Key Verse: 2 Corinthians 4:7
But we have this treasure in jars of clay to show that this all-surpassing power is from God and not from us.

When our son, Brad, was in high school he really enjoyed taking courses in ceramics. Even though I am his mother, I can say he was very good. In fact, many of his prized vases, jars, and pots still adorn our home. Brad loved working in clay. When I looked at a lump of reddish tan clay, I was always amazed that Brad was able to make a beautiful vessel out of it. When he added color and a glaze, it became a masterpiece.

In today's Scripture we read that we are "jars of clay." We have a great treasure in us, and this all-surpassing power is from God and not from us.

We live in a world that tells us that if we are righteous enough we can become little gods. However, our reading says that we (Christians) are jars of clay with this great treasure (Jesus Christ) in us. I can go to any nursery in our area and purchase an inexpensive clay pot. They're not of much value. On the other hand my dictionary defines "treasure" as wealth or riches, valuable things. Isn't it amazing we hide our treasures in vaults or safe deposit boxes, but God trusts His treasure in a common clay pot? The only value our clay pot has is in the treasure inside.

I am continually amazed how God can use me, just an ordinary person who is willing to be used for Christ's sake. Basic Christianity is simply stated as Jesus Christ, the treasure, in a clay pot, the Christian. If that is true, and I believe it to be true, then I want to share that valuable treasure inside of me with others.

We need to show others that this all-surpassing power is from God and not from us. Philippians 4:13 states, "I can do everything through him who gives me strength." Can you trust God today to believe that you, a clay pot with a great treasure inside, can do all things because Christ Jesus has given you the strength and power to do it? If we, as women, could believe this promise, we would change ourselves, our families, our churches, our cities, our country, and the world. Trust God today for this belief.

Thoughts for Action

❧ Jot down in your journal three very large problems facing you. Beside each one state what needs to be done to solve the problem; also write down the date when you want the problem solved.

❧ Pray specifically for the answer to these problems, remembering the treasure, the strength, living within each of us.

❧ Give God, in prayer or public testimony, the credit for these answers.

Additional Scripture Reading

Matthew 10:28,39   John 17:20

Asking the Right Questions

Scripture Reading: Romans 8:28-39

Key Verse: Romans 8:28

> *And we know that in all things God works for the good of those who love him, who have been called according to his purpose.*

In doing radio and TV interviews across America and Canada, I have an opportunity to answer a lot of questions. In my earlier days of ministry, I would just immediately answer the interviewer's questions, assuming I knew exactly what he or she meant. In many cases, I answered the wrong question. Bob would very gently instruct me by saying, "Emilie, you need to ask one more question *before* you answer the question." I started to do that. I know now I'm better able to answer the proper question, and I find my interviews go much more smoothly. There is also definitely clearer communication with my audience.

In our passage for today, Paul asks some very strong questions that need to be answered from the proper perspective. It is one thing to ask a good question, but getting the right answer is extremely important.

Let's take a look at the questions and the answers that were mentioned in today's reading.

1. "What, then, shall we say in response to this?" (verse 29).

Answer: In today's passage Paul writes one of the great promises in the New Testament: "And we know that in all things God works for the good of those who love him, who have been called according to his purpose" (verse 28).

- God foreknew us.
- God predestined us to be conformed to the likeness of His son.
- God called us.
- God justified us.
- God glorified us.

What, then, shall we say in response to this? I'm overwhelmed that we have such a marvelous God, one who would do all this for me.

2. "If God is for us, who can be against us?" (verse 31).

Answer: If I know God, nothing, absolutely nothing, can be taken from me that has any value. We have everything in God through His son Jesus.

3. "He who did not spare his own Son, but gave him up for us all—how will he not also, along with him, graciously give us all things?" (verse 32).

Answer: The blessed answer is that He will graciously give us all things according to His will for our lives. What an assurance to know that what we have has been screened by our heavenly Father.

4. "Who will bring charges against those whom God has chosen?" (verse 33).

Answer: No one—absolutely no one.

5. "Who is he that condemns?" (verse 34).

Answer: No one. Jesus Christ is at the right hand of God and is also interceding for us.

6. "Who shall separate us from the love of Christ?" (verse 35).

Answer: No one.

- Neither death nor life
- Neither angels nor demons
- Neither the present nor the future
- Neither height nor depth
- Nor powers
- Nor anything else in all creation

Nothing will be able to separate us from the love of God that is in Christ Jesus our Lord. We can be assured that our questions will be properly answered in Scripture. Try not to rely on the answers of the world, but go to Scripture to get the best answers. And be assured that all things work for our good if we are called according to His purpose.

Thoughts for Action

❧ In your journal jot down an answer from today's study that you never knew before.

❧ In your journal jot down a question that has been rolling around in your head. Go to Scripture and see if you can't find a biblical answer. Talk with a pastor, a Bible study leader, or another mature Christian you respect.

Additional Scripture Reading

2 Timothy 3:16   1 John 1:5–2:2
Colossians 2:9

Your Family in Christ

Scripture Reading: Ephesians 3:14-21

Key Verse: Ephesians 3:17-19

> *And I pray that you, being rooted and established in love, may have power, together with all the saints, to grasp how wide and long and high and deep is the love of Christ, and to know this love that surpasses knowledge—that you may be filled to the measure of all the fullness of God.*

An old European story tells of a traveler in Germany who saw a peculiar sight in a tavern where he had stopped for dinner. After the meal, the tavern owner put a great bowl of soup on the floor and gave a loud whistle. A big dog, a large cat, an old raven, and a very large rat came into the room. They all four went to the dish and, without disturbing each other, ate together. After they had dined, the dog, cat, and rat lay before the fire, while Mr. Raven, in his black coat, hopped around the room. The tavern owner had trained these animals so that not one of them bothered to hurt any of the others. He thought that if a dog, a rat, a cat, and a bird can live happily together, little children, especially brothers and sisters, ought to be able to do the same.

Yes, you would think that harmony could be established in our families, but somehow it escapes us.

In today's passage we find that through Paul's prayer we can learn some basic principles for praying for our own family.

—————— ❦ ——————

1. *Pray that your family may be rooted and established in love.* Oh, how we need families that really love each other. We see so much evil that originates from the family. Ask God to protect your family from evil and put a big hedge of protection around each member. Continually be on guard for the wolf that tries to enter in and devour members of your family.

2. *Pray that you may have power to grasp how wide and long and high and deep is the love of Christ.* Today there is a lack of commitment, a lack of trust, a lack of love in relationships. Pray that your family may begin to grasp the vastness in Christ's love for them individually and collectively.

3. *Pray that your family may know this love that surpasses knowledge.* We cannot comprehend this love that gives beyond our knowledge. But with a great leap of faith, we believe and live the gospel message first within our own life and then share with our family members this love. There are two things to do with the gospel: one, we believe it; two, we live it.

4. *Pray that you will be filled in measure of all the fullness of God.* Each day that I'm in God's Word, I better understand what the fullness of God is all about. After many years of life, I better understand being filled in measure of God's fullness. And being in His family is so much a part of that fullness. Proverbs 24:3-4 states, "By wisdom a house is built, and through understanding it is established; through knowledge its rooms are filled with rare and beautiful treasures."

I will pray for you and your family, that you may grasp these principles and that your rooms will be filled with rare and beautiful treasures.

Father God, You know that sometimes we have tensions in our family and we're not as united as we should be. I earnestly pray that we are rooted and established in love, and that we might realize how

*wide, how long, how high, and how deep Your love is
for us. Grant me this supplication for my family.
Amen.*

Thoughts for Action

❦ Go to each member of your family today and tell them that
you love them.

❦ Write or phone a friend who lives out of town and express
your love for her.

❦ Do an act out of love for someone today, one that expects
no return or personal gain.

Additional Scripture Reading

Ephesians 4:29   James 2:15-17

What a Father!

Scripture Reading: Matthew 7:7-12

Key Verse: Matthew 7:11

If you, then, though you are evil, know how to give good gifts to your children, how much more will your Father in heaven give good gifts to those who ask him!

Last year I had some extra time at the Dallas Fort Worth Airport waiting for a connecting flight to California, so I decided to purchase a Sunday morning newspaper. While looking through the classified section, I came upon a tribute to a father from a bereaved daughter. As I read this, I commented to myself, "What a Father!"

This is an open letter to my father which I desire to share with those of you who did not have the privilege of knowing him. J.T. Yates was a war hero of the European Campaign fighting in the Battle of the Bulge. He landed in France on D Day and fought his way across Europe not only as a medic but also as a combat soldier putting his life in jeopardy constantly while trying to save others. He was a man of his own will and lived his life according to his own beliefs and convictions.

But he was also a hero to me as only a daughter can know and love a father. He was my teacher, whether it be from learning how to survive in the wilderness, to catching a fish, planting a garden, writing a school drama, making science projects or caring for animals. Unknowingly he strengthened my admiration and appreciation of him. He was my place of safety whenever he held me and cradled me in his big strong arms. Daddy always tried to give me joy. We made every circus that came to town, walked in every parade, rode in every rodeo, played ball in the park or took many walks through the zoo. Even at home, he would play games with me, tell me stories, or camp out in the yard. Every year at Christmas, Santa would come to our house and sit me on his knee yet not one time did I ever suspect that was my dad. They tried to tell me one time that Santa Claus was make-believe but I knew better. I was fortunate to live with him every day for many years. Daddy always let me shine and have all the glory while he stood behind in the shadows. That was his way.

The world may not have considered him a religious man, but he did believe in God. If he couldn't go to church with me, he always provided me a way. Daddy respected men of the clergy and on Sunday afternoons there was always plenty of food for any of God's people that would visit. His love for children was unsurpassed by no one and there were lots of wiener roasts and entertainment for all youth. That foundation stayed with me and carried me through the next forty years of my life.

Daddy was a man of strong convictions. He never turned his head and pretended not to see. He would stand up to any man, stand up for any woman, stand with any child and stand behind his beliefs. Daddy was always there when I needed him and his love was always enough.

If he could, he would have spared me pain, cried my tears to protect all sadness from my eyes. If he could, he would have walked with me everywhere I went to make sure I never chose a wrong turn that might bring me harm or defeat. If he could, he would have shielded my innocence from time, but the time he gave me really wasn't his. He could only watch me grow so he could love me for who I was. But Daddy was a wise man. He knew love couldn't be captured or protected. So he let me take my chances, he gave me my freedom, he let me fight my own battles. I made mistakes but he was always patient.

He was the most generous and giving man of his own self I have ever known and I hope the legacy he left me will be passed to multitudes of generations.

Thank you, Daddy, for all the times and all the nurturing you have given me. The memories will always be in my mind. Now that there will be no more rainbows for us, I will have to let you go, Daddy, but I will always love you. Your daughter. Paula Yates Sugg[13]

This dad certainly reflected great qualities of character, ones that we all could model for our own lives. Yet by looking at our verses for today, we see that our heavenly Father will far exceed the goodness of our earthly fathers! Unfortunately, many of us may not have had a pleasant experience with our earthly fathers. In some cases, this has prevented us from being able to trust an unseen heavenly Father.

We certainly have the opportunity to experience the abundance of God if we are willing to ask Him. Your Father in heaven is waiting to give you good gifts if you will ask Him.

Today would be a great time to begin trusting your heavenly Father for all your needs. Go to Him in prayer with thanksgiving, adoration, confession, and petition. He is able to meet you where you are.

Father God, I lift up my father and my husband to You. Please give them the courage to be the men that You want them to be. May their love abound in our family. Amen.

Thoughts for Action

❦ Write your earthly father a letter expressing your love for him. Don't wait until it is too late.

❦ If your father has passed away, still write that letter in your journal so you can express to him what you have always kept inside.

❦ If your experience with your earthly father wasn't good and you can't write that letter of love, you still might write a letter of hurt and share it with your heavenly Father. Ask Him for the strength to support you while raising your children. Let the pain of the past generation stop in your generation.

❦ If you haven't had a heavenly Father before, open your heart to Jesus today. Know that you have a loving father who wants to give all things to you.

Additional Scripture Reading

John 3:16   Romans 5:8
John 14:6   John 1:12

The way
each tiny flower
reaches up to heaven
with trust,
we, too, should lift
our hearts to God
and know He cares
for us.

□ □ □

Behavior at the Table

Scripture Reading: Deuteronomy 6:1-9

Key Verse: Deuteronomy 6:6-7

> *These commandments that I give you today are to be upon your hearts. Impress them on your children. Talk about them when you sit at home and when you walk along the road, when you lie down and when you get up.*

Raising children with manners seems to be a lost art. The drive-through window at our favorite fast-food restaurant has dramatically affected how our children eat their food. I see a lot of kids using their fingers in the back of a mini-van, licking their hands when the sauce leaks from the fat of the hamburger. They are usually five minutes late to some activity, somewhere.

Whatever happened to sitting down to the dinner table as a family? To evenings with healthy, nutritious foods, with the TV off and with the conversation centering on what happened during the day in each of our lives. Does this sound foreign to your family? Are you saying, "Please, get real. We are living in the '90s. It's not like it use to be"?

Well, if you stand amazed at what I've said, can you imagine how startled the early Shaker settlers would be if they visited in our homes for an evening? While in Ohio doing a seminar last year, I was privileged to visit one of the restorations of an early Shaker village. In the bookstore I saw an early set of rules framed as a picture that gave advice to children on behavior at the table.

As I read this, I was convicted by how far we have deviated from our early beginnings. May we somehow become challenged to reknow the zeal of the training of our children. In our Scripture passage for today, we see that instructions from the Lord are to be upon our hearts, and that we are to impress them upon our children and talk about them when we walk along the road, when we lie down, and when we get up.

Be committed to properly train your children in *all* areas of life.

Advice to Children on Behavior at the Table

First, in the morning, when you rise,
Give thanks to God, who well supplies
Our various wants, and gives us food,
Wholesome, nutritious, sweet, and good.
Then to some proper place repair,
And wash your hands and face with care;
And ne'er the table once disgrace
With dirty hands or dirty face.
When to your meals you have the call,
Promptly attend, both great and small;
Then kneel and pray, with closed eyes,
That God will bless these rich supplies.
When at the table you sit down,
Sit straight and trim, nor laugh nor frown;
Then let the elder first begin,
And all unite, and follow him.
Of bread, then take a decent piece,
Nor splash about the fat and grease;
But cut your meat both neat and square,
And take of both an equal share.
Also, of bones you'll take your due,
For bones and meat together grew.
If, from some incapacity,

With fat your stomach don't agree,
Or if you cannot pick a bone,
You'll please to let them both alone.
Potatoes, cabbage, turnip, beet,
And every kind of thing you eat,
Must neatly on your plate be laid,
Before you eat with pliant blade;
Nor ever—'tis an awkward matter,
To eat or sip out of the platter.
If bread and butter be your fare,
Or biscuit, and you find there are
Pieces enough, then take your slice,
And spread it over, thin and nice,
On one side, only; then you may
Eat in a decent, comely way.
Yet butter you must never spread
On nut-cake, pie, or dier-bread;
Or bread with milk, or bread with meat,
Butter with these you may not eat.
These things are all the best of food,
And need not butter to be good.
When bread or pie you cut or break,
Touch only what you mean to take;
And have no prints of fingers seen
On that that's left—nay, if they're clean.
Be careful, when you take a sip
Of liquid, don't extend your lip
So far that one may fairly think
That cup and all you mean to drink.
Then clean your knife—don't lick it, pray;
It is a nasty, shameful way—
But wipe it on a piece of bread,
Which snugly by your plate is laid.
Thus clean your knife, before you pass
It into plum or apple-sauce,
Or butter, which you must cut nice,
Both square and true as polish'd dice.

Behavior at the Table

Cut not a pickle with a blade
Whose side with grease is overlaid;
And always take your equal share
Of coarse as well as luscious fare.
Don't pick your teeth, or ears, or nose,
Nor scratch your head, nor tonk your toes;
Nor belch nor sniff, nor jest nor pun,
Nor have the least of play or fun.
If you're oblig'd to cough or sneeze,
Your handkerchief you'll quickly seize,
And timely shun the foul disgrace
Of splattering either food or face.
Drink neither water, cider, beer,
With greasy lip or mucus tear;
Nor fill your mouth with food, and then
Drink, least you blow it out again.
And when you've finish'd your repast,
Clean plate, knife, fork—then, at the last,
Upon your plate lay knife and fork,
And pile your bones of beef and pork:
But if no plate, you may as well
Lay knife and fork both parallel.
Pick up your crumbs, and, where you eat,
Keep all things decent, clean, and neat;
Then rise, and kneel in thankfulness
To Him who does your portion bless;
Then straightly from the table walk,
Nor stop to handle things, nor talk.
If we mean never to offend,
To every gift we must attend,
Respecting meetings, work, or food,
And doing all things as we should.
Thus joy and comfort we shall find,
Love, quietness, and peace of mind;
Pure heavenly Union will increase,
And every evil work will cease.

(Reproduced from the original in the Shaker Collection)

Thoughts for Action

❦ Identify two or three areas of your training that need emphasis. Write in your journal how you plan to concentrate on these areas. Think of several activities that will give you an opportunity to strengthen a deficiency. For example, plan an evening meal where the whole family will sit down at the table and partake in home-prepared food. Depending on the age of your family members, you might delegate . . .

- help in selecting the menus.
- help in shopping for the food.
- help in preparing the food.
- help in setting the table.
- help in providing the centerpiece.
- help in serving the food.
- help in removing the dishes when the family is finished eating.
- help in cleaning the dishes.
- help in developing questions that the whole family could talk about. (Try this one: "What is the best thing that happened to you today?")

Additional Scripture Reading

Proverbs 22:6   Proverbs 1:1-7
Luke 12:22-34

Los Angeles Marathon

Scripture Reading: Hebrews 12:1-12

Key Verse: Hebrews 12:1-2

> *Therefore, since we are surrounded by such a great*
> *cloud of witnesses, let us throw off everything that*
> *hinders and the sin that so easily entangles, and let*
> *us run with perseverance the race marked out for us.*
> *Let us fix our eyes on Jesus, the author and perfecter*
> *of our faith, who for the joy set before him endured*
> *the cross, scorning its shame, and sat down at the*
> *right hand of the throne of God.*

Our son, Brad, has always been an athlete. You name the sport and he could do it and do it well. In high school he played football. In college he played volleyball and tennis. After graduation he and some college friends began working out as tri-athletes—swimming, biking, and running. Brad raced and did very well.

When Brad was 30, Maria came into his heart. She was the perfect woman for Brad because she loved athletics too. For their first date they jogged Central Park in New York City. From then on they were running mates for life.

In spring of 1991 Brad and Maria entered the Los Angeles Marathon, a 26.2 mile run. They both worked out hard and long. They needed discipline to get out every day before or after work to run 6 to 19 miles a day—enough to total 75 miles a week.

Finally, the day of the marathon arrived. They had prepared well by eating a large pasta meal the evening before to buff up their energy. The gun went off and over 20,000 runners began a race which lasted 26.2 hard miles.

That spring day of '91 wasn't a great day for Brad. He had prepared for months, had eaten the right high-energy foods, had disciplined himself, and he should have been on top. But by the tenth mile Brad hit the wall. Physically he was Mr. America, but that day that race just wasn't cutting it for him. He continued to run but kept hitting the wall, struggling painfully on. Yes, Brad finished, only because he has always been one to finish what he starts. His time, however, was 3 hours, 50 minutes. He should have completed the race in a little over three hours.

Maria had an up day. She finished in 3 hours, 25 minutes. When she crossed the finish line, she immediately began looking for Brad. "He's been in a long time," she thought, but she couldn't find him. She began to check the stretchers lined with men and women who fell out of the race. No Brad. She grew concerned as she asked friends and others on the sidelines. No Brad! She was amazed later to find that Brad had come in 25 minutes after her. It just wasn't his day. It was an experience they will never forget.

Looking at our text in Hebrews, we see the importance of keeping our eyes on Jesus, running toward the mark He has set for us. No, we won't do it in 3 hours, 50 minutes. It's a lifetime of struggle against sin. Brad could spend a lifetime looking back at a bad race asking "Why?" But he looks at it as just a race past, pressing on to perhaps one day when they may do it again.

Life is like a race. We must discipline ourselves to study and know God's Word, understanding we must endure hardships in life. But the exciting results come later when our hearts begin to produce a harvest of righteousness and peace. We become mature, strong, and able to help others through their struggles.

Thank You, Lord, for discipline in life; help us to daily run the race of life so we might bring glory to Your name. Amen.

Thoughts for Action

❦ In your journal list areas you need discipline in: physical, mental, organizational, eating, financial, etc.

❦ Are there any things in your life from a past race that you are still holding onto? If so, give them to the Lord today. Run ahead to the mark of Jesus' calling in your life.

Additional Scripture Reading

Isaiah 40:31   1 Corinthians 9:24

□ □ □

Create in Me a New Heart

Scripture Reading: Ezekiel 36:24-27

Key Verse: Ezekiel 36:26a

> *I will give you a new heart and put a new spirit in you.*

As you begin to meet with God and spend time with Him regularly, you will realize that, with your old heart, you can't do what is necessary to make you a godly person. In fact, none of us can make that transformation happen under our own power—and, fortunately, we don't have to. In Ezekiel 36:26, God says, "I will give you a new heart and put a new spirit in you." God offers us a heart transplant, one that is even more remarkable than a medical transplant of a physical heart.

Thankfully, not everyone of us will need a new physical heart, but each of us does need a new spiritual heart. Why? Because we are born with a sinful nature. King David acknowledges that fact in the psalms: "Behold, I was brought forth in iniquity, and in sin my mother conceived me" (51:5). The prophet Jeremiah writes: "The heart is deceitful above all things and beyond cure" (Jeremiah 17:9). Jesus teaches that same lesson: "Out of the heart come evil thoughts, murders, adulteries, fornications, thefts, false witness, slanders" (Matthew 15:19). The apostle Paul wrestles with his sin nature:

"For the good that I wish, I do not do; but I practice the very evil that I do not wish. But if I am doing the very thing I do not wish, I am no longer the one doing it, but sin which dwells in me" (Romans 7:19-20). And the apostle John is very direct in his statement about sin: "If we say that we have no sin, we are deceiving ourselves, and the truth is not in us" (1 John 1:8).

So what are we to do? Not even the most skilled physician can cure a sinful heart or give us a new and pure one. But God can and, according to His promise, will. In *Seeing Yourself Through God's Eyes*, June Hunt talks about this process:

> Slowly, after this divine transplant, healing begins and, as promised, your new heart becomes capable of perfect love. Your self-centeredness is now Christ-centeredness. There is healing to replace the hatred; there is a balm for the bitterness. You can face the world with a freedom and a future you have never known before.
>
> "Create in me a clean heart, O God, and renew a steadfast spirit within me" (Psalms 51:10). Once you have a changed heart, you have a changed life. You can love the unlovable, be kind to the unkind, and forgive the unforgivable. All this because you have a new heart—you have God's heart![14]

This kind of heart operation, at the loving hands of your divine Physician, doesn't require major medical insurance. There are no disclaimers or deductibles. God offers this transformation to us free of charge. It costs Him greatly—He gave His only Son for our salvation—but it's a gift to us. All we have to do is accept it—no strings attached.

Father God, You know that I need a new heart—not one that a doctor transplants but one You

change. Give me that newness of spirit that refreshes
like the spring water which flows through the valley.
Amen.

Thoughts for Action

❦ Pray to God in earnest that you truly want a new heart.

❦ In your journal write down five areas of your life where you
want to create a new heart and spirit.

❦ Under each of the areas write down two to three activities
you will do to accomplish these changes. Beside each
activity write a date when you will accomplish each.

Additional Scripture Reading

2 Corinthians 5:17   Romans 5:5

Commit to God and to Your Spouse

Scripture Reading: Ephesians 5:15-21

Key Verse: Ephesians 5:21

Submit to one another out of reverence for Christ.

You've probably never heard of Nicolai Pestretsov, but now you may never forget him. He was 36 years old, a sergeant major in the Russian army, stationed in Angola. His wife had traveled the long distance from home to visit him when, on an August day, South African military units entered the country in quest of black nationalist guerrillas taking sanctuary there. When the South Africans encountered the Russian soldiers, four people were killed and the rest of the Russians fled— except for Sergeant Major Pestretsov.

The South African troops captured Pestretsov, and a military communique explained the situation: "Sergeant Major Nicolai Pestretsov refused to leave the body of his slain wife, who was killed in the assault on the village. He went to the body of his wife and would not leave it, although she was dead."

What a picture of commitment—and what a series of questions it raises! Robert Fulghum, who tells this story, asks these questions:

Why didn't he run and save his own hide? What made him go back? Is it possible that he loved her? Is it possible that he wanted to hold her in his arms one last time? Is it possible that he needed to cry and grieve? Is it possible that he felt the stupidity of war? Is it possible that he felt the injustice of fate? Is it possible that he thought of children, born or unborn? Is it possible that he didn't care what became of him now? Is it possible? We don't know. Or at least we don't know for certain. But we can guess. His actions answer.[15]

What do your actions say about your commitment to your husband? What do your attitudes and your words reveal? Standing by the commitment you made to your spouse—the commitment you made before God and many witnesses—is key to standing by your man.

Picture again Sergeant Major Pestretsov kneeling by the side of his wife's lifeless body, not wanting to leave the woman to whom he'd pledged his life even when his very life was at stake. That is a high level of commitment. We are to be as committed. We who are married are to be as committed to our spouse as Christ is to the church He died for. In fact, as Christians, our marriages are to be a witness to the world of Christ's love and grace. Clearly, marriage is not to be entered into casually.

In light of the importance God places on marriage, Bob and I take the premarital counseling we do very seriously. We never, for instance, encourage two people to get married if one is a Christian and the other is not (2 Corinthians 6:14). A marriage needs to be rooted in each partner's commitment to love and serve the Lord, or else the union will be divided from the start. In addition, only a Christian marriage will result in a Christian home, a home which glorifies God and acts as His witness to the world.

I can vividly remember an evening Bob and I were sitting on the couch in my living room. He cupped my face in his hands and said, "Emilie, I love you, but I can't ask you to marry me." I was stunned. I couldn't understand why two people who were in love couldn't get married.

As Bob looked steadfastly into my eyes, I asked, "Why not?" With all the courage he could muster, Bob answered firmly but gently, "Because you are not a Christian." Very innocently I asked Bob, "How do I become a Christian?" From that moment I began to consider whether Jesus might actually be the Messiah my Jewish people had long waited for.

After several months of seeking answers, I prayed one evening at my bedside, "Dear God, if You have a Son and if Your Son is Jesus our Messiah, please reveal Him to me!" I expected a voice to answer immediately, but God waited a few weeks to reveal Himself to me. Then, one Sunday morning, I responded to my pastor's challenge to accept Jesus Christ as my personal Savior, and that evening I was baptized.

Being obedient to God has meant being blessed by a rich and wonderful marriage that is rooted in His love and dedicated to Him. Furthermore, vowing before God to love Bob through the good times and the bad has reinforced my commitment to him when the times were indeed bad. Had my vows been to Bob alone, they might have been easier to walk away from. But God's witness of our vows and the foundation He gives to Christian couples enables us to stand together whatever comes our way.

"Lord, what joy that we may tell other people that it works."

—Corrie ten Boom

Father God, it's sometimes difficult to stand by the commitment I've made to my spouse. We all want to do our own thing our own way. Help me to stay true to the vow I made before You and other witnesses. I truly want to commit to You and to my husband, and to receive the blessings that You promise in Scripture when we do just that. Amen.

Thoughts for Action

❧ Today in your journal write down a fresh, new commitment to your God and to your spouse.

❧ Make a commitment to be willing to "submit to one another" in all things (Ephesians 5:21).

❧ Touch your marriage ring (if you wear one). Think back to your wedding day and review your wedding vows. Touch your ring regularly and each time think about those vows.

Additional Scripture Reading

Ephesians 5:22-33   Ephesians 6:10-18

The Spirit of a Woman

Scripture Reading: 1 Peter 3:3-6

Key Verse: 1 Peter 3:4

[Your beauty] should be that of your inner self, the unfading beauty of a gentle and quiet spirit, which is of great worth in God's sight.

Oh, if only we could truly capture the spirit of today's passage! Today we are drastically in need of women who are satisfied with themselves inwardly and reflect a soft and tender peacefulness in their lives. Too often as women we have become loud, aggressive, and masculine in manners. We have left God's pattern of womanhood, sometimes trying to be better men than men themselves.

How do I define "feminine"? Not by a particular style of dress or interior decorating. "Feminine" can take on an infinite variety of physical appearances. Instead, I see "feminine" as a softness, a gentleness, and a graciousness. That's not to say, though, that a woman cannot be the president of a corporation or an active participant in the business world. She certainly can, yet a feminine woman will have a softness and graciousness that men simply don't have. To me, "feminine" also means that a woman has a sense of who she is apart from what she does. She nurtures a strong spirituality and manifests the fruit of the Spirit in every aspect of her life (Galatians 5:22-23). "Femininity" also brings to my mind a woman's deep concern for her husband and children, the ability to submit to her husband when appropriate (Ephesians 5:21), and the maternal awareness that she is raising not only her children but generations to come. Finally, a truly feminine woman understands the "mystique" of being a godly wife and mother.

The "gentle and quiet spirit" which Peter refers to—this tranquillity, this sense that a woman is at peace with herself, this ability to share the fruit of the Spirit with people she comes in contact with—results from a woman's relationship with God. When a woman has this inner peace, she doesn't feel any need to prove herself to her husband or to anyone else. Confident in herself and aware of her God-given strengths, she doesn't feel compelled to use those strengths to control other people. She enjoys an inner contentment that isn't based on accomplishments, status, authority, power, or other people's opinions.

As I mentioned earlier, this woman of God has learned the value of *being* as opposed to *doing*. Too many women today have forgotten how to simply *be.* They have bought into the lie of doing and have become highly obsessive-compulsive about getting work done. As a result, they are cut off from their feminine feelings and nature.

A woman who walks closely with her God, however, is free from competitiveness, aggressiveness, and the need to prove her worth. Yes, she may be aggressive and high-energy by temperament or competitive and very capable in the business world, but the fact is that she is affirmed not by other people but by her God. Such a woman "speaks with wisdom, and faithful instruction is on her tongue" (Proverbs 31:26), and her family is blessed: "Her husband has full confidence in her and lacks nothing of value. She brings him good, not harm, all the days of her life. . . . Her children arise up and call her blessed" (Proverbs 31:11,12,28). Such a woman inspires the man of her life to rise to his own greatness, and she supports him unconditionally in his search for fulfillment and achievement. And such a woman—one closely in tune with God—is indeed worthy of praise as she models godly values and high moral standards. A woman's gentle and quiet spirit makes her a blessing to the people around her.

Gentleness, patience, and devotion to God—traits which I view as components of godly femininity—are qualities which hold society together and provide hope for the future. We have an incredible responsibility! History shows that as the woman goes, so goes the family. You give meaning and purpose to a home. You are the heartbeat, pumping vital blood into the family system by setting the spirit and tone. You help others establish and live by moral standards.

The femininity I am describing teaches, inspires, and civilizes. It brings glory to God and hope to His world. And such femininity also has a real "mystique" about it. Men look to women to bring out their gentler natures and their highest ideals, to inflame their passions, and to motivate them to achievement.

One mother, wise about the more practical side of the feminine mystique, offered a piece of advice to her future daughter-in-law. The groom-to-be was a minister and an avid reader who spent large amounts of time in the library studying and preparing for the next Sunday's sermon. The mother said to her son's intended: "John loves to study and often works late into the night at the library. Don't try to change him, but always have his dinner in a warm oven and keep a pot of coffee on the stove." The young lady listened to her future mother-in-law and, at last account, she had been married to Pastor John for over 40 years.

Pastor John's wife was an example of "that kind of deep beauty... seen in the saintly women of old who trusted God and fitted in with her husband's plans" (1 Peter 3:5 TLB). This type of woman can be irresistible to men. This femininity is a rarity in today's culture, and the traditional male still seeks valiantly for it. The mystique works. Are you letting it enrich your marriage?

Thoughts for Action

❧ Write in your journal several activities that help you feel feminine. Consider a few of these:

—Buy some fresh flowers for your home. (Silk flowers will do, too.)

—Light a candle or small oil lamp by the kitchen sink, the nightstand, or the bathtub.

—Get a new haircut or add something new to your makeup collection.

—Read a love story or poem.

—Buy that lacy dress you've been looking at for the last month.

—Pamper yourself with a new bottle of perfume.

—Buy a new set of sheets—the kind with soft ruffles on the edges.

—Start a daily exercise program. (If you don't have access to a gym or aerobics on videotape, walk!)

—Unclutter your bedroom. Reserve it for sleep and romance.

❧ Choose at least one new activity this week and then another one next week.

Additional Scripture Reading

Matthew 6:33   Ephesians 4:32

Her Children Call Her Blessed

Scripture Reading: Proverbs 31

Key Verse: Proverbs 31:28a

Her children arise and call her blessed.

Consider Sarah Edwards, the wife of theologian and preacher Jonathan Edwards and the mother of 11 children. According to one biographer, Sarah's children and her children's children through the generations were a tribute to this woman in their distinguished positions as college presidents, professors, attorneys, judges, physicians, senators, governors, and even a vice president of the United States! What influenced 1400 of Sarah Edwards's descendants to become such fine citizens? One author suggests that Sarah treated her children with patience, courtesy, respect, and love. Being a deeply Christian woman, she taught her children to work and deal with what life brought their way according to biblical principles. Convinced that until children can obey their parents they will never be obedient to God, Sarah was also a firm disciplinarian. But she never resorted to words of anger. Her home emanated love and harmony. And what were the results of her efforts as homemaker and mother?

> As [biographer] Elizabeth Dodds makes
> abundantly clear in her book, a mother is not
> merely rearing her one generation of children.

She is also affecting future generations for good or ill. All the love, nurture, education, and character-building that spring from Mother's work influence those sons and daughters. The results show up in the children's accomplishments, attitudes toward life and parenting capacity. For example, one of Sarah Edwards' grandsons, Timothy Dwight, president of Yale (echoing Lincoln) said, "All that I am and all that I shall be, I owe to my mother."[16]

Have you ever felt discontent in your role as wife and mother, as though what you do makes very little difference? I think we all have. But consider this:

As one ponders this praise [by Timothy Dwight], the question arises: Are we women unhappy in our mothering and wife role because we make too little, rather than too much of that role? Do we see what we have to give our husbands and children as minor rather than major, and consequently send them into the world without a healthy core identity and strong spiritual values?[17]

Are you fulfilled in your role as wife and mother? Do you have purpose? Fulfillment and the peace it offers don't come free. You will work and sacrifice as you live out your purpose and find fulfillment as a woman of God, a wife, and a mother.

Sarah Edwards spent many hours serving her husband and children. Her responsibilities were many and the demands on her great, yet she seemed to offer her family a sense of serenity as she cared for them. And despite how different our world is today, I believe a wife and mother can still make her home a place of serenity, a place where her children will rise up and bless her. It starts when she herself discovers and nurtures a serenity that God alone gives.

Father God, how I want my children to arise and call me blessed! Children today so often criticize and put down their mothers. I so want my children to be different. Give me the wisdom and strength to discern attitudes and behaviors in me which will place in my children's hearts the desire to call me blessed. Amen.

Thoughts for Action

❧ Here are some ways to develop a serenity that will weather the demands of being a wife and mother:

—Sit in a quiet room for 5, 10, or 15 minutes and reflect on what God is doing in your life.

—Wait upon the Lord. Listen for Him to direct, encourage, guide, and teach.

—Just sit and hold hands with your husband and think about God's love, power, and peace.

—Turn on some peaceful music. Avoid loud sounds and high volume.

—Take a walk—at the beach, on a mountain trail, in a snowy meadow. Ski down a hill or watch the leaves fall off the trees.

—Take a warm bubble bath.

—Draw a picture.

—Find a new hobby.

—Eliminate some of the confusion in your life.

—Don't drive over the speed limit.

—Ride a bicycle instead of driving a car.

—Feed the ducks in the park.

—Tell your husband that you love him.

❧ Write in your journal several activities that help you feel serene.

❧ Do at least one of these activities this week and then another one next week.

Additional Scripture Reading

Genesis 2:18-24   Luke 1:39-49

Little Jelly Beans

Scripture Reading: John 3:16-21

Key Verse: John 3:16

> For God so loved the world that he gave his one and
> only Son, that whoever believes in him shall not
> perish but have eternal life.

A friend placed a simple little bag of colored jelly beans in
my hand. A card was attached to the bag. In passing I thought,
"Cute gift." Placing the bag on the table with a quick thank
you, I went on to visit with my friend.

It was actually several days later when I picked up the small
package of colored jelly beans to throw a few into my mouth.
However, in order to get to those silly beans I had to cut the
attached card off. In so doing I noticed the words on the card.
Here is what they said:

Little Jelly Beans

Little jelly beans
Tell a story true
A tale of Father's love
Just for me and you.

GREEN is for the waving palms
BLUE for the skies above

BROWN for the soft earth where
People sat hearing of HIS love.

A SPECKLED bean for fish and sand
RED for precious wine
And BLACK is for the sin He washed
From your soul and mine.

PURPLE'S for the sadness of
HIS family and friends,
And WHITE is for the glory of the
Day HE rose again.

Now you've heard the story
You know what each color means
The story of our Father's love
Told by some jelly beans.

So every morning take a bean
They're really very yummy
Something for the soul, you see.
And something for the tummy.

It's been a year since that gift of jelly beans was put into my hand. I have not eaten them—they sit on my desk as a beautiful reminder of what God has done and given to me. When I see those jelly beans I remember to thank our Lord for the earth and sky, for friends and family, for a family of God that is so big and mighty, for the love and prayers of others. And most of all, for our heavenly Father's love, the love gift of His very own Son, Jesus Christ.

Father God, thank You for the simple reminders of who You are and what You have done. You are a great and awesome God. Help me to remember that always. Amen.

Thoughts for Action

❦ Thank the Lord today for the beautiful world He created.

❦ Meditate on our key verse, John 3:16.

❦ What does that verse mean to you?

Additional Scripture Reading

John 5:24   John 10:28

The True Christmas Spirit

Scripture Reading: Matthew 7:7-12

Key Verse: Matthew 7:12

> So in everything, do to others what you would have them do to you, for this sums up the Law and the Prophets.

———— ❦ ————

Edwin Markham wrote a poem based on a story by Tolstoy that beautifully illustrates how we may demonstrate the true Christmas spirit.

One night Conrad, a cobbler of shoes, dreamed that Christ would come to his shop on the following day. Early the next morning Conrad went to the woods to gather greens and flowers to decorate his simple shop for the Lord's coming.

All morning he waited, but the only visitor was an old man who asked if he might sit down to rest. Conrad saw that his shoes were worn. Before sending the stranger on his way, Conrad put the best pair of shoes in the shop on the old man's feet.

Throughout the afternoon Conrad waited for the Lord's coming, but the only person he saw was an old woman struggling under a heavy load. Out of compassion he brought her in and gave her some of the food he had prepared for Christ. She went on her way refreshed.

Just as evening was falling, a lost child entered Conrad's shop. Conrad carried the child home, and then hurried back, lest he miss the coming of Christ.

Though Conrad waited long and patiently, Christ did not come. Finally, in disappointment, the old cobbler cried:

"Why is it, Lord, that your feet delay?
Did You forget that this was the day?"
Then soft in the silence a voice he heard:
"Lift up your heart, for I kept my word.
Three times I came to your friendly door;
Three times my shadow was on your floor.
I was the beggar with the bruised feet;
I was the woman you gave to eat;
I was the child on the homeless street!"

May you, dear reader, know the true meaning of Christmas. May you know Jesus Christ as your Savior, and may you find the joy of sharing with others in need. Then Christmas for you will not merely be a holiday, but a holy day, a celebration of the love of God and love for others. And that is what Christmas is really all about.

Thoughts for Action

What are some things we can do to help others when holidays come? Start with my list and add some of your ideas to it.

- Take food—homemade if possible—to those who may not have extra.
- Decorate the home of a family who can't afford decorations this year.
- Clean someone's house or fix their car.

❦ Offer your babysitting services free of charge to a single parent.

Additional Scripture Reading

Galatians 6:9

2 Thessalonians 3:13

Colossians 3:17

Ephesians 6:7-8

The Two Shall Become One

Scripture Reading: Genesis 2:20a-25

Key Verse: Genesis 2:24

> *For this reason a man will leave his father and mother and be united to his wife, and they will become one flesh.*

One of Aesop's fables tells the story of a wise father who sensed disharmony among his sons and decided to bring them together to discuss this strife. He told each of his four sons to bring a twig to the meeting.

As the young men assembled, the father took each boy's twig and easily snapped it in half. Then he gathered four twigs, tied them together in a bundle, and asked each son to try to break the bundle. Each one tried to no avail. The bundle would not snap.

After each son had tried valiantly to break the bundle, the father asked his boys what they had learned from the demonstration. The oldest son said, "If we are individuals, anyone can break us, but if we stick together, no one can harm us." The father said, "You are right. You must always stand together and be strong."

What is true for the four brothers is equally true for a husband and wife. If we don't stand together and let God make us one in spite of our differences, we will easily be defeated.

As I studied today's Scripture passage, I saw God calling a husband and wife to:

- *departure* ("A man shall leave his father and mother...")
- *permanence* ("And shall cleave to his wife...")
- *oneness* ("And they shall become one flesh")

All three steps must be taken if a marriage is to stand strong.

In God's sight, we become one at the altar when we say our vows to one another before Him. But practically speaking, oneness between a husband and wife is a process that happens over a period of time, over a lifetime together.

Becoming one with another person can be a very difficult process. It isn't easy to change from being independent and self-centered to sharing every aspect of your life and self with another person. The difficulty is often intensified when you're older and more set in your ways when you marry or, as was the case for Bob and me, when the two partners come from very different family, religious, or financial backgrounds. I, for instance, came from an alcoholic family and was raised by a verbally and physically abusive father. Bob came from a warm, loving family where yelling and screaming simply didn't happen. It took us only a few moments to say our vows and enter into oneness in God's eyes, but we have spent more than 38 years blending our lives and building the oneness which we enjoy today.

Becoming one doesn't mean becoming the same, however. Oneness means sharing the same degree of commitment to the Lord and to the marriage, the same goals and dreams, and the same mission in life. Oneness is internal conformity to one another, not an external conformity. It's not the Marines with their short haircuts, shiny shoes, straight backs, and characteristic walk. The oneness and internal conformity of a marriage relationship comes with the unselfish act of allowing God to shape us into the marriage partner He would have us be. Oneness results when two individuals reflect the same Christ. Such spiritual oneness produces tremendous strength and unity in a marriage and in the family.

The two marriage partners must leave their families and let God make them one. Men help the cleaving happen when they show—not just tell—their wives that they are the most important priority after God. Likewise, a wife needs to let her husband know how important he is to her. Your man cannot be competing with your father or any other male for the number-one position in your life. He must know that you respect, honor, and love him if he is to act out his proper role as husband confidently. Your clear communication of your love for him will strengthen the bond of marriage.

Consider what Paul writes to the church at Philippi: "Make my joy complete by being of the same mind, maintaining the same love, united in spirit, intent on one purpose" (Philippians 2:2). This verse has guided me as I worked to unite my family in purpose, thought, and deed. After many years of trial, error, and endless hours of searching, I can say that we are truly united in our purpose and direction. If you were to ask Bob to state our purpose and direction, his answer would match mine: Matthew 6:33—"Seek first his kingdom and his righteousness, and all these things will be given to you." As we have faced decisions through the years, we have asked ourselves, "Are we seeking God's kingdom and His righteousness?" Will doing this help us find His kingdom and experience His righteousness? Or are we seeking our own edification or our own satisfaction? We both hold to this standard whenever we have to decide an issue, and that oneness of purpose helps make our marriage work.

Larry Crabb points out another important dimension to the oneness of a husband and wife when he writes, "The goal of oneness can be almost frightening when we realize that God does not intend [only] that my wife and I find our personal needs met in marriage. He also wants our relationship to validate the claims of Christianity to a watching world as an example of the power of Christ's redeeming love to overcome the divisive effects of sin."[18]

The world does not value permanence and oneness in a marriage, and much of our culture works to undermine those characteristics. But knowing what God intends marriage to be, working to leave, cleave, and become one with our spouse, will help us shine God's light in a very dark world.

> *Father God, today's reading has made me aware that there are several areas in my life where my husband and I need better unity. Please give me a proper sensitivity to these areas when I approach him. You know that I want total oneness in purpose of spirit. I thank You now for what You are going to do in this situation. Amen.*

Thoughts for Action

- Set a date with your mate and write down five things you agree on regarding family, discipline, manners, values, church, home, etc.

- At the same session write down several items in which you are not one as yet. State what your differences are regarding each. Discuss these differences. Agree to pray about these differences. Set an appointment for your next date to again discuss these items.

- Ways to say "I Love You":

  —Deliver something in a heart-shaped box, be it jelly beans, chocolates, or jewelry.

  —Give a certificate for a massage, facial, or a weekend getaway.

—Have firewood delivered, then deliver yourself and refreshments.

Additional Scripture Reading

Philippians 2:2   Matthew 19:3-6

Three Loves

Scripture Reading: Deuteronomy 6:4-9

Key Verse: Deuteronomy 6:5

> *Love the Lord your God with all your heart and with all your soul and with all your strength.*

Today's Scripture talks about three basic loves:

- Love for God
- Love for your neighbor
- Love for yourself

Our circle of love is full when we are able to love in this way. The whole world would know of Jesus if the Christians in the church would manifest these three basic love relationships. Our passage challenges us by giving a directive to:

- Put these commandments in our hearts.
- Impress them on our children.
- Talk about them continually.
- Tie them as symbols on our bodies.
- Write them on our door frames and gates.

God must be serious about this because He engulfs our lives with continuous reminders of His commandments to love.

How do we manifest these three loves? Paul, in writing to the church at Ephesus, includes a section on a believer's relationship with the Holy Spirit, beginning in Ephesians 5:18: "Instead, be filled with the Spirit." In the verses that follow we learn that we are to be satisfied with self, God, and others.

If we are satisfied with ourselves, Paul teaches us to manifest it in speaking and singing words of joy: "Speak to one another with psalms, hymns, and spiritual songs. Sing and make music in your heart to the Lord" (verse 19). Satisfied lives will be ones of joy, praise, and excitement. They will reflect positive thoughts, ideas, and praises to God. What a great test to see where our personal satisfaction is! Are we known as a person who is fun to be around or as someone who people avoid? God wants us to be satisfied with ourselves and reflect the joy of the Lord in our soul, mind, and spirit.

Paul continues in verse 20, "Always giving thanks for all things in the name of our Lord Jesus Christ to God, even the Father" (NASB). This verse shows *our satisfaction with God.* If we are satisfied, we find ourselves giving thanks for all things. We have an appreciative heart for all that goes on around us. The positive words flow from our lips unto God.

Our third satisfaction is with other people. In verse 21 Paul teaches, "And be subject to one another in the fear of Christ." As women, we find that when we love God and ourselves, we become equipped to be submissive to others. These words, "subject" or "submissive," unfortunately, have taken a beating in today's culture. In essence, these words are telling us to be satisfied with other people to the point that we are willing to step aside in our personal relationships. We are willing to allow another's needs to take precedence over our own. The submission is to be mutual among Christians, among husband and wife, and based on reverence for God. It is impossible to be subject to one another by human desire. It is possible only when we mutually submit to one another out of respect for God.

Ephesians 5:18-21 truly gives us guidelines for being satisfied with God, with ourselves, and with others.

As I have taught this concept over the years, I have used a diagram to illustrate my point:

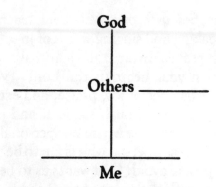

As you can see, we have vertical and horizontal relationships. The vertical relationship is between God and me, and the horizontal relationship is between myself and other people. I find that when God and I have the proper relationship, my relationship with others falls into proper alignment. If I have dissatisfaction with myself and others, I realize that I am not responding to God properly. Over the years, God has taught me to put first things first: to love God, to love self, and to love others.

> *Father God, life is so difficult at times. There seems to be so many things pulling at me that I get exhausted trying to be all things to all people. Let me start each day concentrating on the three loves. It seems so basic, but I know it takes a lifetime to accomplish. Amen.*

Thoughts for Action

❧ In your journal write down several ways you presently express love to:

—God

—Others

—Self

❧ Now write down several new ways to express love in these three areas.

❧ Make or purchase a sign or plaque that states to the world that you are a Christian. Put this sign by your front door. (Make sure you walk your talk and not talk your walk.)

Additional Scripture Reading

Ephesians 5:18-21   Matthew 22:36-40

To Know the Love of Christ

Scripture Reading: Ephesians 3:16-21

Key Verse: Ephesians 3:18b

> . . . *to grasp how wide and long and high and deep is the love of Christ.*

Bob and I are usually not home on Friday evenings, but we were on the night of June 23. We were preparing for a marriage seminar in our home the next morning. After getting everything organized and ready, Bob and I went to the kitchen and began popping popcorn. The phone rang at 9:30 P.M. I remember checking my watch, wondering who would be calling so late to get directions for tomorrow.

After Bob's first few words on the phone, I knew something serious had happened. Our dear friends of 20 years were calling for care, help, support, and prayers. Their son, Jimmy, had been in a terrible car accident on a street near our home. He had hit a palm tree on Victoria Avenue. That's all it took for Bob to say we would be right there.

We had met Jim and Barbara DeLorenzo the first year we moved to Riverside. Jimmy was about 8 years old. They were new Christians, and God truly bonded our hearts and friendship almost immediately. Over the years our families have experienced many memorable times. We still call Jim, Jr. "Jimmy."

But at that moment all we could think of was how dangerous Victoria Avenue is, with palm trees lining both sides of the street and also in a row down the median. The years our children were in high school, eight students had died due to palm tree accidents. We couldn't believe this was happening to Jimmy. He was an excellent driver. He knew very well the danger of Victoria Avenue and how to handle cars in dangerous situations. As we drove to the hospital, all we could do was pray and ask God to spare this child.

The first words that came from Big Jim's mouth when Jim and Barbara met us in emergency was, "Jimmy wasn't driving and the two young men are alive."

The car was going 65 MPH when it lost control on a curve and crashed into a palm tree, literally wrapping itself around the tree. The pictures of the accident later showed that only a miracle of God could explain Jimmy's and his friend's lives being spared. The "jaws of life" were used to cut these young men out of the car, and thankfully drugs and alcohol were immediately ruled out.

Jim and Bob stayed with Jimmy as the doctors stitched up his lacerated head, eyes, and hands. Barbara and I prayed. Rather, I prayed as Barbara cried and shook from shock. We knew the situation was in God's hands. We also knew of other parents who had lost their sons and daughters through similar accidents.

Jimmy is okay today, but only after plastic surgery, a shaved head, hundreds of stitches, and a plastic pin in his eye socket.

As Barbara and Jim reflect on the experience, they see what a precious time of love and friendship occurred. The bond we felt between us will always be there. As Barb says, "It's beyond words, the changes we've made with priorities in our life. The results have been a closer prayer life within the family and such growth of fellowship with God and friends, not to mention the times we've had with our son and his recovery."

Their roots of faith in God's love and protection have deepened. They do realize how wide, how high, and how deep God's love really is.

Yes! So easy to read, but sometimes so very difficult to live out in life.

Thoughts for Action

❦ Write in your journal several incidents or blessings which have happened in your life that reflect God's love for you.

❦ Today be a doer of God's Word and not just a hearer. Go out and unselfishly love someone.

Additional Scripture Reading

Philippians 1:9-11   Colossians 2:2-7

We find God
in so many things,
in flowers wakened
with each Spring,
in butterflies and
sunsets grand,
we see God's love—
we touch God's hand.

□ □ □

Respect Your Husband

Scripture Reading: Ephesians 5:22-33

Key Verse: Ephesians 5:33

However, each one of you also must love his wife as he loves himself, and the wife must respect her husband.

How your family functions can reveal a lot about the respect you and your husband have for each other. How you and your husband communicate can also give an indication of the level of respect you show one another. Today we're going to take a look at a woman's respect for her husband.

Jerry and Barbara Cook suggest that wives read the following message to their husbands. Let it be the catalyst for a discussion about your marriage.

I married a man I respect;
  I have no need to bow and defer.
I married a man I adore and admire;
  I don't need to be handed a list entitled "how to build
    his ego" or "the male need for admiration."
Love, worship, loyalty, trust—these are inside me;
  They motivate my actions.
    To reduce them to rules destroys my motivation.

I choose to serve him, to enjoy him.
We choose to live together and grow together, to stretch
our capacities for love even when it hurts and looks like
conflict.
We choose to learn to know each other as real people, as
two unique individuals unlike any other two.
Our marriage is commitment to love;
   to belong to each other
   to know and understand
   to care
   to share ourselves, our goals,
      interest, desires, needs.
Out of that commitment the actions follow.
Love defines our behavior
   and our ways of living together.
And since we fail to meet not only the demands
   of standards but also the simple requirements of love
We are forced to believe in forgiveness...and grace. [19]

Notice that today's Scripture reading doesn't *suggest* that
you respect your husband; it makes a firm statement, "The wife
must respect her husband." Our culture says it's okay to give
after you receive, but God's principles are usually opposite from
the world's point-of-view. God says give first, then you will
receive. Be a risk-taker in your marriage; don't be afraid to
give. God would never tell you to do something that wasn't
right and that wouldn't bring blessings in your life.

God's design for marriage is for husbands to love their
wives as Christ loved the church and for wives to respect their
husbands. Christ loved the world enough to die for it, and that
kind of love is worthy of respect.

Now consider a passage from H. Norman Wright's *Quiet
Times for Couples* in which he addresses the issue of respect
more specifically. What does this passage show you about your
marriage and the respect you show your husband?

Do you have a respectful marriage? This is part of our calling as believers. [Scripture] instructs both husbands and wives to respond to one another with respect. But do you understand what that means? Respect in marriage means ministering to your partner through listening, a loving embrace, a flexible mind and attitude, and a gracious spirit. It means looking past faults and differences and seeing strengths and similarities. It means sharing concerns mutually instead of attempting to carry the load yourself.

Consider the following questions as you evaluate your respect for one another:

- In a tense situation, do I cut off my partner when he or she holds a view different from mine?

- When I think my partner is wrong, do I become offensive and harsh trying to put him or her in place?

- In trying to get a point across, am I gently persuasive or opinionated and demanding?

- Am I driven so much by the need to be right that I try to pressure my spouse into my position? Do I intimidate my partner?

Yes, these are questions which meddle. But answering them is a good step toward building a respectful marriage. As one author said, respect begins when we "learn to practice careful listening rather than threatened opposition, honest expression rather than resentment, flexibility rather than rigidity, loving censure rather than harsh coercion, encouragement rather than intimidation." How's the respect in your marriage relationship?[20]

When we show our mate respect in the ways that Norm Wright outlines, we do much to strengthen our marriage. And you, as a wife, have an important opportunity to show your respect for your husband each time he makes a decision, good or bad—and some will be bad. Let me remind you that Babe Ruth struck out more times than any other baseball player, but he also hit 60 home runs in a season and set a record that no other player has equaled. Keep in mind, too, that today's baseball players make millions of dollars for batting .300—and batting .300 means getting on base 300 times out of 1000 times at bat. Looked at differently, that statistic means *not* getting on base 700 times. And still the world is willing to pay greatly for a performance like that! So perhaps we can be a little more forgiving and respectful when our mates make a few bad decisions. When you can do that for your husband, you will be showing him your love in a very powerful way.

You will also be loving your husband with the love of Christ. "When we fail," Norm Wright observes, "and often we do—God keeps no record of it. God does not deal with us according to our sins (Psalm 103:10), but He accepts us in Christ. Because of the work of Jesus on the cross, you are accepted as blameless. [So] perhaps one of your most important callings in marriage is to follow the model of Christ by being a living benediction to your partner. Help keep your mate from stumbling, and when he or she does fall, don't keep track of it. Score keeping isn't a part of marriage; however, forgiveness is."[21]

Encourage your man when he makes decisions. Let go of unrealistic standards of perfection and love him for who he is, a fallible human being. Let your home be a place where he isn't constantly evaluated and where he doesn't have to perform in order to be accepted. Focus on his skills and abilities, and let him lead from his strengths. Finally, don't keep track of the poor decisions he makes. Your husband will become a more confident decision maker and a better leader when he knows that you are in his corner no matter what the outcome.

Accept your husband unconditionally (unless he is doing something in violation of God's commands). Encourage your husband to be the unique person God created him to be. Be a source of serenity in his life and grant him the solitude he needs to dream, to recover, and to be with the Lord. Encourage him to develop friendships with other men and welcome the new perspectives, interests, and passions these friends may introduce into your husband's life.

> *Father God, touch my heart. Help me to respect my husband unconditionally. Let me risk rejection and reach out to show him that I do respect him in a godly way. May I be obedient to this command. Amen.*

Thoughts for Action

❦ Write in your journal five expectations you have for your husband.

❦ After each one write, "I release you, and you are free to become the man God wants you to be!"

❦ Also, list in your journal how you are going to respect your husband more.

❦ Leave a surprise love message on his computer or fax machine.

❦ Call your husband every hour one morning or afternoon with one more reason why you respect him.

Additional Scripture Reading

Mark 10:35-45   John 13:1-17

Not on Your Permanent Record

Scripture Reading: Romans 8:1-9

Key Verse: Romans 8:1-2

Therefore, there is now no condemnation for those who are in Christ Jesus, because through Christ Jesus the law of the Spirit of life set me free from the law of sin and death.

Our son-in-law, Dr. Craig Merrihew, relates an incident in his life that vividly illustrates the great promise in today's key verse. When Craig was in the fifth grade, he and a friend rode their bicycles to school each day. School started at 9:00 A.M. and they couldn't get on the playground before 8:30 A.M. One day they had tail winds which had them arriving to the playground before the appropriate time. Of course, no supervision was available, but did that stop them? No! As boys will do, they went on the playground early. They were having a ball when a teacher arrived and firmly stated, "Boys, go to the principal's office!"

Upon arriving at Mr. Fox's office, they had to sit in the reception area. Just imagine two good boys sitting there waiting for the principal to come out of his big office. They didn't know what was going to happen to them, maybe expulsion, a call to the police, a trip to jail, or a phone call telling parents to come get them. Their knees were shaking and their voices were quivering when Mr. Fox appeared and invited the boys into his office.

After hearing the story, Mr. Fox stood up and very authoritatively stated, "This will go on your permanent record." Craig thought he would die. He just *knew* this would probably prevent him from graduating from elementary, junior high, high school, and college, and it would definitely prevent him from becoming a dentist! He also knew that his parents would be very upset.

When Craig got home that evening, he related the incident to his dad. His dad assured Craig that this event would not prevent him from obtaining his academic endeavor.

Have you ever been crippled because of some sin that you have felt has gone on your permanent record of life? In Romans 8, Paul assures us that there is now no condemnation for those who are in Christ Jesus, because through Christ Jesus the law of the Spirit of life has set us free from the law of sin and death.

The truly godly person never forgets that he was at one time an object of God's holy and just wrath. He never forgets that Christ Jesus came into the world to save sinners, and the godly person feels, along with Paul, that he is himself the worst of sinners. But then as he looks to the cross, he sees that Jesus was his atoning sacrifice. He sees that Jesus bore his sins in His own body, and that the wrath of God—the wrath which he, a sinner, should have borne—was expended completely and totally upon the holy Son of God. And in this view of Calvary, he sees the love of God.

The love of God has no meaning apart from Calvary. And Calvary has no meaning apart from the holy and just wrath of God. Jesus did not die just to give us peace and a purpose in life; He died to save us from the wrath of God. He died to reconcile us to a holy God who was alienated from us because of our sin. He died to ransom us from the penalty of sin—the punishment of everlasting destruction, shut out from the presence of the Lord. He died that we, the just objects of God's wrath, should become, by His grace, heirs of God and co-heirs with Him.

Do you have that assurance that your past, present, and future sins are forgiven by Christ Jesus because of what He did on the cross? If not, you can. In 1 John 1:9 we read, "If we confess our sins, he is faithful and just and will forgive us our sins and purify us from all unrighteousness."

Through God's Word you can be assured that your sins will not be on your permanent record as you stand before God on judgment day.

Thoughts for Action

- ❦ Confess any and all sins (past, present, future) and ask God to forgive them and to purify you from all your sins.

- ❦ Record this date in your journal.

- ❦ If you have a Bible, write today's date on the first inside page and write Romans 8:2 and 1 John 1:9 down as references.

- ❦ Tell a friend of your decision.

Additional Scripture Reading

Luke 18:9-14   Romans 5:14-21

□ □ □

Love Is Very Patient and Kind

Scripture Reading: 1 Corinthians 13:4-13

Key Verse: 1 Corinthians 13:4

> *Love is patient, love is kind. It does not envy, it does not boast, it is not proud.*

———— ❧ ————

Our dear friends Bill and Carole Thornburgh know about showing love. In 1987 Bill was diagnosed with leukemia. Eighteen months and three rounds of chemotherapy treatment later, Bill went to be with our Lord. Soon afterward, Carole was reading a novel where the main character, who was dying of cancer, left a letter for her husband and another for her young children to read when they became adults. Carole desperately wished that Bill had left her a note.

Several days later, when she was getting ready to visit Bill's sister, Carole decided to take some of Bill's old books to her. While going through the books, Carole found an envelope addressed to her from Bill. He had written Carole an Easter card two years earlier, and she had tucked it away in a book. Upon rediscovering the card now, she was so thankful to God for her husband's written words. At Christmastime 1989, Carole had a precious Easter card from her beloved husband. It read:

———

192

A Tearful Week
A Long Week
A Hard Week
A Lonely Week
A Painful Week
A Revealing Week
A Recovering Week
A Reassuring Week
A Peace Week
A Rededication Week
A Friendship Week
A Love Week
A Roller Coaster Week
A Renewal Week
A Glorious Week
A Victorious Week
A Life Changing Week
But A Week I Will Never Lose Sight Of

May God be our source of true love and friendship. You have been so good these days. I love you for it. You have been all a husband would desire. Forgive me, Sweet, for not keeping our love fresh. I love you.

Happy Easter and Happy Beginnings,

Bill

Bill and Carole spoke openly of their love for one another, and Bill's words offered Carole a sense of his presence when he was gone.

Learn the language of love. Each of us who is married needs to learn how to say, "I love you." And I'm not talking only about speaking aloud those three powerful words (although that's an important thing to do!). We need to also say, "I love you" through our sensitivity to our spouse, through our manners and our respect. Sometimes, for instance, as Bob is leaving on errands, he will ask if there's anything he can get for me while he's out. Once in a while he might hear me say that I'd like a certain new book and—what do you know?—it shows up unexpectedly for no special reason. These are just some of the ways that Bob shows me that he loves me.

And I show Bob that I love him with an evening at the theater, a new shirt, or his favorite Southern fried chicken for dinner. However I choose to show my love, I say aloud to Bob, "Just another way to say, 'I love you!'" Little acts of kindness like this are powerful and effective ways to strengthen your friendship with your mate. Such little acts of thoughtfulness show that you do not take your loved one for granted.

Certain rituals and traditions in our family also enable us to express our love for one another. We kiss each other goodnight and say, "May God bless your sleep." We celebrate our love on anniversaries and birthdays by giving each other small gifts. We telephone one another when we're apart, visit one of two favorite restaurants on special occasions, go out to lunch, attend the theater, and share hugs and (my contribution) corny jokes. All of these things—spontaneous little acts as well as carefully planned events—make for a special friendship.

One word of caution! Be sure that you are expressing your love in the language—the words and the actions—that your spouse will understand! Just because you feel loved when he plans a special dinner out doesn't mean that he feels loved when you do the same! Be a student of your husband. Know what best communicates to him the love you have. And keep your eyes open for common, everyday events that give you the chance to express that love!

Bob and I continually strive to make sure that our love is patient, kind, that it does not envy, does not boast, or is not proud. It's a lifetime of challenges in developing a Christlike expression of love one to another.

Jerry and Barbara Cook offer another way to tell your

husband—who is, I hope, your best friend—that you love
him.

I Need You

I need you in my times of strength and in my
weakness;
I need you when you hurt as much as when I hurt.
There is no longer the choice as to what we will
share.
We will either share all of life or be fractured
persons.
I didn't marry you out of need or to be needed.
We were not driven by instincts or emptiness;
We made a choice to love.
But I think something supernatural happens at
the point of marriage commitment (or maybe it's
actually natural).
A husband comes into existence; a wife is born.
He is a whole man before and after, but at a point
in time he becomes a man who also is a husband;
That is—a man who needs his wife.
She is a whole woman before and after.
But from now on she needs him.
She is herself but now also part of a new unit.
Maybe this is what is meant in saying,
"What God hath joined together."
Could it be He really does something special at "I
do"?
Your despair is mine even if you don't tell me
about it.
But when you do tell, the sharing is easier for me;
And you also can then share from my strength in
that weakness. [22]

Father God, I sincerely want this type of love for
myself and for all those whom I meet. Give me the

desire and strength to love others as You have loved me. Protect me in this endeavor so that I will only love in an honorable way and express my love in a language that the person I care for will understand. Amen.

Thoughts for Action

❧ Do something for your husband that you hate doing: Iron his shirts, cook him breakfast, make his lunch, wash his car, cook his favorite meal, run an errand.

❧ Send him flowers at work.

❧ Let him warm his cold feet in bed.

❧ Spread rose petals all over the bedroom.

Additional Scripture Reading

    1 Peter 4:7-11   1 John 4:7-21

Your Husband's Friend

Scripture Reading: Genesis 2:18-23

Key Verse: Genesis 2:18

> The Lord God said, "It is not good for the man to be alone. I will make a helper, suitable for him."

Genesis 2:18-23 is a beautiful picture of how God created not only the first woman and wife, but also the first friend. A wife is indeed to be her husband's friend, and that has truly been my experience. Through the years, the love Bob and I have for each other has grown, and we have become each other's best friend. This passage from Genesis suggests that is exactly what God intends for a married couple. Let's look closely at this section of Scripture.

- God gives the woman to the man to be "a helper, suitable for him" (2:18). Do you consider yourself a helper or a hindrance to your husband? To his work? To his time at home? Are you "suitable" or unsuitable when it comes to recognizing and meeting his needs? Where could you be more helpful to him? If you're not sure, why not ask him?

- God creates woman from man's rib (2:21,22). Earlier in Genesis, we learn that God created human beings in His image (1:27). The fact that each of us is created in God's image calls us to honor and respect one another. Consider for a moment that your husband was made by God in His image, just as you were. How, then, should you treat him? Acknowledging that your husband has been created in the image of God calls you, I believe, to respect and honor him and to offer him love and friendship.

• Adam perceived Eve as part of his own bone and own flesh (2:23). If, like Adam, I rightly understand that Bob is actually part of me, I will want to treat him as well as I treat myself. I will want to take good care of him and provide for his every need. This kind of wife's love provides a good foundation for the kind of friendship a wife can give her man.

Consider the following definition of a friend.

> And what is a friend? Many things...A friend is someone you are comfortable with, someone whose company you prefer. A friend is someone you can count on—not only for support, but for honesty.
>
> A friend is one who believes in you...someone with whom you can share your dreams. In fact, a real friend is a person you want to share all of life with...and the sharing doubles the fun.
>
> When you are hurting and you can share your struggle with a friend, it eases the pain. A friend offers you safety and trust...Whatever you say will never be used against you.
>
> A friend will laugh with you, but not at you...A friend will pray with you...and for you.
>
> My friend is one who hears my cry of pain,

who senses my struggle, who shares my lows as well as my highs.[23]

In such a friendship, nothing is hidden. Such friendship is built on trust, and such friendship takes time to grow and develop. What better context for this kind of friendship to grow than your marriage? How does your marriage measure up against this description? If you and your husband don't yet share this kind of friendship, don't wait for him to reach out. Take the initial step and see how he responds. If you have tried before and not been well received, ask God to guide and bless your efforts and then risk reaching out again.

Father God, I want You to know that I want to be a friend to my husband. I want to fulfill the role for which I was made. Let my husband know that my desires for him come from my friendship with him and not from wanting to take away his freedom. Amen.

Thoughts for Action

❧ Do something with your husband that you don't normally like to do: maybe a ball game, a "man's" movie, the theater, fishing, hiking, or the beach.

❧ Write your mate a note expressing how much you enjoy him as a friend.

❧ Add a dimmer to your bedroom light switch.

Additional Scripture Reading

Proverbs 18:24   Amos 3:3
Ecclesiastes 4:9

How to Attract Your Mate

Scripture Reading: 1 Peter 3:3-5a

Key Verse: 1 Peter 3:3

> *Your beauty should not come from outward adornment, such as braided hair and the wearing of gold jewelry and fine clothes.*

What is attractive? Our Scripture today talks about God's perspective on beauty and attractiveness.

Scripture calls women to be godly and to develop an inward beauty, and that's of first importance. But wise women today also work to make themselves pleasing to their husband's eye—and that's right on target. When a wife looks good, a husband looks at her often and likes what he sees. A pleasing appearance will invite your husband to touch and hold you—and no one else. Your husband wants to be proud of you whether at home or in public. Besides, doesn't looking nice make you feel better about yourself?

My mother wore current fashions and popular colors even though we were a low middle-class family. (You don't have to have a lot of money to look attractive!) She always looked fashionable. She never left home with curlers in her hair or a bandanna wrapped around her head—she didn't want to embarrass herself if she ran into friends.

Every married woman needs to ask herself, "Am I looking my best when I am with my husband? Is he proud of my personal appearance?" If you feel you could make yourself more appealing and attractive, there are many resources available, including books and magazines, friends who will give suggestions, color and wardrobe seminars, and department store consultants who can assist you in developing a new you. Or you might follow the example of a friend of mine...

Jan has a specific plan of action to get ready for her husband's arrival home. Each day at 4:00 P.M., she takes a shower or bath, powders and perfumes, combs her hair, and dresses informally. She lives according to the Barnes motto: "A husband should be sad when he leaves for work in the morning, and a wife should be glad to see him come home in the evening." When Jan's husband arrives, her appearance shows that she has been waiting for him and that she cares that he has returned. I encourage you to pay attention to how you look for your husband. You—and he and your marriage—will definitely benefit!

As you strive to look and feel your best, always remember today's key verse. It provides balance when it comes to dress and style. As Christian women we have to be sensitive not to be conformed to the world's standard of beauty, but to look at the inner qualities that develop us into godly women.

Father God, show me how I can be appealing to my husband both inside and out. Guide my efforts at inner beauty and outer attractiveness. Truly let my husband be sad when he leaves home for work, and give me a joy and happiness when he comes home each evening. Amen.

Thoughts for Action

❦ In your journal list several areas where you feel you could be more attractive.

❧ Alongside each entry write what action you will do to get it accomplished.

❧ Try a new way to say, "I love you!" to your husband. Write him a love letter, a poem, or a song. Hiding places for love notes and small gifts: under the pillow, in the glove compartment of his car, in the medicine cabinet near his razor, in his briefcase, under his dinner plate, etc.

❧ Why be romantic? Why bother? Simple. It will improve your quality of life.

Additional Scripture Reading

1 Timothy 2:9-10   Song of Songs 1:1-17

Your Most Important Decision

Scripture Reading: Joshua 24:14-15

Key Verse: Joshua 24:15

But as for me and my household, we will serve the Lord.

———— ❦ ————

Some decisions we make in life are everlasting. We see throughout history how proper and improper decisions have changed the history of mankind.

Joshua faced the same dilemma for his family as we do for our family. Which God to worship? The gods of the world or *the* God—Jehovah?

Choosing whom to worship is the most basic question of our life. Joshua was a man of courage, strength, determination, and faith. He was a leader to his family and nation. As recorded in today's Scripture reading, Joshua states that we worship the gods we want to. For Joshua and his family, they will serve the Lord.

Which of the gods will you serve? Your life today is the consequences of the decisions you made yesterday. Are you tired of being a slave to poor decisions of the past? If so, you can have the freedom and joy of being in Christ. You do not have to continue to suffer the pain of yesterday; today you can commit to turning your life around.

Paul writes in Romans 10:9-10, "That if you confess with your mouth, 'Jesus is Lord,' and believe in your heart that God raised him from the dead, you will be saved. For it is with your heart that you believe and are justified, and it is with your mouth that you confess and are saved."

Can you make a decision today about this promise? It will be the best decision of your life. Don't delay. Don't wait until it's too late. The writer of Ecclesiastes 3:1 states, "There is a time for everything, and a season for every activity under heaven."

Three times a soldier in a hospital picked up the hymn "Will You Go?" which was scattered as a tract. Twice he threw it down. The last time, he read it, thought about it, and, taking his pencil, wrote deliberately in the margin these words: "By the grace of God, I will try to go, John Waugh, Company G, Tenth Regiment, P.R.V.C." That night, he went to a prayer meeting, read his resolution, requested prayers for his salvation, and said, "I am not ashamed of Christ now; but I am ashamed of myself for having been so long ashamed of him." He was killed a few months later. How timely was his resolution!

Today is the appointed time. Make that decision for the first time, or reconfirm a previous decision that you and your family will serve the Lord.

> *Father God, each day I must choose what god I will worship. May I, as Joshua did, choose Jehovah God. I want to serve You with all my heart and soul. Please renew that desire in me on a daily basis. I love You. Amen.*

Thoughts for Action

❦ Make the decision to serve the Lord today.

❦ Record this date in your journal.

❦ If you have a Bible, write today's date on the first inside page and write Romans 8:1 and 1 John 1:9 down as a reference.

❦ Tell a friend of your decision.

Additional Scripture Reading

Romans 3:23	Acts 16:30-31
Romans 6:23	Ephesians 2:8-9

Worthy of Love

Scripture Reading: Matthew 22:36-40

Key Verse: Matthew 22:37-39

> *"Love the Lord your God with all your heart and with all your soul and with all your mind." This is the first and greatest commandment. And the second is like it: "Love your neighbor as yourself."*

Jesus' words in today's key verse are from Deuteronomy 6:4-9. The Jewish nation used these words as part of their Shema, which became Judaism's basic confession of faith. According to rabbinic law, this passage was to be recited every morning and night. This passage stresses the uniqueness of God, precludes the worship of other gods, and demands a total love commitment.

In Matthew 22 Jesus was asked, "Teacher, which is the greatest commandment in the Law?" Jesus gave two commandments which stress three loves: the love of God, the love of your neighbor, and the love of self. We know we ought to love God and to be kind and love our neighbors, but somehow we have a difficult time knowing how to love ourselves. I have met many women who do not understand this concept. As women, we always seem to be giving so much to others in our family that there is no time left for us.

As a young woman and a new bride, then as a new mother, I was always tired. I had no energy left over for me and we most certainly didn't have any money left over from our budget to give me anything. So what did I do for myself? Not very much. After studying this passage of Scripture, I was challenged to study the subject of personal worth. I was careful not to put an overemphasis on self, but to take a balanced and moderate approach that would let me grow as an individual. I knew if God was going to make me a complete and functioning person in the body of Christ, I had to develop a wholesome approach to this area of caring for myself.

As I began to look about me, I discovered women who had a mistrust of themselves and who had begun to withhold love and self-acceptance, women who had no idea that God had a plan for their life, women whose lives reflected fear, guilt, and mistrust of other people. These women did not understand that God had given them certain divine dignity which could make it possible for them to love themselves, and realize they are worthy of love. I also noticed that women would relate to their friends, their husbands, and their children either positively or negatively depending how well they understood this principle.

I can remember one Friday morning in a home Bible study. We were studying a marriage book, and Amy spoke up and said that she didn't take care of her personal self because her father had told her at a young age that pretty girls with good clothes and nice figures stood a better chance of being molested by older boys and men as they grew up. At that time Amy decided she would not let herself be molested by an older man, so she began to gain weight and wear sloppy clothes. She even remarked that her husband liked her this way because other men didn't try to flirt with her. He felt safe from any competition.

Over the next several months in our weekly study, I began to share with Amy how this fear was put there by Satan and not by God. I took extra time encouraging her to be all that God had for her. We looked at her eating habits and why she chose certain foods. After a while she began to seek professional counseling to understand what she was hiding behind. If you could see Amy today, you would see a fine young woman who has a totally new image and who shares with other women in full confidence. Because of Amy's appropriate self-appraisal, her husband has also joined a support group at church and has lessened his fears from his own insecurities.

What is anger? What is hatred? It is really fear. And what is fear? It is a feeling of being threatened, a deep feeling of insecurity. And what causes that feeling of insecurity? It is a lack of confidence in our ability to cope with threatening situations. And lack of self-confidence is the result of too low a value of yourself. You aren't able to love yourself because of what you think you are!

R.C. Sproul says that "lack of faith" is a "lack of trust" that God is capable of doing what He has promised He will do.

It takes a lot of faith to love. People who cannot love themselves do not dare to love. They are afraid they'll be spurned or rejected. Why do they have that fear? Because they do not trust themselves or rate themselves high enough to believe they'll be loved. And why do they fear rejection? Because rejection will only put salt in the wounds, proving again that they aren't worthy.

In Genesis 1:26-27 it says, "Then God said, 'Let us make man in our image, in our likeness...' So God created man in his own image, in the image of God he created him; male and female he created them." In verse 31 the Scripture says, "God saw all that he had made, and it was very good." We were spiritually designed to enjoy the honor that befits a prince of heaven. There is a basic need to recognize the dignity of the human being to be a child of God.

George Gallup, Jr., of the Gallup organization, conducted a poll on the self-esteem of the American public. The poll conclusively demonstrated that people with a positive self-image demonstrate the following qualities:

1. They have a high moral and ethical sensitivity.

2. They have a strong sense of family.

3. They are far more successful in interpersonal relationships.

4. Their perspective of success is viewed in terms of interpersonal relationships, not in crass materialistic terms.

5. They're far more productive on the job.

6. They are far lower in incidents of chemical addictions. (Current research shows that 80 percent of all suicides are related to alcohol and drug addiction.)

7. They are more likely to get involved in social and political activities in their community.

8. They are far more generous to charitable institutions and give far more generously to relief causes.[24]

As contributing members of our family, church, community, and society, each of us wants these positive qualities.

It seems the majority of our churches struggle in implementing the three loves of Deuteronomy and Matthew. But people who view God as a personal, loving, and forgiving Being, and relate to Him in such a personal way, do develop a strong, healthy sense of self-worth. Make sure you are in a church that teaches these aspects of the gospel.

Paul teaches in Philippians 4:13 that, "I can do everything through him who gives me strength." Using this principle, we can realize that Christ gives us the inner strength to care for ourselves. We must choose to love ourselves. There are many who say that self-love is evil and wrong, but I don't believe that's true. I want to encourage you to take time for yourself each day. Time for yourself gives you time to renew your mind, body, and spirit. Not only will you be rewarded, but so will those who come in contact with you daily.

Father God, I don't want to become self-centered, but I do want to understand the value You

*have given me because You gave Your Son. Please
reveal to me those areas of my life that I find difficult
to love, nurturing through time with just You, or
maybe a fresh flower or even a relaxing massage.
Help me to base my sense of self-worth on You.
Amen.*

Thoughts for Action

❦ In your journal write down five things you like about your-self.

❦ Also, write down five things you want to improve about yourself.

❦ After each item on the second list write one or two things you are going to do to improve that area of your life.

❦ Take a stroll at the beach, in the woods, through the snow, on a windy trail. Ponder how wonderfully you are made (Psalm 139).

Additional Scripture Reading

Deuteronomy 6:4-9   Philippians 4:13

Martha and Mary and Me

Scripture Reading: Luke 10:38-42

Key Verse: Luke 10:41-42

> *"Martha, Martha," the Lord answered, "you are worried and upset about many things, but only one thing is needed. Mary has chosen what is better, and it will not be taken away from her."*

———— ❧ ————

Confession of a Clutter Bug

Lord, bless this mess—
All of it's mine.
It keeps me in distress
All of the time.
Each item I save,
And think I may need,
Is an outward sign
Of inner greed.
Help me to let go and
Quit keeping everything.
I'm a clutter bug I know,
But You are the King of Kings!
By Your power I ask

For freedom—yes release.
Help me in my task
To let go of things, please?

—Tina Posey
Alabama

I have a confession to make: I've been more like Martha than like Mary. I desire to be like Mary, but my Martha side keeps getting in the way.

With a basic knowledge of people differences, we can see that Martha is the doer. Author and speaker Florence Littauer would identify her as a Powerful Choleric ("Let's do it my way"). Martha has a desire to control the situation. She has the ability to take charge of anything instantly. She is valuable in work because she can accomplish more than anyone else in a shorter time, and she's usually right. But she has weaknesses too. She's often bossy, domineering, autocratic, insensitive, and impatient. She is usually unwilling to delegate or to give credit to others.

On the other hand, Mary would be identified as Peaceful Phlegmatic ("Let's do it the easy way"). Mary wants to avoid conflict and to keep peace. She has a balance in life, an even disposition, and usually a dry sense of humor. Her personality is pleasing. She is valuable in work because she cooperates and is a calming influence. She keeps peace, mediates between contentious people, and objectively solves problems. However, she will often lack decisiveness, enthusiasm, and energy.

Many of my readers express this frustration of the struggle between Martha and Mary. They can relate to the following:

My Martha Side

My house is a tyrant, demanding each hour. Imperiously ordering: "Sweep, mop and scour! Do the dishes, the laundry, then iron, dust and cook! And there's mending to do if you'll just take a look. Now, Martha, get busy and don't waste a minute; dirt is a sin, and you're wallowing in it!"

My Mary Side

My housework can wait . . . there's a friend I must see, who's lonely and frightened, she's looking for me. Then I'll tidy up quickly and hurry to hear that fine missionary we support every year. Home again, "Father, thank You, please help me to care for the hungry and homeless who live in despair."

Mary—Martha—Me

Martha nags me to keep my house spotless each day; and Mary says gently, "I need time to pray." Martha's concerned with "what neighbors might think if they dropped in and found dishes stacked in the sink." While Mary chides, "Selfish! I think it's a crime if you don't share with others your talents and time."

My Prayer

Oh God, in compassion, so order my days that Mary might serve Thee and Martha may praise Thee.

Father God, I desire a balanced life. Reveal to me how I can be a Martha and a Mary. They were both virtuous in the way they ministered to You, and I have only pure desires to serve You as well. Please show me the way. Amen.

Thoughts for Action

❦ Write down in your journal the struggles you have with being a Martha.

❦ Write down in your journal the struggles you have with being a Mary.

❦ In each case state what you might do to come to a middle ground. Pray to God that He will give you the desires of your heart to serve God and family in a more balanced lifestyle!

Additional Scripture Reading

Luke 9:57-62   Matthew 4:4

Continually Seek God's Wisdom

Scripture Reading: Proverbs 1:1-7

Key Verse: Proverbs 1:7

*The fear of the Lord is the beginning of knowledge,
but fools despise wisdom and discipline.*

Most of what I really need to know about how to live, and what to do, and how to be, I learned in kindergarten. Wisdom was not at the top of the graduate school mountain but there in the sandbox at nursery school.

These are the things I learned: Share everything. Play fair. Don't hit people. Put things back where you found them. Clean up your own mess. Don't take things that aren't yours. Say you're sorry when you hurt someone. Wash your hands before you eat. Flush. Warm cookies and cold milk are good for you. Live a balanced life. Learn some and think some and draw and paint and sing and dance and play and work some every day.

Take a nap every afternoon. When you go out into the world, watch for traffic, hold hands, and stick together. Be aware of wonder. Remember the little seed in the plastic cup. The roots go down and the plant goes up and nobody really knows how or why, but we are all like that.

Goldfish and hamsters and white mice and even the little seed in the plastic cup—they all die. So do we.

And then, remember the book about Dick and Jane and the first word you learned, the biggest word of all: LOOK. Everything you need to know is in there somewhere. The Golden Rule and love and basic sanitation. Ecology and politics and sane living.

Think of what a better world it would be if we all—the whole world—had cookies and milk about 3 o'clock every afternoon and then lay down with our blankets for a nap. Or if we had a basic policy in our nation and other nations to always put things back where we found them and cleaned up our own messes. And it is still true, no matter how old you are, when you go out into the world it is best to hold hands and stick together. [25]

Solomon's wise sayings offer us advice on how to conduct ourselves in various situations in everyday life. His fundamental instruction is to fear and trust the Lord. Solomon challenges us to continually seek God's wisdom in the decisions we must make each day.

This type of knowledge goes beyond academic accomplishments to moral responsibility. It focuses in on decision-making and shows itself best in the disciplining of our character. We raise our children to be lawyers, doctors, teachers, salespeople, musicians, but do we ever purposefully raise our children to be good? We need a country where parents want to raise children to be good. Our country and world are desperately in need of good people.

We must begin to think clearly and scripturally if we are to survive the present cultural war in America. In regard to right and wrong, we must arrive at consistent answers that go along with our theological understanding of Scripture. We can't be swayed by what the secular world says. We must go to Scripture to see what God instructs us to do (see Romans 12:1-2). We must continually seek God's wisdom.

> *Father God, I want to be a woman who seeks after Your knowledge. Show me Your ways that I might acknowledge You as God. Help me to see that You are all that I will ever need. Amen.*

Thoughts for Action

❦ List in your journal five decisions that need to be answered today. On what basis will they be answered? Scriptural or secular?

❦ Get in the habit of answering basic questions from a theological framework.

❦ Select a verse of Scripture that will be your theme verse for life. I use Matthew 6:33.

Additional Scripture Reading

Romans 12:1-2   James 3:13-18
Proverbs 3:1-18

Memories of the Garden Bench

Scripture Reading: Philippians 1:3-11

Key Verse: Philippians 1:3

I thank my God every time I remember you.

It was a warm sunny day for January in Riverside, California. Two of our four grandchildren were helping us enjoy this fine day. Ten-and-a-half-year-old Christine was helping her Grammy Em plan and cook the dinner. She was picking flowers to arrange for our dinner table. PaPa Bob and Bevan were raking the garden, and picking oranges, avocados, and lemons off our trees that surround our property.

As the afternoon progressed, our working men became warm and tired.

Christine said, "Grammy, let's have tea." That's all it takes for me to stop whatever I'm doing and put the kettle on for Christine and me to have tea. In the process, we poured the men a tall glass of fresh juice on ice and prepared some yummy-for-the-tummy snacks. We carried the treats up the hill to PaPa and Bevan. How happy they were to receive the refreshment. They thanked us and headed for the bench that sits under a large shady avocado tree overlooking the grounds and our quaint, tree-lined little Rumsey Drive which winds by our barn.

As Christine and I left them, we headed back toward the house. Christine took my hand and said, "Grammy, I love you." "I love you, too, Christine," I said.

I prepared the tea kettle, and Christine pulled down the tea pot and put the teacups on the table with our special silver tea spoons. We toasted thick sourdough bread that we spread with jam and butter. It was an instant tea party—just Christine and me.

That night as my Bob and I crawled in bed, we began to share about our day with the oh-so-wonderful grandchildren.

"What do a PaPa and seven-year-old grandson talk about on the bench under the big avocado tree?" I asked.

"Oh, very special things," Bob replied. "Boys talk just like you girls talk."

I could still picture PaPa Bob and seven-year-old Bevan— with smudges of dirt on both their faces—sitting on that bench.

Bob continued, "I told Bevan, 'Someday, Bevan, when PaPa's in heaven and you drive down Rumsey Drive as a man, you'll look at this bench we are sitting on and you can remember the day that Grammy Em and sister Christine served us jam and toast with a glass of juice.' Then Bevan said, 'Not only will I remember, but I will bring my son and someday he will bring his son and point to the bench and tell him about the toast and jam we ate on the bench under that big avocado tree over there.'"

How does a little boy understand and think through the process of generations?

How blessed we are to have the God-given opportunity to teach our children and grandchildren about the beauty of God's creations, life and death, and most of all about God the Father, God, the Son, and God, the Holy Spirit.

Father God, we think we only live for today but
Scripture tells us to look to the future and eternity.

The world wants us to conform to the pressures of the here and now and focus on the temporal. Help me to take time to develop a future orientation for myself and my family. What You have done for us in the past gives us hope for the future. Amen.

Thoughts for Action

❦ Take a child's hand. Take a walk and talk to each other.

❦ Give a cup of refreshment to someone today—a cup of tea or a glass of juice.

❦ Tell someone, "I Love You."

Additional Scripture Reading

1 Corinthians 1:4   Deuteronomy 6:7

Psalm 67:1

Keeping a Tight Rein

Scripture Reading: James 1:19-27

Key Verse: James 1:26

> *If anyone considers himself religious and yet does not keep a tight rein on his tongue, he deceives himself and his religion is worthless.*

In *All I Really Need to Know I Learned in Kindergarten*, Robert Fulghum suggests that serenity and a quiet spirit is very much needed in our noisy world. He tells of villagers in the Solomon Islands who felled a tree by screaming at it for 30 days. The tree died, confirming the Islanders' theory that hollering kills a living thing's spirit. Fulghum then considers the things that he and his neighbors yell at: the wife, the kids, the telephone, the lawnmower that won't start, traffic, umpires, machines. Then he offers this observation:

> Don't know what good it does. Machines and things just sit there. Even kicking doesn't always help. As for people, well, the Solomon Islanders may have a point. Yelling at living things does tend to kill the spirit in them. Sticks and stones may break our bones, but words will break our hearts.[26]

Oh, if we could only remember this each time we want to overpower someone with a loud voice. How much better a quiet and gentle spirit! How much better tranquillity and serenity!

One of the ways we try to get control over a person or situation is by raising our voices. However, that is just the opposite of what we need to do. Try lowering your voice next time you're tempted to raise it. The world already has people who are dead in spirit because someone didn't realize that loud voices can kill. You can have a tremendous positive effect upon those who are near you. Let others remember you as a loving person, not a screamer.

Thoughts for Action

❦ Plant a tree today; water it and give it some vitamin B-1. It's a positive experience to see things grow.

❦ In your journal evaluate how you use your words and your voice in your life. If you aren't satisfied with your behavior, list several areas where you want to change. At the same time, list what actions you are going to do to make changes.

❦ Today practice lowering your voice when you feel like raising it.

❦ Apologize to someone in person, by phone, or in a letter to whom you have talked too harshly.

Additional Scripture Reading

Ephesians 4:29   Psalm 34:12-13

A Wife of Noble Character

Scripture Reading: Proverbs 12:1-7

Key Verse: Proverbs 12:4

> *A wife of noble character is her husband's crown,
> but a disgraceful wife is like decay in his bones.*

Major Sullivan Ballou wrote this letter to his devoted wife, Sarah, a week before Manassar, the first battle of Bull Run. Sarah must have been a wife of noble character that truly was a crown to her soldier husband.

July 14, 1861
Camp Clerk, Washington, D.C.

My very dear Sarah,
    The indications are very strong that we shall move in a few days—perhaps tomorrow. Lest I should not be able to write again, I feel impelled to write a few lines that may fall under your eye when I shall be no more . . .
    I have no misgivings about, or lack of confidence in, the cause in which I am engaged, and my courage does not halt or falter. I know how strongly American

Civilization now leans on the triumph of the Government, and how great a debt we owe to those who went before us through the blood and sufferings of the Revolution. And I am willing—perfectly willing—to lay down all my joys in this life, to help maintain this Government, and to pay that debt.

Sarah, my love for you is deathless; it seems to bind me with mighty cables that nothing but Omnipotence could break; and yet my love of Country comes over me like a strong wind and bears me unresistibly on with all these chains to the battlefield.

The memories of the blissful moments I have spent with you come creeping over me, and I feel most gratified to God and to you that I have enjoyed them so long. And hard it is for me to give them up and burn to ashes the hopes of future years, when, God willing we might still have lived and loved together, and seen our sons grow up to honorable manhood, around us. I have, I know, but few and small claims upon Divine Providence, but something whispers to me—perhaps it is the wafted prayer of my little Edgar, that I shall return to my loved ones unharmed. If I do not, my dear Sarah, never forget how much I love you, and when my last breath escapes me on the battlefield, it will whisper your name. Forgive my many faults, and the many pains I have caused you. How thoughtless and foolish I have often times been! How gladly would I wash out with my tears every little spot upon your happiness...

But, O Sarah! if the dead can come back to this earth and flit unseen around those they loved, I shall always be near you; in the gladdest days and in the darkest nights... *always, always,* and if there be a soft breeze upon your cheek, it shall be my breath, as the cool air fans your throbbing temple, it shall be my spirit passing by. Sarah, do not mourn me dead; think I am gone and wait for thee, for we shall meet again.[27]

Sullivan Ballou was killed at the first battle of Bull Run, leaving his wife these few, beautiful lines of love. She undoubtedly thought of her beloved husband whenever a soft breeze touched her cheek. Her husband had been both strong and sensitive, both tough and tender. As his letter reflects, he faced death with courage, standing strong in his convictions and unwavering in his commitment to his country, his wife, and his God. And I would guess that some of his courage resulted from a wife who believed in him, encouraged him, and made him her hero.

Supporting your man will indeed encourage him to be the man—and husband and father—that God wants him to be. Like Sullivan Ballou, who was both tough and tender, your husband can come to know the strength of his masculinity. He can know the balance between strong and sensitive that God intended when He made man. I'm sure God looked down upon Major Ballou and said, "It was good." You can help your man earn those same words of praise, and he will praise you at the gates.

May we all strive to be a wife of noble character and our husband's crown.

Father God, I desire to be a woman of character. I want to find pleasure in Your sight, and I want to be a crown unto my husband. Please bring into my life those women who will show me how to develop Christian character. May my husband be receptive to my changes. I so want him to know that I love him very much. I never want to be a disgrace to him. Amen.

Thoughts for Action

🦋 Do you consider yourself to be a woman of noble character?

🦋 What makes you answer yes?

❧ What makes you answer no?

❧ What changes need to be made in your life to become a wife of noble character?

❧ List a few activities that you will undertake to make these changes.

❧ Meditate on these:

—Find good men and women to emulate.

—Carry no grudges. They'll weigh you down.

—Every day look for some little thing you can do to improve how you do your job.

Additional Scripture Reading

Philippians 4:8   Romans 14:17-19

Don't Be Afraid

Scripture Reading: Mark 16:1-8

Key Verse: Mark 16:6a

Don't be afraid.

Steven R. Covey, in his book *The Seven Habits of Highly Effective People,* tells a story that reflects the need for renewal and reawakening in our lives.

Suppose you come upon a man in the woods feverishly sawing down a tree.

"You look exhausted!" you exclaim. "How long have you been at it?"

"Over five hours," he replies, "and I'm beat. This is hard."

"Maybe you could take a break for a few minutes and sharpen that saw. Then the work would go faster."

"No time," the man says emphatically. "I'm too busy sawing."

To sharpen the saw means renewing ourselves in all four aspects of our natures:

Physical—exercise, nutrition, stress management;
Mental—reading, thinking, planning, writing;
Social/Emotional—service, empathy, security;
Spiritual—spiritual reading, study, and meditation.

To exercise in all these necessary dimensions, we must be proactive. No one can do it for us or make it urgent for us. We must do it for ourselves.[28]

If we are to stay on top of the pile rather than under the pile, we must take time to sharpen the saws of our lives. As I speak in front of various groups, I find many women who are defeated and burned out from their roles in life. Many women express to me, "If I only had time for myself, I would stop and smell the roses!"

Below I have given you several ideas that will help you care for yourself. When we renew our lives, we are better equipped to handle stress and fear. If you are afraid, uptight, tense, or short-tempered, maybe you need a touch of renewal for yourself.

In the "Thoughts for Action" section, you will find several activities that will give you a fresh approach to life.

Reach out, risk, and try several of them.

Thoughts for Action

Physical

❧ Get a professional massage, sauna, and steam bath.

❧ Have your hair and nails done. Get a pedicure.

❧ Exercise regularly by walking, jogging, doing aerobics, etc.

❧ Read a book on nutrition and begin to change your eating habits.

❧ Take a stress-management class.

❧ Take a quiet bubble bath by candlelight.

❧ Take a stroll on the beach, by the lake, or along a mountain trail.

❧ Plant a flower and/or vegetable garden.

❧ Walk or run in the rain.

Mental

❦ Listen to good music.

❦ Read a good magazine or book.

❦ Retreat to a spot for a quiet time of meditating and reflecting.

❦ Spend time alone.

❦ Write a poem.

❦ Write a letter to an old friend.

❦ Plan your next three months' goals.

❦ Enroll in a class at your local college.

❦ Think of possible changes in your life.

❦ List everything for which you are thankful.

❦ Memorize a poem.

❦ Learn to play an instrument.

❦ Go to the beach and listen to the waves.

❦ Reach back to joyful times as a child and think about them.

Social/Emotional

❦ Have a good cry.

❦ Have breakfast or lunch with a friend.

❦ Go to the mall and people-watch.

❦ Have a friend over for tea or coffee (decaffeinated preferably).

❦ Spend a day doing anything you want.

❦ Spend a weekend with your husband in a quiet setting just to regroup.

❧ Visit a friend.

❧ Develop friendships with new people.

❧ Buy a bouquet of flowers for yourself.

❧ Donate time to a school, hospital, or church.

❧ Volunteer to collect money for United Way, the Cancer Society, or the Heart Association.

❧ Serve a friend in need.

Spiritual

❧ Read the Psalms.

❧ Meditate on Scripture.

❧ Read a spiritual book that you have had lying on your kitchen table for some time.

❧ Write your worries in the sand at the beach.

❧ Join a women's Bible study.

❧ Visit someone at the hospital or nursing home.

❧ Give of yourself.

❧ Examine your motives. Are they self-serving or serving others?

❧ Listen to good Christian music.

Make up your own lists of ideas under each of the headings. Learn to care for yourself. God felt it was such a valuable concept that He stated it as part of one of the two great commandments in Matthew 22:37-38. Jesus says, "Love the Lord your God with all your heart and with all your soul and with all your mind. . . . Love your neighbor as yourself." The world needs to witness us Christians living these two great commandments. Begin today to walk your talk. Jesus went on to say that on these two commandments depend the whole law and prophets.

Yes, it's okay to care for yourself because Jesus said it was. Let's plan time in each of our days to care for ourselves.

Additional Scripture Reading

Isaiah 41:10,13   Exodus 20:2-18

❑ ❑ ❑

Dwelling in the Sanctuary

Scripture Reading: Psalm 15:1-5

Key Verse: Psalm 15:1-5

> *Lord, who may dwell in your sanctuary? Who may live on your holy hill? He whose walk is blameless and who does what is righteous, who speaks the truth from his heart and has no slander on his tongue, who does his neighbor no wrong and casts no slur on his fellowman, who despises a vile man but honors those who fear the Lord, who keeps his oath even when it hurts, who lends his money without usury and does not accept a bribe against the innocent. He who does these things will never be shaken.*

———— ————

In today's passage David describes the character of the person who qualifies to be a guest of God's sanctuary. The two parallel questions of verse 1 are answered in the following four verses by an eleven-fold description of the righteous person who is upright in deed, word and attitude, and finances. These qualities, which aren't natural, are imparted by God and by his Holy Spirit.

Let's see what we can learn from this great psalm about the person who may dwell in the Lord's sanctuary:

1. He walks blameless.

2. He does what is righteous.

3. He speaks the truth from his heart.

4. He has no slander on his tongue.

5. He does his neighbor no harm.

6. He casts no slur on his fellowman.

7. He despises a vile (evil) man.

8. He honors those who fear the Lord.

9. He keeps his oath even when it hurts.

10. He lends his money without usury.

11. He does not accept a bribe against the innocent.

These are honorable characteristics! We certainly can appreciate the virtue of this type of person. However, many times we look upon the life of a righteous person and say to ourselves, "It must be easy for her to be a Christian. She evidently doesn't have the struggles with sin like I do!" Yet anyone who is trying to live a righteous life knows that we must choose each day to serve the Lord. It isn't any easier for any of us. We must decide moment by moment to do what is right.

David closes this psalm by stating, "He who does these things will never be shaken." What a great promise. Now let's live it with great faith.

> Father God, the Scripture tells me to dwell on those things which are honorable and pure in deed. I willfully decide today to believe and live the Scriptures as the saints of old, beginning with precept unto precept and line upon line. I want to be your woman. Amen.

Thoughts for Action
❦ Think on these things:

1. Compliment someone today.

2. Begin reading a good book.

3. Find five things every day to thank God for.

4. Lose no opportunity to develop relationships with wise men and women whose outlook will rub off on you.

❧ Choose one of the 11 points in today's study and concentrate on improving this area of your life.

Additional Scripture Reading

Psalm 27:5   Psalm 24:3-4
Joshua 24:14-15   Philippians 4:8

The Power of the Chocolate Chip Cookie

Scripture Reading: Proverbs 31:10-26

Key Verse: Proverbs 31:15

She gets up while it is still dark; she provides food for her family and portions for her servant girls.

When our son, Brad, started thinking about that special woman who God had for him as a wife, he naturally looked for someone like the woman he knew at home—his mother, ME.

Every once in a while he would bring a girlfriend home for dinner. These girls were foreigners to the kitchen. They didn't seem to understand what would attract a young man who had been raised in a family with our values. When I asked about these girls, Brad often told me, "I would really be more interested in them if they could cook and maybe even ask me over for dinner. But they don't even know how to cook."

One day Brad called with an excitement in his voice. He told me about this young woman named Maria who had brought him a plate of chocolate chip cookies that she had personally made. He was so thrilled that I knew this woman had captured Brad's attention. You guessed it, she eventually became our daughter-in-law. What a gem she is! We are so glad that her mother took the time to teach her how to bake chocolate chip cookies.

There is power in chocolate chip cookies. There is power in finding out what pleases a man. I know from experience, and I know from the mail I receive, specifically letters from husbands whose wives make great improvements in their homemaking and organizational skills after attending one of our seminars. What happens in three hours that changes a wife? The secret isn't a little pill or a magic word. Instead, I offer a biblical perspective on being a wife and homemaker, holding out the hope that women can indeed change the way their home is functioning. I share ideas about how to lighten the load and even make homemaking fun. This kind of message is important because, for one reason, men need to know that their wives can handle the household and children in an organized and efficient way. The stereotypical male fantasy of coming home to a well-cooked meal, cooperative and well-behaved children, and a kiss at the door is not too far off from what men really do want!

Why is an organized, smoothly functioning home important to a man? Because he needs a place to unwind after a day at work. When Bob arrived home, he used to always say to me, "You think I'm home, but I just sent my body ahead of me!" In reality, he wouldn't be home for another 30 minutes. During that half-hour he regrouped. He didn't handle any emergencies or deal with any bad news. I'd often get him a cold drink, let him sit in his favorite chair, and even take a brief nap. That time allowed him to change gears. After 30 minutes, he was truly home and able to function as a member of the family.

Bob was able to unwind because our home was well-organized and functioning smoothly. If I had not taken the time over the years to put some good practices into our home, we too would fall victim to disorganization.

As our Scripture teaches today, the woman of the home has some very challenging roles for her. The woman who comments, "The homemaker role isn't stimulating enough for me and I have to get a job outside of the home to find purpose," hasn't ever considered Proverbs 31 as a role model.

There is a whole lifetime to implement these tasks, so roll up your sleeves and begin today.

> *Father God, thank You for reminding me that it's the little things that count in life. Let me dwell on this truth today. I sometimes get so caught up in the big things that I forget the preciousness of simplicity. Amen.*

Thoughts for Action

❦ Make your loved ones a batch of their favorite cookies.

❦ Share your extra cookies with a friend or neighbor.

❦ In your journal, write down two or three new areas of your home-management skills that need attention. After each area write down what you will do to improve these areas of your home.

Additional Scripture Reading

Proverbs 12:4   Ruth 3:11
Proverbs 19:14   Romans 12:10-13

Earthquake

Scripture Reading: Matthew 24:6-13

Key Verse: Matthew 24:7b

> There will be famines and earthquakes in various places.

On January 17, 1994, at 4:31 A.M. in Southern California, the Los Angeles area was rocked by a 6.6 earthquake. Living one hour east of the epicenter, we felt the quake quite well. This quake shook up and down, not the rolling motions we've felt in the past. Almost all of Southern California awoke out of a dead sleep. Many ran into the streets or crawled under beds, desks, tables, and doorways. Our phone rang. It was our son Brad, "Dad, this was a bad one. Los Angeles has been hit hard." He was correct. Fatalities mounted and damages rose to billions of dollars. Freeways fell, fires broke out, and much, much more.

Only three months earlier Southern California had been hit by major fires, then rain caused mud slides in multi-million-dollar home areas. Within the past year we have experienced most of what the Scripture talks about from riots, quakes, fire, and flooding. The safety factor in this part of the country has dropped dramatically, with drive-by shootings, gangs, carjackings, murders, and thefts of all kinds.

Yet, why are we surprised? Our text tells us that before the Lord returns these things will happen. We must be ready. Residents here keep bottled water, earthquake kits, gas shut-off valves, etc.—trying to prepare for the big hit. Well, January 17 was almost it. The cleanup and rebuilding will take months, perhaps years. Yet time will pass, people will forget, and we'll proceed on with the fast pace of L.A. life.

More importantly, though, we must be ready in an eternal way. We need to prepare ourselves, spiritually and eternally, for the future quake of Jesus' return. He is coming again—just as the earth trembles at times. We don't know time, day, or place. Our Lord will come when we least expect Him.

I'll tell you from experience that when the earth quakes the fear flies through your body. But it will not be near the heated fear and trembling of those who are not ready upon the Lord's return. Jesus says in John 11:25-26 "I am the resurrection and the life. He who believes in me will live, even though he dies, and whoever lives and believes in me will never die." This is what we must believe to be ready. So simple, yet so many reject.

Remember, when comes the last call, we'll know that the Bible was true after all.

Believing is receiving.

> *Father God, I pray for those who do not believe in You as Savior of the world. May Your Spirit touch those hearts and open them to Your words. May we, as believers, be ready, taking the preparation time to pray for those who we know in our jobs, communities, and yes, even churches. Amen.*

Thoughts for Action

❧ Read 1 John today.

❧ Write in your journal the time you invited the Lord to be your Savior.

❧ Read this devotion to someone today.

Additional Scripture Reading

Isaiah 29:5-7   Acts 16:26
John 3:16

Life with Joy

Scripture Reading: Psalm 40:1-4

Key Verse: Psalm 40:3

> *He put a new song in my mouth, a hymn of praise to our God.*

What would our life be without joy? Without joy, we can do nothing. We would be like a violin out of tune; it yields such harsh sounds. Life without joy is like a bone out of joint; it doesn't function properly. We can do nothing well without joy.

Yes, God will give us a new song in our mouths and a hymn of praise to our God. When we come before God with an open heart and a voice of confession, He is just and will forgive us of all unrighteousness. With this emptying of our old self, He will give us a new song. He will give you a new song. One written just for you.

As a family, we can take this promise and turn our joy and song into laughter. We are a country that has forgotten how to laugh. We greatly need people who have a good sense of humor between Mom, Dad, and the children. In his poem "Laughter in the Walls," Bob Benson captures the essence of spending time together in laughter as a family.

> I pass a lot of houses on my way home—
>   some pretty,

some expensive,
  some inviting—
but my heart always skips a beat
  when I turn down the road
and see my house nestled against the hill.
  I guess I'm especially proud
of the house and the way it looks because
  I drew the plans myself.
It started out large enough for us—
  I even had a study—
two teenaged boys now reside in there.
  And it had a guest room—
my girl and nine dolls are permanent guests.
  It had a small room Peg
had hoped would be her sewing room—
  the two boys swinging on the dutch door
have claimed this room as their own.
  So it really doesn't look right now
as if I'm much of an architect.
  But it will get larger again—
one by one they will go away
  to work,
    to college,
  to service,
  to their own houses,
and then there will be room—
  a guest room,
    a study,
  and sewing room
for just the two of us.
But it won't be empty—
  every corner
    every room
    every nick
      in the coffee table
will be crowded with memories.

Memories of picnics,
    parties, Christmases,
bedside vigils, summers,
    fires, winters, going barefoot,
leaving for vacation, cats,
    conversations, black eyes,
graduations, first dates,
    ball games, arguments,
washing dishes, bicycles,
    dogs, boat rides,
getting home from vacation,
    meals, rabbits and
a thousand other things
    that fill the lives
of those who would raise five.
And Peg and I will sit
quietly by the fire
    and listen to the
    laughter in the walls. [29]

When the children are gone, when there are no lunches to be made, when retirement sets in—what will you hear in your walls? I pray it's laughter, for God created laughter. May your life truly reflect joy and laughter.

Father God, let me take time to build precious memories with my family and friends. We are here for a very short while and then we are gone—gone from those who are so dear to us. How will I be remembered? As someone who is angry, screaming, bitter? Or as a loving, laughable, joyful person? May my laughter echo strong in the walls long after I'm gone. Show me the way. Amen.

Thoughts for Action

❦ Buy a clean joke book and tell a new joke every night at the dinner table for one week. Begin to laugh at home.

❦ Loan the book to another member of the family and let him or her tell a joke for each dinner meal next week.

❦ Realize that the children will only be home for a short period of your life. Create your own laughter in the walls.

❦ Rediscover and nurture the "child" in you. It's the key to your creativity, your sense of wonder and joy.

Additional Scripture Reading

Habakkuk 3:17-18   Luke 15:9-10
Acts 2:46-47   1 Chronicles 29:9

Believe What God Believes About You

Scripture Reading: 1 Corinthians 13:4-13

Key Verse: 1 Corinthians 13:4-13

> *Love is patient, love is kind. It does not envy, it does not boast, it is not proud. It is not rude, it is not self-seeking, it is not easily angered, it keeps no record of wrongs. Love does not delight in evil but rejoices with the truth. It always protects, always trusts, always hopes, always perseveres.*
>
> *Love never fails. But where there are prophecies, they will cease; where there are tongues, they will be stilled; where there is knowledge, it will pass away. For we know in part and we prophesy in part, but when perfection comes, the imperfect disappears. When I was a child, I talked like a child, I thought like a child, I reasoned like a child. When I became a man, I put childish ways behind me. Now we see but a poor reflection as in a mirror; then we shall see face to face. Now I know in part; then I shall know fully, even as I am fully known.*
>
> *And now these three remain: faith, hope and love. But the greatest of these is love.*

It's important to believe that we have value and that we

are worthy to give of ourselves. This begins by knowing and accepting what our heavenly Father believes about us. Christian psychologist Dr. Dick Dickerson has written a paraphrase of 1 Corinthians 13 which beautifully summarizes how God looks at us. Read this aloud to yourself each morning and evening for the next 30 days, then evaluate how your feelings about yourself have changed:

Because God loves me, He is slow to lose patience with me.

Because God loves me, He takes the circumstances of my life and uses them in a constructive way for my growth.

Because God loves me, He does not treat me as an object to be possessed and manipulated.

Because God loves me, He has no need to impress me with how great and powerful He is because He is God. Nor does He belittle me as His child in order to show me how important He is.

Because God loves me, He is for me. He wants me to mature and develop in His love.

Because God loves me, He does not send down His wrath on every little mistake I make, of which there are many.

Because God loves me, He does not keep score of all my sins and then beat me over the head with them whenever He gets a chance.

Because God loves me, He is deeply grieved when I do not walk in the ways that please Him because He sees this as evidence that I don't trust Him and love Him as I should.

Because God loves me, He rejoices when I experience His power and strength and stand up under the pressure of life for His name's sake.

Because God loves me, He keeps working patiently with me even when I feel like giving up and can't see why He doesn't give up with me too.

Because God loves me, He keeps on trusting me when at times I don't even trust myself.

Because God loves me, He never says there is no hope for me, rather, He patiently works with me, loves me and disciplines me in such a way that it is hard for me to understand the depth of His concern for me.

Because God loves me, He never forsakes me even though many of my friends might. [30]

"Please be patient with me. God isn't finished with me yet." That is certainly true! As we look at a particular area in our lives, we can be tempted to break into tears of discouragement because we feel so defeated. But God is still working in our lives, and He will never give up on us.

There is a void in each of our lives that cannot be filled by the world. We may leave God or put Him on hold, but He is always there. He patiently waits for us to run our race, becoming fatigued in the process, and then to turn back to Him.

As you become secure in God's love, you will discover that you need not surrender your caring for yourself to the opinions and judgments of others. *God is for you!*

> *Father God, negative inner voices would love to convince me that I am a nobody, but the Holy Spirit continually challenges me to believe that I am of value to God and will be with Jesus in Paradise. Can I believe God when He tells me that I was so important to Him that He gave His only Son, Jesus Christ, to die on the cross for my sins? Yes, I can! I am special to God. Let me believe it and live it. Amen.*

Thoughts for Action

❦ Buy 100 "Love" postage stamps.

❦ Buy a new recording of your favorite musical artist.

❦ Buy yourself a new novel by your favorite writer.

❦ Write in your journal, "God loves me and so do I" 25 times. Read it through twice. Believe what you write and read.

Additional Scripture Reading

1 John 4:10   Song of Songs 8:6-7
1 John 4:12

Not Ashamed of the Gospel

Scripture Reading: Romans 1:1-17

Key Verse: Romans 1:16

I am not ashamed of the gospel, because it is the power of God for the salvation of everyone who believes; first for the Jew, then for the Gentile.

Ashamed of the gospel of Christ! Let the skeptic, let the wicked profligate, blush at his deeds of darkness, which will not bear the light, lest they should be made manifest; but never let the Christian blush to own the holy gospel. Where is the philosopher who is ashamed to own the God of Nature? Where is the Jew that is ashamed of Moses? or the Moslem that is ashamed of Mahomet? and shall the Christian, and the Christian minister, be ashamed of Christ? God forbid! No! Let me be ashamed of myself, let me be ashamed of the world, and let me blush at sin; but never, never, let me be ashamed of the gospel of Christ!" [31]

Dr. R. Newton was passionate in his plea of not being ashamed of the gospel. As I reflect upon my life, I have to confess that I have had an easy time of sharing the gospel due to the religious climate in America over the years. Lately, however, I have begun to realize that the religious freedom of the past may not be the same freedom of the future.

In our passage today, we see seven principles about the gospel that Paul is trying to teach the believers in Rome—and to us.

Point 1: We are all set apart for the gospel (verse 1). What an awesome thought that we are set apart! That makes us something special in the sight of God. With this thought, it helps me establish my daily priorities. It's not sports, politics, knowledge, business, or finances, but the gospel that goes to the top of the list.

Point 2: This gospel was promised beforehand through His prophets in the Holy Scripture (verse 2). I must realize that this precious gospel has a historical background that has been documented in the Bible. It's not something that was just recently thought up by a group of men in a dark backroom.

Point 3: We are to share the gospel with our whole heart (verse 9). With a passion and a zeal we are to share this good news with our friends and acquaintances.

Point 4: We are to share this good news with everyone (verses 14-15). Paul says he was obligated and eager to preach the gospel to both the Greeks and non-Greeks, to the wise and to the foolish—to the whole spectrum of life. The message of Jesus can make a difference in anyone's life.

Point 5: We are to take a stand for the gospel (verse 16). Paul very powerfully states, "I am not ashamed of the gospel." Oh, do we ever need individuals and families who can stand together and exhibit a lifestyle that reflects the love of Christ. We need to show the world that we aren't ashamed of this gospel.

Point 6: We need to see the power of the gospel for salvation (verse 16). This gospel is a change agent, giving people real purpose and meaning to life, helping us struggle against the power of sin. Each of us not only knows of this miracle in our own lives, but also in the testimonies of those around us.

Point 7: We are to live a life of righteousness by faith (verse 17). In studying the gospel, the righteousness of God is revealed to us, so we can go out and live a righteous life by the power of the Holy Spirit.

May today's study help us focus on the eternal values of life and not only the temporal. There are a lot of good things to use up our energies and passions, but are they the best priorities for our time and energy? One of our Barnes' mottos is: "Say 'No' to good things and save our 'Yeses' for the best." Know what's important and act on it.

Thoughts for Action

❧ Read a good biography of one of the great pillars of the church who reflects the power of the gospel in his or her life.

❧ Share the "good news" with someone you have been hesitant to do so because of various reasons.

❧ Evaluate your love for the Lord. How might you be more focused on sharing the gospel? Write this down in your journal.

❧ Pray to God, thanking Him for sending Jesus Christ to fulfill the prophecies of the Old Testament.

❧ Thank God for your own salvation.

Additional Scripture Reading

1 Corinthians 15:1-6   Luke 24:27-32
Hebrews 11:1

Declare God's Power and Might

Scripture Reading: Psalm 71:14-18

Key Verse: Psalm 71:18

> *Even when I am old and gray, do not forsake me, O God, till I declare your power to the next generation, your might to all who are to come.*

As I get older, I think more and more about what comes next. I know there's got to be something else after this life is over, because I can't grasp the alternative. I can't imagine that through all eternity I'll never see anyone I love again, that my whole awareness will just be obliterated. I can't believe that we're only bodies passing through.

When I muse about this, I think of all the great moments I had with my father. It's inconceivable that I had this wonderful period in life with him and then suddenly the curtain dropped. Instead, I want to believe I'm going to meet up with him again. I also want to have the opportunity to catch up with Mary, if only to tell her what I forgot to tell her, and to meet all my lifelong friends who have died. I do think they're out there someplace.

I haven't yet formed a clear idea about what the hereafter might be like. I don't know if everyone's an angel. Or an apparition. Or it's just all beyond comprehension. But I do hope that it's going to be better than here, because life on this planet is not exactly peaches and cream. I mean, this life is tough. I suppose that's the promise religion holds out. If you can take this life as it comes and give it your best, there will be something better afterwards.

I've always marveled at how belief in the hereafter gets accentuated as people grow older. Until their deathbeds, many of the great minds in science thought that because their soul and being were wrapped up in their body—the old ninety-eight cents' worth of chemicals—and that because after death these would no longer be a body, that was it. But now when they have to go, suddenly they want to believe in somebody up there because they don't know where they're going and they are scared.[32]

There is a season of life which challenges our belief of the hereafter. What happens when we die? The psalmist pleads for God not to forsake him until he declares the power of God to the next generation. Wow! What a great prayer. I guess that's why I do what I do. I want to tell everyone, starting with my immediate family and branching out to others, about the power and the might of God.

> Lord, I have so much to tell. Just continue to give me a message, give me a passion for the message, give me power to tell the message, and give me an audience who wants to hear the message.

One of my favorite passages that gives me a vision for that all-important message is found in Titus 2:3-6: "Likewise, teach the older women to be reverent in the way they live, not to be slanderers or addicted to much wine, but to teach what is good. Then they can train the younger women to love their husbands and children, to be self-controlled and pure, to be busy at home, to be kind, and to be subject to their husbands, so that no one will malign the word of God."

If only we could grasp the vastness of these words. And some say that being a wife and homemaker isn't exciting and challenging!

Don't wait until you are old and gray-haired. Begin today to share the message of Jesus Christ with the whole world.

Perhaps you're unsure of the message. Read this chain of Scripture to gain God's revelations for salvation.

- Romans 3:23
- Romans 6:23
- Acts 16:30-31
- Ephesians 2:8-9
- Romans 10:9-10
- Luke 18:13
- Luke 23:43
- John 10:28
- John 14:2-3

You can receive Christ right now by faith through prayer.

> Lord Jesus,
>
> I need You. Thank You for dying on the cross for my sins. I open the door of my life and receive You as my Savior and Lord. Thank You for forgiving my sins and giving me eternal life. Take control of the throne of my life. Make me the kind of person You want me to be.[33]

If you prayed this prayer, read the following Scriptures for your assurance.

- Revelation 3:20
- 1 John 5:11-13
- Hebrews 13:5
- John 14:21

Thoughts for Action

❦ If you have never prayed a prayer of salvation before and you want to now, kneel before God and repeat these simple words of acceptance.

❦ Read the Scriptures listed which support your decision.

❦ Write in the front page of your Bible today's date. Never doubt the decision you made.

❦ If you have already made this decision for your life, choose a message to be shared with the world. Develop it by starting with your own life and your own family. Then when you have lived it, share it with others.

Additional Scripture Reading

Read the Scriptures mentioned in today's devotion.

□ □ □

Becoming New, Becoming Strong

Scripture Reading: 2 Corinthians 5:15-18

Key Verse: 2 Corinthians 5:17

> *Therefore, if anyone is in Christ, he is a new creation; the old has gone, the new has come!*

———— ❦ ————

Becoming a woman of God begins with making a personal commitment to Jesus Christ. Only He can give us the strength to change. Only He can give us the fresh start that allows the spirit of godliness to grow strong in us.

Second Corinthians 5:17 reminds us, "If anyone is in Christ, he is a new creation; the old has gone, the new has come!" That's what I discovered many years ago when I, a 16-year-old Jewish girl, received Christ into my heart. My life began to change from that moment on, and the years since then have been an exciting adventure.

It hasn't always been easy. I've had to give up much bitterness, anger, fear, hatred, and resentment. Many times I've had to back up and start over, asking God to take control of my life and show me His way to live. But as I learned to follow Him, God has guided me through times of pain and joy, struggle and growth. And how rewarding it has been to see the spirit of godliness take root and grow in my life! I give thanks and praise for all His goodness to me over the years.

I'm not finished yet—far from it. Growing in godliness is a lifelong process. And although God is the one who makes it possible, He requires my cooperation. If I want the spirit of godliness to shine in my life and in my home, I must be willing to change what God wants me to change and learn what He wants to teach me. How? Here are some of the ways I've learned to keep myself open to the spirit of godliness.

God's Word is the foundation of my security and strength. Only through daily prayer and meditation can I tap into God's strength and love and get a handle on what He wants for my life.

Because I sometimes need a nudge to keep these disciplines regular and meaningful, I have gotten in the habit of keeping a prayer basket close at hand. This pretty little carryall (I like to use a soft, heart-shaped basket in pastel colors) keeps in one place the tools I need to keep in regular touch with God. My prayer basket contains:

1. A *Bible* to prepare my mind and heart to communicate with God.

2. A *daily devotional* or other inspirational reading.

3. My *prayer notebook* (more on this later).

4. A *bunch of silk flowers* to remind me of the beauty and fragrance of the Lord Jesus Himself.

5. A *small box of tissues* for the days I cry in joy or pain.

6. A *pen* for journaling my prayers and writing notes.

7. A few *pretty postcards or notes* for when I feel moved to communicate God's love to someone I'm praying for.

Seeing my basket waiting for me is a wonderful invitation to times of prayer, and a reminder when I haven't taken the time to pray. And it is so convenient to pick up and take to my prayer closet for a quiet time of communion with my heavenly Father.

Where is my closet? It may be a different place every day. (That's the beauty of the portable prayer basket.) Sometimes I settle down at my desk for a quiet time with God. Other times I use the bed, the breakfast room table, the bathtub, a chair by the fireplace, the front yard by the pond, or under a tree—anywhere where I can enjoy privacy.

The actual content of my devotional times varies according to how much time I have available. But generally I start by reading a brief inspirational message from a book. And then I pray. Next I open my Bible and read a chapter or more. (If time is really short, it may be only a verse.)

Next, I turn to my prayer notebook. This is a tool I developed many years ago to help me remember prayer requests and pray more effectively for others. My prayer notebook is a simple 8½" x 11" loose leaf notebook divided into seven sections—one for each day of the week. I've divided all the people and projects I want to pray for—family, friends, church, finances, and so on—into the various sections. For instance, I reserve Mondays to pray for my family, Tuesdays for my church and its servants and activities, Wednesdays for my personal concerns, and so on. (I reserve Sunday for sermon notes and outlines.) Organizing my prayer times in this way keeps me from being overwhelmed while reminding me to be faithful in my prayer life.

I have filled my prayer notebook with photos of people I'm praying for, information about their interests and needs, and special things to remember about them. When I receive prayer requests, I assign them a place in my prayer notebook. I also go through my notebook from time to time and weed out old requests so I don't become overwhelmed. This little book has become a creative, colorful companion that is so close to my heart.

In the back of my prayer notebook, I keep a supply of blank paper for journaling my prayers. This has not been an easy habit for me to develop. I do so much writing for magazine articles, books, letters, and such that writing feels like more work. But for the past few years I have made the effort to write down my praises, my confessions, my thanks, and my requests. I give the Lord my hurts, my pain from the past, my disappointments, and all the questions my mind can think of—in writing. I also write down the convictions of what I hear God saying to me. I'm learning firsthand the benefits of putting my conversations with God in written form:

1. *I am able to verbalize things I've held in my heart but never spoken about.* The act of writing somehow seems to bring up my thoughts, feelings, and desires and to expose them to the light of God's love.

2. *Writing out my confessions helps me get honest with the Lord.* Somehow a confession feels more real when it's down there in black and white. But this means that God's forgiveness feels more real, too.

3. *I can see concrete evidence of my spiritual life*—and my spiritual growth—when I read back over past prayers.

4. *My faith grows as I see God's answers more clearly*— God's "yeses," "nos," and "waits." Writing down the answers I think I hear helps me discern which ones really are of God.

5. *My obedience is strengthened.* Once again, written promises are harder to ignore than mental ones. Once I have written down my sense of what God wants me to do, I am more likely to follow through.

There is another kind of writing that I often do during my prayer times. Often while I am praying, God will bring to mind someone who needs my love or care. That's what the note cards are for. When God brings someone to mind, I try to stop right there and drop that person a line, assuring him or her of God's love and my prayers. Having the materials right there at hand makes this encouraging habit easy to maintain. It takes 21 days to form a habit. Start today.

Father God, instill in me the desire to commune with You each day in prayer. My days are busy and I often can't get done what I already need to do, but, God, I beg You to touch my life in a marvelous way so I can find time to be with You. Please be near to me and bless me when I'm in Your presence. Amen.

Thoughts for Action

- Locate and name your prayer closet.

- In your journal write a prayer to God today.

- Spend 15 minutes today in your prayer closet. Set your timer. (Make it longer if you want to.)

Additional Scripture Reading

Philippians 4:13

Psalm 55:22

John 11:40

Psalm 37:5-6

Stillness

Scripture Reading: Psalm 46:1-11

Key Verse: Psalm 46:10

> *Be still, and know that I am God; I will be exalted among the nations, I will be exalted in the earth.*

"Be still, and know that I am God," our heavenly Father urges. Easier said than done, right? The complaint I hear from so many women these days is, "I'm just dying for a little peace and quiet—a chance to relax and to think and to pray. And somehow I just can't seem to manage it."

"Stillness" is not a word that many of us even use anymore, let alone experience. Yet women today, perhaps more than at any other time in history, desperately need the spirit of stillness. We are constantly on the move, stretched to our maximum by all the hats we wear, all the balls we juggle, and all the demands our lives bring. In order for the spirit of loveliness to live in us, we must seek out opportunities to rest, plan, regroup, and draw closer to God. And we do that when we deliberately cultivate the spirit of stillness in our homes and in our lives.

As I write these words, Bob and I are at a condo in the California desert. It's July, and the temperature is 109°. But the air is sparkling clear, and a breeze is ruffling the palm tree fronds. As I gaze out over the rippling pool, a deep sense of peace descends upon me.

We've just spent two days of rest, reading, and enjoying each other—letting our conversation roam to cover family, ministry, food, goals, God's love, His Word, and our writing. The conversation has quieted, and I can almost feel my bones relaxing as the spirit of stillness steals over us.

I would say the ideal balance between outward and inward pursuits should be about fifty-fifty. By "outward" I mean working toward goals and deadlines, negotiating needs and privileges, coping with stress, taking care of daily chores, striving toward retirement—getting things done. "Inward" things include tuning in to my spiritual self, talking to God, exploring the sorrows, hopes, and dreams that make up the inner me, and just relaxing in God's eternal presence.

When I was younger, my life was tilted more outward and less inward. As I grow and mature (and perhaps reach another stage of my life), I find I'm leaning more toward the inward. I want my life to be geared more toward heaven. I want to lift my life, my hands, my head, and my body toward God, to spend more time alone with Him—talking, listening, and just being. I want to experience the fragrance of His love and let that love permeate my life, to let the calmness of His spirit replenish the empty well of my heart, which gets depleted in the busyness and rush of the everyday demands and pressures.

I want those things for you, too. That's why I urge you: Do whatever is necessary to nurture the spirit of stillness in your life. Don't let the enemy wear you so thin that you lose your balance and perspective. Regular time for stillness is as important and necessary as sleep, exercise, and nutritional food.

But I know the objection that is already bubbling up in your mind: Who has time?

It's the common complaint—and a valid one.

It's true that the battle is on between Satan and the spirit of stillness. (The father of lies absolutely thrives on chaos and misery!) And it really isn't easy to eliminate all the distractions—the dust, the dirty clothes, the orders that need filling; timers buzzing, phones ringing, children needing us.

Bob and I purposely set aside chunks of our yearly schedule just to be alone with each other and rethink our lives. We work hard all year, fulfilling more than a hundred speaking engagements all over the country. Schedules, interviews, and travel keep us on the move. We have to make space for the spirit of stillness, or we would quickly lose track of each other... and grow out of touch with God.

The door to stillness really is there waiting for any of us to open it and go through, but it won't open by itself. We have to choose to make the spirit of stillness a part of our lives.

I don't mean we need to be monks or hermits. The Scriptures tell us that if we are to live wisely, we must learn to balance the time we spend in quiet and calm with the time we spend in the fray of everyday existence. Ecclesiastes 3:1 says, "There is a time for everything." But that includes a time and a place to cultivate the spirit of stillness in the midst of your busy, productive life.

Thoughts for Action

- ❦ Read Ecclesiastes 3—yes, the whole chapter. List in your journal from that chapter what time in life it is for you now.

- ❦ If you find it difficult to develop a habit of quiet time, find a prayer partner with the same problem and hold each other accountable.

Additional Scripture Reading

Isaiah 30:15   Psalm 116:7

Do You Love Me?

Scripture Reading: John 21:15-19

Key Verse: John 21:15b

> *"Simon son of John, do you truly love me more than these?" "Yes, Lord," he said, "you know that I love you." Jesus said, "Feed my lambs."*

Dear Emilie,

Before I share with you a letter I received from my dad, I wanted to give a little background so you would realize just how much it meant to me. A few years ago my parents divorced after nearly 30 years of marriage. (I am the oldest of four children.) Needless to say, so many things changed, particularly my role as a daughter. My life seemed turned upside down. The relationship between my dad and I was strained for a while. Although I never stopped loving him, our relationship would never be the same again. I have done a lot of growing and learning over the years since.

Just before Christmas, I received an unexpected package in the mail. Enclosed in the package was a letter with the following instructions: "Sheri, you wanted one of these a long time ago! Explanation enclosed, read *before* opening." Here is the letter:

Dear Sheri,

You didn't know it but last night you and I shared a *magic* moment together...I stopped at a very small "shoppe" in town to browse. It was pretty cold and breezy, and the owner had a fire going in her potbellied stove in the corner. The room wasn't too well lit and everything was old (well if not old, at least used) and it smelled a little musty...the kind of place you might envision in a movie.

After finding nothing of real interest, I spotted the enclosed item on my way out. I was immediately transported back in time to a similar evening when just you and I went "looking"...(I couldn't afford to buy anything then)...and I *remembered* that wonderful way you had of seeing all the beautiful parts of the world with big, bright eyes and smiles (you were maybe five or six months old). That made me feel as if we were both in a fairy tale...(one nice thing about being older is that you can let a tear fall in public and people seem to understand)! Well, in short, this obviously *belongs to you*...Sorry it took so long! I guess you will always be my bright-eyed baby.

Love, Daddy

Although my dad wasn't aware of all I had been going through with the changes in our family and the confusion I felt, I'm sure he somehow sensed my need for this declaration of love. I will cherish the letter always. (By the way, the gift was a musical "Dickens" box, the kind you shake up and it snows.)

Sheri

No matter how old we become, we seem to always ask this basic question, "Do you love me?" I see it in the market when a child is misbehaving. I see it when a couple is engaged in a nasty shouting match. I see it when a friend is discouraged and depressed at life's turn of events. We all cry out, "Do you love me?"

Many times these irregular behaviors are ways that mankind reaches out and says, "Won't someone reassure me that they love me? I need a touch, a sign, a signal, a hug. Just let me know that I'm loved."

In 1 John 4:7-12 we find another great example of how much God loved us:

> Dear friends, let us love one another, for love comes from God. Everyone who loves has been born of God and knows God. Whoever does not love does not know God, because God is love. This is how God showed his love among us: he sent his one and only Son into the world that we might live through him. This is love: not that we loved God, but that he loved us and sent his Son as an atoning sacrifice for our sins. Dear friends, since God so loved us, we also ought to love one another. No one has ever seen God; but if we love one another, God lives in us and his love is made complete in us.

Let's love so the world can see how much God loves mankind.

Father God, put a special message in my heart today to let me know with definite assurance that You love me. Help me to cry out with confidence, "My God loves me so much." May I also realize that there are others around me, my mate, children, relatives, fellow workers, who let me know that I am

*loved. May I also reach out and assure these same
people that they are loved by me. Since You are love,
I want to be love to those around me. Amen.*

Thoughts for Action

🍎 Go out and feed lambs (real ones and Jesus' lambs).

🍎 Write a note to someone who needs a little extra love.

🍎 Give a telephone call to someone who needs encouragement.

🍎 Does that friend have a special theme for her life (lace, thimbles, teacup/saucer, gardening)? Send her a little gift with an uplifting note inside.

Additional Scripture Reading

Matthew 5:44   John 3:16
Matthew 22:39   Ephesians 5:1-2

☐ ☐ ☐

The Pain of Rejection

Scripture Reading: John 3:16-21

Key Verse: John 3:16a

> *For God so loved the world that he gave his one and only Son.*

Oh, how often we have been rejected in our life! That first date, first marriage proposal, first college entrance application. That first promotion, that first home we didn't qualify for. We have all experienced the hurt and pain of rejection. Let your mind race quickly through that long list of rejections. We often cried. We sometimes called a close friend to let her know of our hurt. Our mom and dad heard our crying out to God, asking, "Why, why, why?"

Jesus faced the pain of rejection even unto death. The people He came to save were the very ones who nailed Him to the cross (John 1:10). Isaiah the prophet stated that the Messiah would be despised and rejected by men (Isaiah 53:3). Even knowing this outcome, Jesus bore the pain of rejection.

On the cross, Jesus shouted to God in heaven, "My God, my God, why have you forsaken me?" (Matthew 27:46). Even His father had rejected Him.

Jesus' life is a reflection of how He met this rejection:

- He never abandoned the mission that God had given to Him.

- He never fought against His tormentors.

- He responded in love.

Paul writes in Hebrews 4:15-16 that Jesus sympathizes with our weakness, that we may receive mercy and grace in our time of need. What a great Savior! He has experienced our pain and can help us.

Scripture has given us some tremendous promises to hang on to during times of rejection:

- "Never will I leave you, never will I forsake you" (Hebrews 13:5).

- "Praise be to God who comforts us in all our troubles, so that we can comfort those in any trouble with the comfort we ourselves have received from God" (2 Corinthians 1:3-4).

- "Having believed, you were marked in Him with a seal, the promised Holy Spirit" (Ephesians 1:13).

It's natural to dwell on the pain of rejection. You can choose bitterness, depression, anger, fear, doubt, or loneliness to dominate your life. But these negative emotions can destroy you. Don't let Satan get a foothold in your Christian growth.

There is a better way—God's way. He asks you to forgive and to do good to those who hurt you. He knows these actions aren't just for the benefit of the one who hurt you, but for your benefit as well.

God set the model of forgiveness in Matthew 5:44-45 when He tells us to:

- Love our enemies.

- Pray for those who persecute us.

It's only when we adopt His attitude that we can fully experience His healing of our hurts. If you've been hurt by the poison arrow of rejection, then for your own sake, forgive. This forgiveness prevents even greater pain.

When we respond to rejection with God's love, others will notice the difference. Some will be so moved that they will be drawn to Christ and be saved. God will be glorified, and you will experience the wonderful feeling of spiritual victory. It will not be easy, but it is always worth the effort.

Don't be dragged down to defeat. Let rejection be an opportunity to develop Christian character in your life.

Thoughts for Action

🌰 Write in your journal the various remembrances of rejection. Beside each one write the word "Defeat" or "Victory." Praise God for the victories! What could have been done to make your defeats into victories?

🌰 If you still have the pain of rejection in your life, go to God in prayer to see what direction He would have you go—maybe a personal visit, maybe a telephone call, maybe a letter. You take the first step.

🌰 Be assured of God's love for you during this rejection.

Additional Scripture Reading

Luke 9:54-55   1 Samuel 10:19

Humility— God's Characteristic

Scripture Reading: 1 Peter 5:5-11

Key Verse: 1 Peter 5:5b

> *All of you, clothe yourselves with humility toward one another, because, "God opposes the proud but gives grace to the humble."*

As I walk past the Monday Night Football games on television, I see all kinds of strange dances. Most of them occur after a player has scored a touchdown. These guys actually look like they want to destroy the ball, throwing it to the ground as hard as they can! I can't help but think that a person doing such antics hasn't learned the first step in humility. I was always taught to let your skills do your talking and to act in a calm, reserved fashion. And it's not just football players on Monday night. The world has gone mad with pride.

I believe humility is a foundational character quality at the heart of every successful relationship. Those who exhibit great pride usually don't have strong interpersonal relationships.

Peter writes, "Clothe yourselves with humility toward one another, because 'God opposes the proud, but gives grace to the humble.' Humble yourselves, therefore, under God's mighty hand, that he may lift you up in due time." In present-day management books we read about climbing the corporate ladder, upward mobility, self-assertion, winning through intimidation, moving on up. It's always *up*. However, God seems to have a different program. The way up with God is always *down*. Peter's exhortation to be "clothed with humility" is a command, not a mere suggestion. God opposes the proud. The moment we allow pride to raise its ugly head, the resistance of God begins.

In Isaiah 2:12 we read, "The Lord detests all the proud." God not only resists and opposes the proud, but He is clear in His teachings that the proud will be humbled. Proverbs 29:23 states, "A man's pride brings him low."

Peter teaches us this truth: When you are clothed with humility, God terminates His resistance against you. As God's children, we should be smart enough to stay on the good side of God by staying on the side of humility.

God always opposes the proud, yet if we are humble, He will exalt us at the proper time.

- "Humility comes before honor" (Proverbs 15:33).

- "Humble yourself before the Lord and He will lift you up" (James 4:10).

- "He has brought down rulers from their thrones, but has lifted up the humble" (Luke 1:52).

Then what is humility?

- It is moral realism, the result of a fresh revelation of God.

- It is esteeming others as better than ourselves.

- It is the fruit of repentance.

- It is the attitude which rejoices in the success of others.

- It is the freedom from having to be right.

- It is the foundation of unity.

- It is the mark of authenticity.

- It is the fruit of brokenness.

- It is the quality which catches the attention of God.

The end result is holiness. Our only response to God's holiness, and that of His Son Jesus, is humility. If you are interested in developing a long-term relationship with both God and others, make humility your goal. As we kneel at the foot of our Lord, He will lift us up.

Father God, I want to be humble in all that I say and do. Please make me aware of any false pride in my life. Amen.

Thoughts for Action

❦ In your journal, list three or four areas of your life which tend to reflect pride. It might be in dress, friendship, business, attitude, talents. Beside each area write what you plan to do to change your attitude.

❦ Why do you think pride ruins relationships? Jot down a few thoughts.

Additional Scripture Reading

Proverbs 22:4   Philippians 2:8
Psalm 45:3-4   1 Peter 2:21

From Clutter to Contentment

Scripture Reading: Psalm 37:3-7a

Key Verse: Psalm 37:6

He will make your righteousness shine like the dawn, the justice of your cause like the noonday sun.

James Truslow Adams states, "No form of society can be reasonably stable in which the majority of the people are not fairly content. People cannot be content if they feel that the foundations of their lives are wholly unstable."

There may be nothing wrong with you,
The way you live, the work you do,
But I can very plainly see
Exactly what is wrong with me.
It isn't that I'm indolent;
I work as hard as anyone,
And yet I get so little done,
The morning goes, the noon is here,
Before I know, the night is near,
And all around me, I regret,
Are things I haven't finished yet.
If I could just get organized!

I often times have realized
Not all that matters is the man;
The man must also have a plan.
With you, there may be nothing wrong,
But here's my trouble right along;
I do the things that don't amount
To very much, of no account,
That really seem important though
And let a lot of matters go.
I nibble this, I nibble that,
But never finish what I'm at,
I work as hard as anyone,
And yet, I get so little done,
I'd do so much you'd be surprised,
If I could just get organized!

—Douglas Malloch

Caring for our homes brings a great feeling of accomplishment. Our belongings will last longer and those drop-in visitors will not send us scurrying around to clean up. We'll feel proud to have family and guests arrive anytime.

I have found that when you have a mess organizationally, everything in your physical environment and how it's managed and maintained holds you at your current level of effectiveness. For example, when you're overwhelmed, you can't see anything else. You can't see new opportunities, challenges, or even how to care for another person. You protest, "Are you kidding? I've got too much to handle already."

The messes in the home many times reflect messes in someone's personal life. I honestly believe that if you don't know what you want out of life, it's hard to prioritize the activities of your life. My book *Survival for Busy Women*[34] goes into great detail showing how you can establish lifetime goals and theme verses. Taking the time to establish goals for your life is very basic to helping you clean out the messes that prevent you from doing the things you want to do but don't have time to do.

There are seven basic questions that we need to ask ourselves as we prepare to eliminate the mess and clutter from our lives on our way to contentment.

- Who are you?

- Where are you going?

- What do you need to get there?

- Does this activity, commitment, etc. make you money?

- Does this save you money?

- Does this save you time?

- Does this improve the quality of your life?

These are some very penetrating theological and philosophical questions, but we must answer them before we begin tossing things out of our lives. You might be saying, "I didn't want to get this complicated! I just wanted to get rid of my messes." Believe me, you'll find it nearly impossible to get rid of your messes until you come to grips with who you are first.

The ultimate goal, of course, is contentment. In Philippians 4:11 Paul reminds us to be content in whatever state we find ourselves. One of the by-products of our Western culture is people who are not content with their jobs, husbands, children, churches, homes, clothes, food, freeways, and life in general. We are a society of malcontents just waiting for retirement or the rapture, whichever comes first.

Thomas Fuller says, "Contentment consists not in adding more fuel, but in taking away some fire; not in multiplying of wealth, but in subtracting men's desires."[35] I have a motto: "Less is best." When you don't have something, you don't have to dust it, paint it, repair it, or replace it. When we are young, we strive to consume. As we get older, we try to cut back and eliminate possessions from our lives which rob us of being content. If we can't find contentment within ourselves, it is useless to seek it elsewhere. It's just not there! You *choose* to be "content" or "discontent." Which will it be? Whichever option you choose will determine if you are ready to eliminate the messes and clutter from your life, home, and work.

As long as you choose "discontent," you will have clutter in your personal affairs. Only when you get right with God and find His plan for your life will you be able to muster up the desire and discipline to make a new *you*!

After you come to grips with who you are and why you are here, you are ready to eliminate some of the time and money robbers from your home. As you evaluate some of these areas, you will be amazed at how this process will change your life. Finding the answer to these basic questions is a lifetime pursuit in growing into the woman God wants you to become.

Develop a battle plan for attacking the various areas of your home. Keep the following points in mind to help you move toward your level of contentment.

A practical and effective motto we follow in our home is "Do the worst first." In many homes that means the garage, the closets, the kitchen cupboards, or just general paper messes.

I adhere to several rules when I'm in the "attack mode" around my house:

- Turn on good, upbeat music.
- No telephone calls.
- No visitors unless you can recruit a friend to help you.
- Have the total family help on the big projects (particularly on children's bedrooms, bathrooms, and garages).
- Concentrate on one project or area at a time.
- Don't attempt to keep everything. Some things have to go (garage sales, church, Salvation Army). Some things must succumb to the trash can.

• No TV or any other distractions.

As you organize, you will find more contentment, and God will be able to make your righteousness shine like the dawn, the justice of your causes like the noonday sun.

With this new-found peace you will be able to take control of your life, and that makes life more meaningful.

Thoughts for Action

❦ Develop a plan for cleaning up your messes. List in your journal what you plan to do. After each statement, write down a completion date.

❦ Thank God for your blessings of contentment.

❦ List one area of your life in which you aren't content. What can you do to make that a positive statement?

Additional Scripture Reading

1 Corinthians 7:17   1 Timothy 6:6
Hebrews 13:5

Thank You, God,
for quiet places
far from life's
crowded ways,
where our hearts
find true contentment
and our souls
fill up with praise.

Hospitality That Cares

Scripture Reading: 1 Peter 4:8-11

Key Verse: 1 Peter 4:9

Offer hospitality to one another without grumbling.

Hospitality is caring. We can entertain all we like, but not until we care does it become hospitality. It doesn't take much—just the heart to care for your guests.

Too many times we feel things have to be perfect: the right time, the right house, the right food. But who says what is right? In my mind a warm, caring attitude makes any time together right.

We have some affluent, fancy friends who have everything "right": silver, china and crystal, candelabras, matching linens and napkins. Inviting Jim and Georgia over to our house is intimidating, to say the least. I can't possibly meet their level of perfection. In my heart I care and love these friends, but my "self" says, "I can't do it. Why am I having them over?"

I was visiting on the phone one day with Georgia and, before I could catch myself, I invited them over for dinner. "Come tonight," I said, "and I hope you don't mind soup and salad." It was a chilly California January day, and I'd put on a pot of homemade chicken vegetable soup. I must say I got excited about being able to have fellowship with such special people. Bob built a fire in the living room fireplace. I threw a checkered cloth over the coffee table, picked what flowers I could find, lit two candles, and served my famous tossed green salad, chicken soup, and crusty bread. We were all on diets, so for dessert we had sliced fruit with a tablespoon of granola on top. Here's Georgia's thank-you note:

> Dear Bob and Em,
>
> I don't know when Jim and I have had a greater evening. It truly was an evening from soup to nuts. The food and sitting on the floor by the fire was a fun change. In fact, Jim wants me to do the same thing next time we have friends over. Thank you for the great idea and a memorable evening.
>
> Love, Georgia

I later heard from mutual friends what a great evening Jim and Georgia had in our home.

Some people complain they don't have enough room. When our children were in high school, we lived in a very small condo for two years. Brad played varsity football, and Jenny was a cheerleader. Bob and I wanted to get acquainted with the young people our children would be involved with, so we suggested having a tostada feed for all 50 football players and cheerleaders after their first game. Our kids thought it was a neat idea. We called it a Mexican Mountain Fiesta.

Jenny and Brad were thrilled and excited to have everyone over. However, we had a couple of obstacles. First, our condo complex had little guest parking. Second, 50 people simply could not fit into our 1300-square-foot-condo—especially 200-plus-pound players and jumpy, giddy, cute cheerleaders. We had perfectly good reasons to say, "Forget the whole idea," but here's what we did. The school bus dropped all the players off at our front door. We converted our two-car garage into a serve-yourself food buffet, set up long tables for the food, and decorated the walls with sheets of butcher paper, pom-poms, and construction-paper footballs. We had each guest sign the paper with his or her name and a cute saying. Many wrote a big, "Thank you!" or "Great fun!" or "Let's do it again next year."

That evening those young people sang school songs and stayed on and on. Bob and I sat in our little family room and the students came in and out to visit with us. We genuinely cared about those kids. One young football player named Scott came in, sat on the floor, and didn't stop talking for almost one hour. He told us things we didn't even want to know, but we just listened. When Scott got up to leave, he shook Bob's hand and said, "Mr. Barnes, this has been a super evening. I don't know when I enjoyed talking to someone as much as I have you." We laughed later because Bob hadn't said more than 20 words to Scott.

Look what we would have missed if we used the excuse that our home was too small! I've found over the years that we *can* do whatever we *care* to do. We still know many of those students, and they continue to remind us of the Mexican Mountain Fiesta.

The Living Bible paraphrases today's passage this way: "Cheerfully share your home with those who need a meal or a place to stay for the night." Hospitality goes beyond friends and neighbors. Invite a visiting missionary or evangelist home for a meal and sleep. Host members of a visiting choir or a work team that's away from home. Whatever the need, reach out and extend your hand of hospitality.

> *Father God, create in me a heart that wants to open my home to others. Remind me not to grumble when I think about having family, friends, or even strangers in my home for rest and food. Let my family have joy in their hearts as we share what You have so abundantly given us. Amen.*

Thoughts for Action

❦ Pick up your phone today and invite a person, couple, or family over for dinner. Set a date on the calendar. (You might even try potlucking and let your guests bring something if they offer.)

❦ Be available to host someone in need from church.

❦ Purchase a good cookbook that emphasizes simple meal preparation.

Additional Scripture Reading

1 Timothy 3:2   Hebrews 13:2

God Has a Plan

Scripture Reading: Genesis 2:20-25

Key Verse: Genesis 2:23

> *This is now bone of my bones and flesh of my flesh;*
> *she shall be called "woman," for she was taken out*
> *of man.*

—————— ❧ ——————

In his bestselling book *Straight Talk*, Lee Iacocca expresses the importance and priorities of the family:

> My father told me that the best way to teach is by example. He certainly showed me what it took to be a good person and a good citizen. As the old joke has it, "No one ever said on his deathbed, I should have spent more time on my business." Throughout my life, the bottom line I've worried about most was that my kids turn out all right.
>
> The only rock I know that stays steady, the only institution I know that works, is the family. I was brought up to believe in it—and I do. Because I think a civilized world can't remain civilized for long if its foundation is built on anything but the family. A city, state or country can't be any more than the sum of its vital parts—millions of family units. You can't have a

country or a city or a state that's worth a damn
unless you govern within yourself in your day-to-
day life.

It all starts at home.[36]

In our Scripture reading today we see that God institutes
the family. Unfortunately, our secular world is trying its hard-
est to minimize the family as an institution. We know, however, that God will not abandon what He has begun.

Woman was created for man; she was to be his helper. Man
and woman were designed for each other. That was God's plan.
Do you have a plan for your family? Have you and your mate
taken time to determine what values, what guidelines, what
aspirations you have for you and your children?

Marriage causes a man to leave his mother and father, be
united with his wife, and become one flesh with her. Is this a
description of what happened to you?

Scripture then states, "The man and his wife were both
naked, and they felt no shame." Nakedness isn't always physical; it can also include the emotional, spiritual, and psycho-
logical aspects of our lives. One of the biggest challenges for
Bob and me is to stand before each other "naked" and know
that we aren't ashamed. If we've followed God's plans for our
family, we can do just that.

If we are to survive as a society, our foundation must be
built on healthy families. Let's make it our goal to follow God's
plan!

Father God, create in me a hunger to search out
Your plan for my life. Let me have the wisdom to
major on the major and not get sidetracked by the
minors. It's easy to get distracted from Your plan, but
I so want to follow Your master plan for me. When
life is over I want You to say, "Well done, good and
faithful servant." Help me today. Amen.

Thoughts for Action

❦ Meet with your mate and design a master plan for your family.

❦ Write this plan in your journal and write specific goals for each family member.

❦ Begin today to raise good children.

Additional Scripture Reading

Genesis 18:19   Acts 18:8

□ □ □

Femininity

Scripture Reading: Song of Songs 4:1-15

Key Verse: Song of Songs 4:15
All beautiful you are, my darling; there is no flaw in you.

———— 🍎 ————

When I was a little girl, I used to dream of being a "lady." The world of *Little Women*, with its gracious manners and old-fashioned, flowing dresses, fascinated me. Softness and lace, tantalizing fragrance and exquisite texture, a nurturing spirit and a love of beauty—these images of femininity shaped my earliest ideas of loveliness.

Is that kind of femininity a lost value today? I don't believe it. The world has changed, and most of us live in simple skirts or business suits or jeans instead of flowing gowns. But I still believe that somewhere in the heart of most of us is a little girl who longs to be a lady.

I also believe that today's world is hungering to be transformed by femininity. What better antidote for an impersonal and violent society than warm, gentle, feminine strength? What better cure for urban sprawl and trashed-out countrysides than a love of beauty and a confidence in one's ability to make things lovely? What better hope for the future than a nurturing mother's heart that is more concerned for the next generation than for its own selfish desires? All these qualities—gentle strength, love of beauty, care and nurturing—are part of femininity.

Being a woman created by God is such a privilege—and the gift of our femininity is something we can give both to ourselves and to the people around us. Just one flower, one candle, can warm up a cold, no-nonsense atmosphere with an aura of "I care." Women have always had the ability to transform an environment, to make it comfortable and inviting. I believe we should rejoice in that ability and make the most of it.

This doesn't mean we have to follow a set pattern or adopt a cookie-cutter style. The specific expressions of femininity vary greatly. When I think "feminine," I usually think of soft colors, lace, and flowers. I love ruffled curtains and flower-sprigged wallpaper, delicate bone china and old-fashioned garden prints. And I feel especially beautiful when I'm dressed up in soft and colorful fabrics.

But I know women with vastly different styles who still exude that special quality I call femininity—women who wear their tailored tweeds or their casual cottons (or their gardening "grubbies") with an air of gentleness and sensitivity. Women who fill their sleek modern kitchens or their utilitarian office cubicles with that unmistakable sense of warmth, caring, and responsiveness. Women who combine self-confidence and an indomitable spirit with a gracious humility and a tender teachability. Women who wear femininity with the grace and confidence with which they wear their favorite elegant scent.

Femininity is so many things. To me, it is objects chosen for their beauty as well as their usefulness... and lovingly cared for. It is people accepted and nurtured, loveliness embraced and shared. More important, femininity is the spirit of care and compassion. In my mind, the most feminine woman is one with an eye and ear for others, and a heart for God.

At its best, our femininity arises naturally, out of who we are, and finds its natural expression in the way we live our lives and make our homes. But in our hectic, hard-driving society, it's easy to lose track of our gentle, feminine side. Femininity is something we must nurture in ourselves and in our homes, and celebrate as God's gift to us.

Femininity can be cultivated in many ways. A fragrant oil or a few drops of perfume in the bathwater. A daisy on your desk. A lace scarf or an embroidered hanky in your pocket. A crocheted shawl around your shoulders. Whatever awakens the calm and gentle spirit within you will nurture the spirit of loveliness in your life.

The expression of femininity is a very personal thing, an expression of a woman's unique self. It is closely tied with identity and with style. Many of the most feminine women I know develop a signature or trademark that marks their distinctiveness. One woman always wears hats. Another enhances her distinctive presence with a favorite fragrance. Still another adopts a theme or motif that becomes part of her identity.

My friend Marilyn Heavilin's theme is roses. All her correspondence is "rosy," whether with a sticker, a rubber stamp, or her own distinctive stationery. Her home, too, is full of roses—on everything from bedspreads to dessert dishes to rose-scented potpourri.

Marita Littauer-Noon, one of my publicists, loves rabbits. When she was little her nickname was "Bunny," and she has carried this trademark into adulthood. Marita and her husband, Chuck, have bunny T-shirts, bunny candle holders, even a ten-year-old live bunny as a pet. Anytime I see anything with a rabbit on it I think of Marita, and at Christmas or on her birthday she always gets a bunny gift. Finding the personalized presents is fun for me and Marita. It's one way of celebrating her unique, feminine personality.

Femininity includes a wholesome sensuality—a rejoicing in the fragrances and textures and sounds of God's world. We honor God and express the spirit of femininity when we get excited.

Look at your body. How unlike a man's it is! The rest of you is different, too—even the structure of your brain. Did you know that women have a higher pain threshold, a keener sense of smell, and better integration between the right and left sides of our brains? I believe we are meant to rejoice in those special feminine qualities that God has gifted us with.

Song of Songs celebrates feminine beauty with wonderful poetry. The woman described there had bouncy, flowing hair (like a flock of goats), sparkling teeth, lips like scarlet ribbons, glowing cheeks, a round and smooth neck, gently swelling breasts, and clothing with the fragrance of Lebanon.

Does that describe me? I hope so. At least, I hope I am taking the trouble to make the best of what God has given me. I may not have time for the 12 months of beauty treatments that transformed a little Jewish girl named Esther into the Queen of Persia. I may never look like a model or a movie star or even my best friend. But I can honor God's gift of my femininity by taking care of the unique me that He has created.

That's one reason I try to be faithful to my exercise program. My daily walks not only help me keep my figure under control, but they restore my energy, lift my spirits, and give me a sense of well-being that makes it easier for me to reach out to others.

That's also why I make the effort to eat healthful foods and prepare them for my family. Shining hair, healthy nails, fresh skin, strong teeth, stress control—all relate directly to the food I put in my body.

And that's why I take that little bit of extra time to pluck and color and brush and cream. A fresh haircut, well-shaped nails, soft lips and hands, pink cheeks, curled eyelashes, pressed and mended clothing—these things help me feel more beautiful, and they tell the world that I care enough to cultivate the spirit of femininity in my life.

And that's why I make the effort to surround myself with beauty. When I do, I myself feel more beautiful. I experience the joy of sharing beauty with those closest to me. And I am motivated to reach out to others with gentleness and care.

Surely that beautiful woman in Song of Songs did that. Solomon speaks often of perfume filling the air, of lush wildflowers and morning breezes. Beauty was all around her, from the wildflowers in Sharon to the lily in the mountain valley.

I imagine that this woman kept fresh flowers around her home, the fragrances permeating the atmosphere. I imagine that she kept the petals and pods from the dried flowers and piled them in a container, adding fragrant oils to make what today we call potpourri. This was sprinkled in her clothing, which perhaps sat stacked neatly in piles. It's hard to say what life was like then—what homes, rooms, furniture, and cooking areas were like. But I'm sure it was simple yet beautiful. I'm sure it nurtured the spirit of femininity in her and helped her extend a spirit of caring to others.

Yet as much as I believe in taking care of myself and my environment, I know that if I put all my energy into self-care I have missed the whole point. The true beauty of femininity comes from within. If that beauty is lacking, no exercise program, eating plan, wardrobe update, or beauty treatment can put it there. No interior decorating scheme can give it to me. Ruffles and perfume are no substitute for inner beauty.

The true spirit of femininity comes from the *heart*, and I nurture it when I pay attention to what is truly important in life. That's why I need the message of 1 Peter 3:3-5:

> Your beauty should not come from outward adornment, such as braided hair and the wearing of gold jewelry and fine clothes. Instead, it should be that of your inner self, the unfading beauty of a gentle and quiet spirit, which is of great worth in God's sight. For this is the way the holy women of the past who put their hope in God used to make themselves beautiful.

> *Father God, You know that my heart's desire is to be a godly woman, one who other women see as a*

reflection of what God describes in Scripture as a beautiful woman. Show me Your way today. Let me be that beautiful fragrance that others want to emulate. Amen.

Thoughts for Action

❧ Write in your journal what makes you feel feminine.

❧ List what you need to do to feel feminine.

❧ Do one of the things you listed above today.

Additional Scripture Reading

1 Peter 3:4   Proverbs 31:30
Psalm 27:4

We Do What We Want to Do

Scripture Reading: Genesis 18:18-19

Key Verse: Genesis 18:19

> *For I have chosen him, so that he will direct his children and his household after him to keep the way of the Lord by doing what is right and just, so that the Lord will bring about for Abraham what he has promised him.*

My parents spent a lot of time with me, and I wanted my kids to be treated with as much love and care as I got. Well, that's a noble objective. Everyone feels that way. But to translate it into daily life, you really have to work at it.

There's always the excuse of work to get in the way of the family. I saw how some of the guys at Ford lived their lives—weekends merely meant two more days at the office. That wasn't my idea of family life. I spent all my weekends with the kids and all my vacations. Kathi was on the swim team for seven years, and I never missed a meet. Then there were tennis matches. I made all of them. And piano recitals. I made all of them too. I was always afraid that if I missed one, Kathi might finish first or finish last and I would hear about it secondhand and not be there to congratulate—or console—her.

People used to ask me: "How could somebody as busy as you go to all those swim meets and recitals?" I just put them down on my calendar as if I were seeing a supplier or a dealer that day. I'd write down: "Go to country club. Meet starts at three-thirty, ends four-thirty." And I'd zip out. [37]

We have to make so many choices in each of our twenty-four-hour days. How do we establish what's important? By reconfirming day by day what's of value to us. Our Scripture reading today makes us realize that as children of God we have been chosen and are directed by God to keep the way of the Lord by doing what is right and just. The Lord will bring about for you what He has promised you.

Do you really realize that you have been chosen by God? What a tremendous revelation! We are living in an age of irresponsibility, but as children of God we have responsibility. What are you doing to be directed by God? You can start by always having a teachable spirit. Since you are reading this book, I'm going to guess that you are a learner and want to grow. Each day choose to be a learner and to be directed by God to do what is right and just. We do what we want to do!

Notice that today's key verse points out that the reward for stewardship in the family is that the Lord will bring about what He has promised.

In Proverbs 24:3-4 we learn more about these promises: "By wisdom a house is built, and through understanding it is established; through knowledge its rooms are filled with rare and beautiful treasures." Is the writer of Proverbs talking about furniture, carpets, crystal, vases, paintings? I don't think so.

These rare and beautiful treasures are God-fearing, God-respecting children, with good and moral values, children who honor their mother and father and respect others. God has promised these rewards and blessings if only we would abide by His directions. Begin today a new and renewed passion for God's direction in your life.

> *Father God, let me build my house with wisdom, establish it with understanding, and through knowledge fill its rooms with rare and beautiful treasure. Amen.*

Thoughts for Action

❦ Is God giving you specific directions for raising your children? If "yes," what are they?

❦ Write down in your journal what these directions are. Beside each one state what you plan to do to implement these directions.

❦ Share with someone today what one or two of these directions might be.

❦ List a few of the blessings that God has so abundantly given you.

Additional Scripture Reading

Proverbs 27:17   Proverbs 22:6
Proverbs 20:11   Proverbs 19:18

❑ ❑ ❑

You're Special

Scripture Reading: Psalm 139:13-18

Key Verse: Psalm 139:14

> *I praise you because I am fearfully and wonderfully made; your works are wonderful, I know that full well.*

You're special. In all the world there's nobody like you.
Since the beginning of time there has never been another
    person like you.
Nobody has your smile, nobody has your eyes, your nose,
    your hair, your hands, your voice.
You're special. No one can be found who has your hand-
    writing.
Nobody anywhere has your tastes for food, clothing, music
    or art.
No one sees things just as you do.
In all of time there's been no one who laughs like you, no
    one who cries like you, and what makes you cry or
    laugh will never produce identical laughter and tears
    from anybody else, ever.
You're the only one in all of creation who has your set of
    abilities.
Oh, there will always be somebody who is better at one of

the things you're good at, but no one in the universe can reach the quality of your combination of talents, ideas, abilities and feelings. Like a room full of musical instruments, some may excel alone, but none can match the symphony sound when all are played together. You're a symphony.

Through all of eternity, no one will ever look, talk, walk, think or do like you.

You're special...you're rare. And in all rarity there is great value. Because of your great value you need not attempt to imitate others...you will accept—yes, celebrate your differences.

You're special and you're beginning to realize it's no accident that you're special.

You're beginning to see that God made you special for a purpose.

He must have a job for you that no one else can do as well as you.

Out of the billions of applicants, only one is qualified, only one has the right combination of what it takes.

That one is you, because...you're special.[38]

In today's key verse the psalmist shares his feelings to God for why he is special. Oh, do we ever need people who know that God created them and loves them!

We have a "You Are Special" red plate that we use constantly. We use it for breakfasts, lunches, dinners, birthdays, anniversaries, and various special occasions. We've served it at home, in restaurants, at the park, at the beach. You name it, we've done it. There are several things we do extra to reinforce the idea that someone is special. We:

• Take a photograph of the person with the plate and put it in a special album just for our special friends.

• As we eat together with our honored guest, those present

go around the table and tell why the person is special to them.

• The special person also gets to share with us why he (or she) thinks he is special. Often this person has never thought through why he is special.

Our red plate has become a very valuable tradition in our family. We all need to be reminded every once in a while that we truly are special.

> *Father God, help me to realize that I am truly and marvelously made and that, in Your sight, I am very special. Amen.*

Thoughts for Action

❧ Write down in your journal three things that make you special.

❧ Write down who you are: color of eyes, hair, shape of lips, what makes you smile and laugh, etc.

❧ Now thank God for you. Write this prayer in your journal.

❧ Write a note to a friend telling her why she is special to you.

Additional Scripture Reading

Psalm 40:5　　　　　　　　　Psalm 119:73

Notes

1. Emilie Barnes, *Things Happen When Women Care* (Eugene, OR: Harvest House Publishers, 1990), pp. 161-162.
2. *6000 Sermon Illustrations*, edited by Elon Foster (Grand Rapids, MI: Baker Book House, 1992), p. 286.
3. Books by Marilyn Willett Heavilin (published by Thomas Nelson): *Roses in December; Becoming a Woman of Honor; When Your Dreams Die; December's Song; I'm Listening, Lord.*
4. Patrick Morley, *The Man in the Mirror* (Brentwood, TN: Wolgemuth and Hyatt, 1989), pp. 5-7.
5. June Masters Bacher, *Quiet Moments for Women* (Eugene, OR: Harvest House Publishers, 1979), March 5 devotion.
6. Lee Iacocca, *Straight Talk* (New York: A Bantam Book, 1988), p. 67.
7. Ed and Carol Nevenschwander, *Two Friends In Love* (Portland, OR: Multnomah Press, 1986), p. 175.
8. Gigi Graham Tchividjian, *Women's Devotional Bible, NIV Version* (Grand Rapids, MI: The Zondervan Corporation, 1990), p. 1307.
9. Bruce Narramore, *You're Someone Special* (Grand Rapids, MI: Zondervan Publishers, 1978), adapted from pp. 61-62.
10. Charles R. Swindoll and Lee Hough, *You and Your Child* (Nashville, TN: Thomas Nelson Publishers, 1977), a study guide to accompany a series of topics on this subject, 1993, p. 33.
11. James Dobson, *The Strong-Willed Child* (Wheaton, IL: Tyndale House Publishers, 1971), p. 30.
12. James Dobson, *Hide or Seek*, rev. ed. (Old Tappan, NJ: Fleming H. Revell Co., 1979), p. 95.
13. Paula Yates Sugg, *The Dallas Morning News*, In Memoriam (September 26, 1993).
14. June Hunt, *Seeing Yourself Through God's Eyes* (Grand Rapids, MI: Zondervan, 1989), p. 33.
15. Robert Fulghum, *All I Really Need to Know I Learned in Kindergarten* (New York: Ballantine Books, 1986), pp. 29-31.
16. Brenda Hunter, *Where Have All the Mothers Gone?* (Grand Rapids, MI: Zondervan, 1982), pp. 108-111.

17. Ibid.
18. Larry Crabb, *The Marriage Builder* (Grand Rapids, MI: Zondervan, 1982), p. 22.
19. Jerry and Barbara Cook, *Choosing to Love* (Ventura, CA: Regal Books, 1982) pp. 78-80.
20. H. Norman Wright, *Quiet Times for Couples* (Eugene, OR: Harvest House, 1990), p. 35.
21. Ibid., p. 100.
22. Jerry and Barbara Cook, *Choosing to Love* (Ventura, CA: Regal Books, 1982), pp. 78-80.
23. Alan Loy McGinnis, *The Friendship Factor* (Minneapolis, MN: Augsburg, 1979), p. 23.
24. Robert H. Schuller, *Self-Esteem, The New Reformation* (Waco, TX: Word Publishing, 1982), pp. 17-18.
25. Robert Fulghum, *All I Really Need to Know I Learned in Kindergarten* (New York: Ballantine Books, 1986), pp. 4-6.
26. Ibid., pp. 17-18.
27. Source unknown.
28. Adapted from Stephen R. Covey, *The Seven Habits of Highly Effective People* (New York: Simon and Schuster, 1989).
29. Bob Benson, *Laughter in the Walls* (Nashville: Impact Books, 1969).
30. Jan Congo, *Free to Be God's Woman* (Ventura, CA: Regal Books 1985), adapted from p. 94.
31. Dr. R. Newton, *6000 Sermon Illustrations*, edited by Elon Foster (Grand Rapids, MI: Baker Book House, 1992), p. 309.
32. Lee Iacocca, *Straight Talk* (New York: A Bantam Book, 1988), p. 27.
33. Bill Bright, *Four Spiritual Laws* (San Bernardino, CA: Campus Crusade for Christ, Inc. 1965), p. 10.
34. Emilie Barnes, *Survival for Busy Women* (Eugene, OR: Harvest House Publishers, 1992).
35. Wirt and Bechstrom, *Topical Encyclopedia*, p. 42.
36. Lee Iacocca, *Straight Talk* (New York: A Bantam Book, 1988), p. 17.
37. Ibid., p. 270.
38. Source unknown.

15 Minutes of PEACE WITH GOD

Emilie Barnes

Peace with God is a process of growing in the quiet places of our hearts by spending time alone with God.

I dedicate this book to the women who have passed through my life and placed in my heart a little bit of themselves. They have contributed to this book in ways that they know not.

Florence Littauer, Jackie Johnson, Jan King, Donna Otto, Jane Englund, Yoli Brogger, Joan Chambey, Barbara DeLorenzo, Ruth West, Sue Boydstun, Gertie Barnes, Judy Brixley, Susan Beck, Arlene Garret, my daughter Jenny, my daughter-in-love Maria, and many women across the country have all allowed me to be a part of their lives.

My prayer for you is found in John 14:27: "Peace I leave with you. My peace I give to you; not as the world gives do I give to you. Let not your heart be troubled, nor let it be fearful." Amen.

Peacefully,

Emilie

Emilie Barnes

15 Minutes of Peace with God

Traveling across America 20-plus times a year speaking to women has given me a real heart for their hurting hearts. "No time, no time!" they cry. "I have no time left for family, friends, housework, or meals—let alone time to spend a quiet moment with God."

I've written this devotional book for every busy woman who wants to get in touch with her Lord and her life. Each quiet time is designed to take 15 minutes or less. That's not a huge commitment, but it's an important one. You'll spend some time in God's Word, and you'll find helps and direction for your everyday life.

Another unique feature is that you don't have to start at the beginning and go chapter by chapter. You can skip around if you would like. In the top corner of each devotion you will see three boxes. Put a checkmark in one of the boxes each time you read that chapter. This way you can keep track of those devotions which you have read previously.

The 15-minute concept works! You just have to be willing to give it a try. Fifteen minutes a day for 21 days and you are on your way to devotions every day.

Allow God to hold your hand and lead you today to many quiet times with Him.

The only hope to the busy woman's cry is God Almighty Himself:

God the Father
God the Son
and
God the Holy Spirit.

I love you all. May the Lord touch each quiet time with Him.

—Emilie

Look to the Left, Look to the Right

Scripture Reading: Matthew 9:35-38

Key Verse: Matthew 9:36

> *He felt compassion for them, because they were distressed and downcast like sheep without a shepherd.*

Each new day as I exit my front door and look to the left and to the right I find the world full of people who are distressed and downcast.

As I watch the morning news on my favorite TV channel I hear nothing but stories of people who are in distress and are downcast. As my Bob and I eat breakfast and go over the morning newspaper we are stunned by the articles in the paper:

- Pakistan blast kills 40
- Tens of thousands of Brazilians are reported toiling in bondage
- Boy six years old arrested for assaulting a month-old baby to near-death
- Gunman caught after killing 33 in Australia
- Apartment fire leaves 12 dead in Tijuana
- Bus bombed in protest of election; 15 dead
- Bus crash kills 31

- Trials set in killings of Brazilian street children
- $20 million frees abducted millionaire
- Zulu princess' body found at soccer field

After reading all of these depressing headlines, it's hard for us to finish eating breakfast. Yes, the world is full of people who are distressed and downcast.

In our passage for today we find Jesus teaching in all the cities and villages and proclaiming the good news of the gospel. As He looked at the multitudes He felt compassion for them. Yet in today's culture of violence we become desensitized to all the bad news we see, read, and hear. If it doesn't affect us and our friends we have a tendency to turn our heads and look the other way.

Maybe instead of looking to the left and to the right we should look *up toward God* and utter a prayer for all of those caught up in distress. We can't always do anything about people in foreign countries who face terrible problems, but we can look around and find people close to us in similar situations. Ask God to show you people you can help who face such dilemmas.

As Jesus showed compassion to those around Him, we too should show compassion. John Andrew Holmes is credited with saying, "There is no exercise better for the heart than reaching down and lifting people up."

This could mean a love basket of food, payment of a utility bill, a phone call of encouragement, babysitting while the person looks for a job, or a note saying you are praying for their situation.

Let's go beyond our comfort zone today and lift someone up who is down!

Father God, let me become aware of people
in my immediate surroundings who are distressed
and downcast. I'm not by nature a compassionate

person, but let me today take on one of Jesus' character traits: compassion. I thank You for what You are doing in my life regarding concern for others. Amen.

Taking Action

- ❦ Make a love basket of food for a friend in need.

- ❦ Write a note to a friend who has a particular need and tell her you are praying for her today.

- ❦ Babysit for a friend who needs some free time to solve some of her problems.

- ❦ Call someone in need and lift her up with good thoughts of encouragement.

Reading On

Matthew 28:19,20	Deuteronomy 30:3
1 John 3:17	Lamentations 3:22,23

Should we feel at times disheartened and discouraged, a simple movement of heart toward God will renew our power. Whatever He demands of us, He will give us at the moment the strength and the courage that we need.

—*Francois de La Mothe-Fenelon*

❑ ❑ ❑

Where Can Wisdom Be Found?

Scripture Reading: Job 28:12-22

Key Verse: Job 28:12

Where can wisdom be found?

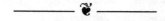

Not long ago my friend Florence Littauer wrote a book titled *Looking for Love in All the Wrong Places.* We are a culture which has a difficult time in reading the instruction manual. For some reason we want to invent the wheel by ourselves; we have trouble seeking the truth from the wise. We look for love in the wrong places, and we also seek wisdom in places where there is no wisdom. We talk to friends, read magazines, listen to talk shows, and attend seminars—all the wrong places.

The writer of the book of Job struggled with this same question of life. In Job 28:12 he asked, "Where can wisdom be found?" He too was perplexed with this question. All through chapter 28 he searched for the answer.

- Man doesn't know its value (verse 13a).
- It is not found in the land of the living (verse 13b).
- The inner earth says, "It's not in me" (verse 14a).
- The sea says, "It's not in me" (verse 14b).
- You can't buy it with gold or silver (verse 15).
- Precious stones don't have it (verse 16).

- It can't be equated with gold (verse 17).

- Pearls don't have it (verse 18).

- It is hidden from the eyes of all living creatures (verse 21a).

- Birds of the sky don't have it (verse 21b).

- Destruction and death say, "We have heard about it with our ears" (verse 22).

- God understands its way and He knows its place (verse 23).

- God looks to the ends of the earth and sees everything under heaven (verse 24).

- God saw wisdom and declared it (verse 27a).

- God established it and searched it out (verse 27b).

In verse 28 God told man, "Behold, the fear of the Lord, that is wisdom" (showing holy respect and reverence for God and shunning evil).

Job and his friends claimed wisdom of themselves, but wisdom is clearly an outgrowth of God and not merely something to be obtained. Although we can know and understand many things, we cannot attain to the level of Creator-wisdom. There will always be unanswered questions, for which only God the Creator will know the answer. Solomon knew that true wisdom is not found in human understanding but is from God alone (Proverbs 1:7; 9:10).

I challenge you to learn this basic truth of Scripture. If you want to know God's perspective, read your Bible daily; don't look in all the wrong places for your answers in life. Start with the manual that tells you step-by-step how to live life.

In John 10:10 we are told that Jesus came so we could have abundant lives. May our lives be richly blessed because of our faithfulness to the Scriptures. We don't have to wonder if God will trust us with His wisdom; the good news throughout Scripture is that the Lord gives wisdom liberally and without reproach to all of us who ask Him (James 1:5,6). If we approach the Lord in faith to show us what to do, what to say, and how to live, we can count on Him to give us His wisdom.

> *Father God, thank You for revealing to me where the true source of wisdom comes from. I truly want to show holy respect and reverence for You. As I read Your Word daily, I pray that Your truths will pop out to me and that I will continue to seek Your wisdom. May I never get to the point where I think I know everything about You. Thank You, Lord, for continuing to work in my life. Amen.*

Taking Action

- In what areas of your life are you seeking wisdom?
- Where can you go to find the answer?
- Is there a person you know who seems wise? If so, seek her out for godly counsel.
- Pray for the specifics of your need; let God know that you are seeking His guidance.

Reading On

Proverbs 1:7	James 1:5,6
Proverbs 9:10	Proverbs 8:18-21

Knowledge is horizontal.
Wisdom is vertical—
it comes down from above.
—*Billy Graham*

Stand By Your Convictions

Scripture Reading: Daniel 1:1-21

Key Verse: Daniel 1:8b

> *He sought permission from the commander of the officials that he might not defile himself.*

———— ❦ ————

A mother's joy would be complete if she heard that her son was making requests for healthful food. She would probably praise her son for actually wanting to eat nutritious foods and not just food from the fast-food restaurants.

In the book of Daniel we see a son who was raised by the teachings found in Leviticus 11. Daniel did not want to defile his body by eating foods that were unclean or had been offered to pagan idols before being put on the king's table. (Eating food offered to a pagan god was an indication of loyalty to that god.)

Notice the deep commitment of faith which enabled these young men to take the stands they took. They bore testimony to the faithfulness of mothers and fathers who taught them the central issues of obedience and faithfulness to biblical principles.

Because of this, Daniel was able to withstand the forces he faced in a hostile land. But since he was captured by the Babylonians and taken from his Israeli homeland, his mother may never have known the results of her early training while he was still in her home.

This value of teaching future generations has been impressed on me since I have two children and five grandchildren. We as mothers may never live to see how our children will respond as adults, but we must be faithful in raising our children to be responsible adults. I'm sure Daniel's mother prayed for him when he was young. She also continued to pray for him during the time of exile.

Whether or not she knew what Daniel had achieved, she had done the best job she could do as a mom: to raise a son who as an adult would follow the leading of the Lord.

As we look at our children we never know of their potential or what they will be as adults. But like Daniel's mother, we must continue as best as we know how to raise and prepare our children for God's calling.

> *Father God, at times I become so discouraged as a mom, because it seems like I'm the only one who cares. At times I sound like a squeaky wheel around my children and family. But You know that I want the very best for them. I want them to know of Your love for them, how to live a disciplined life, to be responsible for their actions, and how to have a healthful selection of foods. Even though I may not live to see them grown, I want You to know that my desire is to make them the children You would have them be. Thank You for putting that desire in my heart. Amen.*

Taking Action

- Do you have a plan to raise your children? What do you want them to become? How are they going to get there?

- Are you raising your children so they can think for themselves or are you still making all their decisions for them? Cut the cord early.

ꗩ What areas of your life do you want to change so that your children are better equipped to face adulthood? Write them in your journal. What are you going to do to get there?

Reading On

Leviticus 11	Hebrews 11:23-28
Luke 2:41-52	Exodus 34:15

Discipline is demanded of the athlete to win a game. Discipline is required for the captain running his ship. Discipline is needed for the pianist to practice for the concert. Only in the matter of personal conduct is the need for discipline questioned. But if parents believe standards are necessary, then discipline certainly is needed to attain them.

—*Gladys Brooks*

Two Wisdoms

Scripture Reading: James 3:13-18

Key Verse: James 3:13

Who among you is wise and understanding? Let him show by his good behavior his deeds in the gentleness of wisdom.

My husband, Bob, has an identical twin brother named Bill. When our children, Jennifer and Bradley, were very young and couldn't tell the men apart, they would address them as "two Daddies." When our grandchildren arrived, they also were confused when the two men were together. They would say "two PaPa's."

That's the way it is with wisdom. Both kinds are called wisdom, but they come from different sources, have different means, and most definitely have different ends. James talks about these two wisdoms in chapter 3:

• one which comes from above (verse 15).

• one which is earthly, natural, and demonic (verse 15).

The one that comes from above is—

• pure
  • peaceable
    • gentle
      • reasonable

- full of mercy
  - full of good fruits
    - unwavering (verse 17).

The second wisdom produces—

- bitter jealousy
  - selfish ambition
    - arrogance
      - lies against the truth (verse 17).

Notice the difference in the fruit that each produces:

- The first produces the fruit of righteousness and peace (verse 18).
- The second produces the fruit of disorder and every evil thing (verse 16).

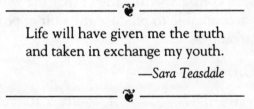

Life will have given me the truth
and taken in exchange my youth.

—*Sara Teasdale*

Wouldn't it be nice to have both wisdom and youth at the same time? Life, however, doesn't work that way.

Luci Swindoll states, "The good life is peace—knowing that I was considerate instead of crabby, that I stood by faithfully when all the chips were down for the other guy, that I sacrificially gave to a worthy cause, that I showed impartiality when I really wanted my preference, that I was real in the midst of phonies, that I was forgiving, that I had the courage to defer reward for something better down the road. Why couldn't I have learned this when I still had a young body?"[1]

Father God, I don't like my gray hair that reflects back to my eyes in the morning through the mirror. But my friends tell me I have wisdom in counseling and speaking. But why the gray hair? It doesn't seem fair that the two must go together. It seems like the world is drowning in knowledge, but we are starved for wisdom. Let me stand back and look at the real priorities of life. I don't want to chase rainbows that have no pot of gold at the end. Let me tell the difference. I want to say no to merely good things and save my yes for the very best. Amen.

Taking Action

 Which of the two wisdoms do you want to pursue?

 Meditate on your actions and see if they produce the right kind of fruit. If not, why not? What needs to be changed?

❦ Make a contract with a friend that she will hold you accountable to produce the fruit of peace and righteousness.

Reading On

Proverbs 4:5-7   Proverbs 9:10
1 Corinthians 2:6-13

There can be no wisdom
disjointed from goodness.
—*Richard C. Trench*

Who Fixed the Roof?

Scripture Reading: Luke 5:17-26

Key Verse: Luke 5:24b

> *He said to the paralytic, "I say to you, rise, and take up your stretcher and go home."*

In our biblical study today we see several strands of truth. The passage opens with some friends of a crippled man who want to bring him to Jesus to be healed. When I was still a teenager my Bob invited me to his church to hear the gospel of Jesus proclaimed. Being raised in the Jewish faith and having just recently graduated from our synagogue's Hebrew school, I couldn't understand why Bob was so interested in having me come to church. In my heart I truly believed that I was perfect and was not a sinner.

Have you ever met anyone like that? As I look back, I see that Bob wanted me to be healed as a sinner and to become obedient to God's Word. Little did I know then that my future husband was willing to take me to the rooftop and lower me through the roof if that had been necessary. Bob truly cared for me, just as this sick man had friends who cared.

The sick man couldn't walk, so they carried him on his personal bed. Can you imagine how the people of the city stared as they watched a man being carried on his bed to see Jesus? As the group arrived at the house where Jesus was teaching they saw a large crowd of people and couldn't even get close to Jesus for the healing of their friend.

So one of the friends said, "Let's go over the crowd and take him up on the rooftop." Then they climbed up some outside stairs with the sick man on his bed. They reasoned that they had to take off some of the flat roof to lower the man and his bed inside the house near Jesus. I can just hear the dialogue that went on between the friends:

- This will be fun—like a party.
- We can't tear into a roof.
- The debris will fall down on top of Jesus.
- Who will fix the roof when we're finished?

Fortunately for the sick man, someone took control and started taking off a section of the roof. Then they tied ropes to the corners of the bed and let the man and his bed down through the hole in the roof.

You can imagine the amazement that Jesus and those in the crowd experienced as they saw a man and bed being lowered through the roof. Some could have thought:

- The nerve of them!
- Can't they take their turn?
- Gate crashers!
- Escort them out!
- Make them wait in line and take their turn like we did.

But Jesus looked at the man who had come down through the roof. Then He smiled and said, "Your sins are forgiven."

Some of the scribes and pharisees (Jewish leaders) were very upset. "Who does this Jesus think he is? Only God can forgive a man's sin!"

But Jesus replied, "You're right. Only God can forgive sins. I will show you that I can forgive sins." So He turned to the sick man and said, "Rise and take up your stretcher and go home."

At once the paralytic man rose up before them all and took up his bed and went home glorifying God. All the crowd watched in amazement and began to glorify God, for they truly had witnessed some remarkable things.

Fortunately, the friends hadn't spent time debating who would fix the roof. They just earnestly wanted to get their friend healed. Jesus also was open to a very unorthodox way in which the sick man was brought to Him, and the sick man was obedient to Jesus' command when He said, "Stand and walk."

The Bible clearly commands us to always obey the Lord (Acts 5:29; Daniel 7:27). In James 1:22 we are specifically required to hear His Word and do His will. We should be obedient to God because of our love for Him (1 John 2:3,4). These acts are to be a reflection of the inner reality that we truly love the Lord and are committed to His ways.

We know from raising children that obedience is not automatic. It must be taught and learned (Deuteronomy 6:7-9). We have security and peace when we are obedient to those in authority. (Maybe our disobedience is why we have so much unrest and violence today in our world, country, states, cities, families, and churches.)

I thank the Lord that my Bob cared for me so much that he took me to Jesus and I was healed. I'm also thankful that in childlike faith I said yes to the call of the gospel and made a conscious commitment to follow Jesus. It has been the most meaningful decision I have ever made in my life. Because of that submission to God and His Word, I am who I am today. Thank You, Jesus!

Father God, again I thank You that my Bob loved me so much that he wanted me to meet You and be healed. It was the event of my life. I can't imagine where I would be today without You. You have made all the difference. I'm glad to experience Your peace and restfulness. May I in turn be a caring friend who will reach out to someone who needs You. Amen.

Taking Action

- Can you think of a friend who needs to be lowered through the roof?

- Invite that person to go with you to tea, a luncheon, shopping, a Bible study, a church event, etc. Even offer to come and get her.

- Minister to the needs (physical, social, emotional, and spiritual) of your friend.

Reading On

Acts 5:29	1 John 2:3,4
Daniel 7:27	Deuteronomy 6:7-9

The difference between perseverance and obstinacy is that one often comes from a strong will and the other from a strong won't.

—*Henry Ward Beecher*

Do You Love Me?

Scripture Reading: John 21:15-22

Key Verse: John 21:15a

Jesus said to Simon Peter, "Simon, son of John, do you love Me more than these?"

It seems as though we go through life wondering if our husbands, our children, and our friends love us. We feel insecure about the other people in our lives, and we're not sure where we stand. Even though we tell and show everyone we love them, they don't seem to catch the answer, because they're always reaching out to test our love for them.

Sometimes our children wear crazy clothes, put rings in their ears, color their hair in strange colors, and use foul language to see if we really love them. Our whole culture is continually testing us to see if we really love them.

In our passage today Jesus asks Peter three times (after His crucifixion and resurrection and Peter's recent denial of Him) whether Peter really loves Him.

I believe that these basic questions . . .

- Do you love Me? (verse 15)
- Do you love Me? (verse 16)
- Do you love Me? (verse 17) . . .

correspond to Peter's three denials of Jesus (John 13:38). Jesus in all His love for Peter wanted to give him a second chance to follow Him. He didn't want Peter to go all through life with the stigma of denying Jesus before His crucifixion. He wanted Peter to know that he was forgiven for his wrongdoings and that he could have a valuable ministry in spreading the gospel throughout the world.

But before Peter was able to confirm his love for Jesus, Jesus stated in verses 18 and 19 that the decision was going to cost him a price. In fact Peter and his wife were crucified upside down approximately 40 years later. After stating that there would be a price for following Him Jesus said, "Follow me," and Peter did.

> In repentance and rest is your salvation, in quietness and trust is your strength.
>
> —Isaiah 30:15 NIV

Yes, love has its price, not always to the extreme of Peter's, but a price of time, energy, commitment, money, and devotion. Selfish people take without giving back, but a true lover of people is always giving and giving and giving.

Is there someone in your life who is asking the very basic question "Do you love me?" What is your reply?

Father God, I know there are times when You ask me, "Do you love me?" I want to answer yes, and, like Peter, I want to follow You. Give me the courage to put my love into action. We can all answer yes, but it is only when we move into action that true love for You is demonstrated. Amen.

Taking Action

❦ Write in your journal what actions of love you are going to do today for:

Jesus	Neighbor	Husband
Child	Friend	

❧ Do what you stated above. Be known as someone who does what she says she is going to do.

Reading On

1 John 4:7   1 Corinthians 13:1-8,13

1 John 4:10,11   John 14:21

When iron is rubbed against a
magnet it becomes magnetic.
Just so, love is caught, not
taught. One heart burning with
love sets another on fire. The
church was built on love; it
proves what love can do.

—*Frank C. Laubach*

Great Family Blessings

Scripture Reading: Ecclesiastes 4:8-12

Key Verse: Ecclesiastes 4:12

A cord of three strands is not quickly torn apart.

"I wish I had some good friends to help me in life!" cried lazy Dennis. "Good friends? Why, you have ten!" replied his master. "I'm sure I don't have half that many, and those I have are too poor to help me." "Count your fingers, my boy," said his master. Dennis looked down at his strong hands. "Count thumbs and all," added the master. "I have; there are ten," replied the lad. "Then never say you don't have ten good friends to help you on in life. Try what those true friends can do before you grumble and fret because you do not get help from others."

—Source unknown

Many times we look to others to help us out and complain when we don't receive the help we think we deserve. But help starts within ourselves, then moves outward. We need to take an inventory of all the skills and tools that God has so graciously given us at birth. We tend to take for granted those attributes of success which were given to us at the very beginning of our life. Our fingers and thumbs are such valuable tools for work. They truly are our dearest friends. In addition, King Solomon in all his wisdom told us that friends are great blessings to our family. He emphasized in Ecclesiastes chapter 4:

- Two are better than one because they have a good return for their labor (verse 9).
- Woe to the one who falls when there is not another to lift him up (verse 10).
- If two lie down together they keep warm (verse 11).
- Two can resist one who tries to overpower them (verse 12a).
- A cord of three strands is not quickly torn apart (verse 12b).

Are you working on relationships that build these kinds of blessings? Begin at home with your family members. Throughout Scripture we are told to be united with one another. Unity should be our goal as husband/wife, parent/child, child/sibling.

Begin to develop those traits that have eternal worth, not the temporal traits that live for such a short time.

In Ecclesiastes 4:8 Solomon asks one of the most basic questions of life: "For whom am I laboring and depriving myself of pleasure?" Is it all for vanity? Does it have redeeming value to you and your family? If not, do something about it.

> *Father God, in my heart and soul I want my family to be a blessing to me, and likewise I want to be a blessing to them. At times it seems to be in vain. Bring to mind those traits that are so important for friendships. I do want to be counted as a friend to those around me. Let me be a discerning person when it comes to doing my best for the people You have placed in my life. Let me major on major issues and minor on minor issues of life. Amen.*

Taking Action

❧ If you are married, discuss with your husband this question: "For whom am I laboring and depriving myself of pleasure?"

🍎 What kind of friend are you? What qualities do you look for in a friend? Who would you consider your best friend? Why?

🍎 Would you have wanted someone like yourself as a mother? Why or why not?

🍎 Whom do you feel very comfortable around? Why?

Reading On

Proverbs 18:24	John 15:13
James 4:4	1 John 1:7

How little do my countrymen
know what precious blessings
they are in possession of, and
which no other people on earth
enjoy.

—*Thomas Jefferson*

Who Is Going to Bell the Cat?

Scripture Reading: Joshua 1:1-9

Key Verse: Joshua 1:9

Have I not commanded you? Be strong and courageous!
Do not tremble or be dismayed, for the Lord your God is
with you wherever you go.

Once upon a time all the mice met together in council and discussed the best means of protecting themselves against the attacks of the cat. After several suggestions had been debated, a mouse of some standing and experience got up and said, "I think I have hit upon a plan which ensures our safety in the future, provided you approve it and carry it out. It is that we should fasten a bell around the neck of our enemy the cat, which will by its tinkling warn us of her approach."

This proposal was warmly applauded, and it had already been decided to adopt it when an old mouse finally got up on his feet and said, "I agree with you all that the plan before us is an admirable one, but I ask: Who is going to bell the cat?"

—Adapted from Aesop

Wouldn't it be wonderful if all we had to do in order to be brave is to talk about it? But true courage and bravery require *action*. Our society today hungers to find people with courage. We look for our heroes in sports, politics, movies, business, and church, but many of them fail the test. We hunger for the character trait of courage, but few people are able to deliver on it.

As parents we are continually tested by the decisions we must make. Are we able to stand alone and make hard decisions on what we as a family are going to do? It's hard to be in the minority as a friend, a neighbor, or a parent, to just say no. Unfortunately, the greatest pressure often comes from those we love the most!

In Joshua 24:15 the writer had a similar dilemma, but he stood tall and delivered this statement:

> If it is disagreeable in your sight to serve the Lord, choose for yourselves today whom you will serve: whether the gods which your fathers served which were beyond the River, or the gods of the Amorites in whose land you are living; but as for me and my house, we will serve the Lord.

Joshua was willing to stand up and be heard. He had the courage to bell the cat. Are you facing a similar difficulty in your life? If so, look to God to find the answer. He says He will never leave us or forsake us. That is a promise we can take to the bank.

We have some friends in Northern California who have made a "Valor Ribbon" for each of their two sons. When the parents are aware that the sons have taken some action that requires courage, bravery, or valor they recognize this fact by letting the boys wear their ribbon that evening at home. It might be for—

- not smoking, drinking, or taking drugs when someone offers them;

- not cheating on a test when the opportunity arises to do so;

- saying no to premarital sex;
- returning found money;
- assisting someone who is in need of help.

These parents recognize the importance of praising their sons' acts of courage.

Our reading today (Joshua 1:8,9) states:

- The law of Scripture shall not depart from your mouth.
- You shall meditate on it day and night.
- Be careful to do according to all that is written in it.
- This will make your way prosperous.
- You will have success.
- Be strong and courageous.
- Do not tremble or be dismayed.
- The Lord your God is with you wherever you go.

Let us not only talk the talk, but walk the walk, for God is always with us and we are never alone.

> *Father God, oh how I want to have courage enough to stand up and be counted in difficult situations. I really want to have the courage to bell the cat. Support me as I stand strong with my convictions. Don't let me waver as I stand tall. Let those around me gain strength from my strength which I receive from You. Let me not only believe the gospel but also behave the gospel. Amen.*

Taking Action

❦ In what areas of your life do you need to show courage? What are you going to do about the situation?

❦ You are offered a great buy on a beautiful jacket. You suspect it is stolen. Will you still buy it?

❦ The bank ATM gives you 60 dollars instead of the 20 dollars you asked for. What will you do?

❦ If you knew that a neighbor was abusing his wife and/or children, what would you do?

Reading On

Isaiah 41:10   Deuteronomy 33:27
Psalm 118:17   Philippians 4:13

❦

Courage is doing what you're afraid to do. There can be no courage unless you're scared.

—*Eddie Rickenbacker*

❦

Use Wisely What He Has Given You

Scripture Reading: Matthew 25:14-30

Key Verse: Matthew 25:29

To everyone who has shall more be given, and he shall have an abundance; but from the one who does not have, even what he does have shall be taken away.

God has given each of us specific talents—to some more than others, but to each of us *something*. What kind of stewards are we to become in using these talents? Some of us know from personal experience how a stuttering child can become an eloquent speaker and how a brilliant debater can become homeless when he uses his talent slothfully.

In today's passage we find Jesus telling His disciples that the kingdom of heaven is like a man who called his servants to delegate to them a portion of his property. To one servant he gave five gold coins, to another two coins, and to the third one coin. Each servant was given according to his ability.

The first man traded with his five coins and made five more. The man with two coins did likewise and made two more. But the one-coin man dug a hole in the ground and buried it.

After awhile the owner of the land came to settle the accounts with his three servants. The first servant brought with him the original five coins plus five additional ones. The

331

master said, "Well done, good and faithful slave; you were faithful with a few things, I will put you in charge of many things" (verse 21).

The second man, who had been given just two coins, brought forth the original two plus the two he had made. The master likewise said, "Well done, good and faithful slave; you were faithful with a few things, I will put you in charge of many things; enter into the joy of your master" (verse 23).

The third servant came forward with the one gold coin and said, "Master, I knew you to be a hard man, reaping where you did not sow and gathering where you scattered no seed. And I was afraid and went away and hid your talent in the ground; see, you have what is yours" (verse 24,25).

But the master replied, "You wicked, lazy slave, you knew that I reap where I did not sow and gather where I scattered no seed. Then you ought to have put my money in the bank, and on my arrival I would have received my money back with interest. Therefore take away the talent from him and give it to the one who has the ten talents" (verses 26-28).

Then Jesus stated, "For to everyone who has shall more be given, and he shall have an abundance; but from the one who does not have, even what he does have shall be taken away" (verse 29).

This third man didn't mean any harm to the master, but he didn't understand the principles of stewardship and faithfulness. When we are faithful we are reliable: appearing on time, doing what we say we are going to do, finishing the job we started, and being there when we need to be there.

Everyday life operates on the laws of faith and trust. We assume that people are going to honor their word, stop at red lights, pay monthly mortgage payments, pay the utility bills, show up for an appointment, be faithful in marriage. Throughout Scripture God shows His attribute of being faithful.

We need women who will reach out with one or two or five talents and invest them wisely in their home, marriage, church, family, and community. We need women who will take the little they have and double it so that when we stand before Jesus He will say, "Well done, good and faithful servant; enter into the joy of my father's mansions." What a glorious day that will be!

> *Father God, I live in a world of comparisons, and I only see people who have five talents, while You seem to have neglected me by giving me only one. I feel, "how can I be as good as that person, since she has so much more than I do?" I pray that You would clearly show me how I can be faithful to the one talent that I have. Thank You, Lord, for all You have given to me. Amen.*

Taking Action

- In your journal list three to five strengths that you have. Also list two or three weaknesses that you are aware of.

- Develop a plan of action to see how you will maximize your strengths. Likewise with your weaknesses, list actions that need to be taken to make these stronger.

- Ask a friend to help you with these ideas.

- Realize that you are special in the eyes of God.

Reading On

Psalm 127	Psalm 145:14
Psalm 139	Psalm 150

We make a living by what we get,
but we make a life by what
we give.

—*Winston E. Churchill*

Christians Are to Persevere

Scripture Reading: James 1:2-8

Key Verse: James 1:4

Let endurance have its perfect result, that you may be perfect and complete, lacking in nothing.

———— ❦ ————

A hare was one day making fun of a tortoise for being so slow on his feet. "Wait a bit," said the tortoise; "I'll run a race with you, and I'll wager that I win." "Oh, well," replied the hare, who was much amused at the idea, "Let's try it and see." They agreed that the fox should set a course for them and be the judge. When the time for the race came, both started off together, but the hare was soon so far ahead that he thought he might as well have a rest; so he lay down and fell fast asleep. The tortoise, meanwhile, kept plodding on, and in time he reached the goal. At last the hare woke up with a start and dashed on at his fastest, only to find that the tortoise had already won the race.

—Adapted from Aesop

Too many of us only see the start of the race and aren't around to see the end and find out who the real winners are. So much of life is painted with speed, flash, and sizzle that we get intimidated by everyone else's flash.

A few years ago our family went to Lake Tahoe to snow ski during the Christmas break. As I walked on the icy slopes of this beautiful resort my eyes were full of the best: the best of cars, of ski racks, of clothing, of beauty, of laughter. I couldn't believe my eyes—I had never seen so much sizzle in one place. Everyone was perfect!

So I said to myself, "No way am I going to compete with them." But after being coaxed into my group ski lesson I found that many of the "sizzle group" were also in my class and that they couldn't ski any better than I could!

The Scripture for today teaches that perseverance is *enduring with patience*. We will experience many trials in life that can discourage and defeat us. In the Bible, "perseverance" is a term used to describe Christians who faithfully endure and remain steadfast in the face of opposition, attack, and discouragement. When we persevere with patience, we exhibit our ability to endure without complaint and with calmness.

As believers we need to daily commit ourselves to godly living. Our daily commitments lead us to lasting discipline. I tell my ladies at our seminars, "It takes only 21 consecutive days to create a new habit."

Commitment and *discipline* are not words that the world is comfortable with. The nineties decade wants everything to feel good, and these words don't always feel good. They are words that demand denial of self and pain. "Feeling good" people don't like pain or testing; it makes them very uncomfortable, particularly when they don't trust the Tester.

Scripture is very clear when it teaches that we are to persevere—

- in prayer (Ephesians 6:18);
- in obedience (Revelation 14:12);
- in faith (Hebrews 12:1,2);

- in service (1 Corinthians 15:58);
- in self-control (2 Peter 1:5-7).

Scripture promises us certain blessings if we endure till the end:

- final deliverance (Matthew 24:13);
- rewarded faith (Hebrews 11:6);
- eternal inheritance (Revelation 21:7).

As we live out this life daily and are able to persevere in all its trials and temptations, we will be rewarded by the Lord with the fruit of His Spirit now and for all eternity (Galatians 5:22,23):

love	goodness
joy	faithfulness
peace	gentleness
patience	self-control
kindness	

Father God, please open my eyes to see that life is a laboratory that is developing Christian character in my life. Let me not get sidetracked by all the hares of life. I want to stay true to You during all the ups and downs of daily living. In life's difficulties I want to look heavenward to see what You are trying to teach me in these particular situations. May I always be faithful to Your Word. Amen.

Taking Action

- In your journal list six blessings that God has given you.

- Also, jot down several struggles you are having in life. Beside each one list several things that God is trying to teach you through them.

❦ Write down one desire of your heart. What are you and God going to do to make it a reality?

Reading On

Romans 5:3-5	2 Corinthians 4:14
Colossians 3:2	James 5:11

❦

Great works are performed not
by strength, but by perseverance.

—*Samuel Johnson*

❦

A Yielding of the Heart

Scripture Reading: Luke 1:46-56

Key Verse: Luke 1:52
He has brought down rulers from their thrones, and has exalted those who were humble.

In the New Testament we find the word "humility" to mean a personal quality of dependence on God and respect for other people. It is not a natural human instinct but is a God-given virtue acquired through holy living.

While the mind of the natural man is selfish and proud, the essence of Jesus' mind is unselfish and loving toward others. Christ was our great example of a proper walk: pleasing to God.

Our hearts must be transformed by the Holy Spirit so that we can reflect God's love to others through the humble example of Jesus.

Corrie ten Boom, an unbelievable Dutch woman who survived the horror of World War II while in the confines of the German death camps, received a lot of praise for what she did during her confinement, and yet she remained unfazed by all the tributes. When asked how she managed to stay so humble among all these honors she humbly replied, "I accept every compliment as a flower and say thank you, and each evening I put them in a bunch and lay them at Jesus' feet, where the praise belongs."

Our world is full of men and women who are eager to take God's honor and heap it on their own heads. But God has a way of humbling us. From my own experience in life I know that I need to come before His throne with open arms and humbly bow before Him, seeking whatever He has for my life. We all need to learn this lesson of humility in life, because God has promised that if we don't humble ourselves, He will do it for us.

> To learn humility is to learn contentment in all circumstances. Humility is not in what we own or achieve, but in maintaining a teachable attitude, a willingness to bend to the will of the Father.
>
> —*Jan Silvious*

When Christ entered into the Greek world, they hated the quality of humility, but Jesus entered as a humble Savior. He became obedient to God's will, which led to His death on the cross. Throughout Jesus' walk on this earth He taught people to be humble before God and man.

In today's passage we see that God will exalt those who are humble. Humility comes from God and results in the praise of God.

Father God, You know how I want to lay down my bouquet of flowers at Your feet and give You all the praise. I know I am nothing without You. You have taken an ordinary woman and exalted her to a point at which I don't feel adequate. Thank You for fulfilling Your promise in me. Through my life may You be richly praised and lifted up. I am humbled that You can use me in life. Let me touch people so they know they have seen and felt Jesus. Amen.

Taking Action

- Ask God for a heart of humility.

- List in your journal three areas of pride that you have in your life. Beside each, state what you are going to do to turn pride into humility.

- Ask a friend to share with you those areas of your life where you need specific rearranging.

Reading On

James 4:10	Colossians 2:18
1 Peter 5:6	Romans 5:15

Unless you humble yourself before God in the dust, and confess before Him your iniquities and sins, the gate of heaven, which is open only for sinners saved by grace, must be shut against you forever.

—*Dwight L. Moody*

A Psalm of Thanks

Scripture Reading: 1 Chronicles 16:23-34

Key Verse: 1 Chronicles 16:34

O give thanks to the Lord, for He is good; for His lovingkindness is everlasting.

I can't tell you how excited I get for fall to start—it's such an exciting time of the year! It also brings cooler temperatures in Riverside and we get to celebrate Thanksgiving Day. When I was a young Jewish girl we did not celebrate Christmas in our home, though Thanksgiving was acceptable. At home and in the neighborhood I could talk with my friends about this holiday.

However, for most of us it just meant that we had a day out of school (where we had reviewed all about the Pilgrims and Indians), we ate roasted turkey with all the trimmings, and of course we visited at one of our families' homes. This was a very festive occasion for a young girl. It wasn't until later in life that I really started to think about the blessings we receive when we are thankful.

Not until I met my Bob and his family did I begin to see all that I had and to mentally count these things with thanksgiving.

In our reading for today we see that we are to give thanks to the Lord, and not some other object. Why? because He is good and His love endures forever. Those are two things I was looking for in life:

- GOODNESS
- EVERLASTING LOVE

Our home certainly didn't reflect either of those. Instead, there was constant upheaval, with doors slamming and with waking at all hours of the night because of my father's drinking. I couldn't count on a love that was unconditional. I was loved when I performed, but it would be withdrawn for the slightest reason.

But Bob was different. He was a good person who seemed to have an everlasting ability to stand by his commitments. His family was so fun and easy to be around, one that modeled what I was so earnestly seeking. Here was a man that walked his talk.

I can still remember that first Thanksgiving feast in their home. The selection of foods was much different from ours, they prayed to tell God how much they appreciated all that they had (we always just dug in, with no time to thank God for what we had), and after the meal was over we went around the table expressing what we were thankful for. You mean to say that people actually thought about such things?

That evening as I got into bed I knew I was truly among a very special family, one much different from my past.

Later in life I discovered today's passage in 1 Chronicles:

> Sing to the Lord, all the earth;
>   proclaim his salvation day after day.
> Declare his glory among the nations,
>   his marvelous deeds among all peoples.
> For great is the Lord and most worthy of praise;
>   he is to be feared above all gods.
> For all the gods of the nations are idols,
>   but the Lord made the heavens.
> Splendor and majesty are before him;
>   strength and joy in his dwelling place.
> Ascribe to the Lord, O families of nations,
>   ascribe to the Lord glory and strength,
>   ascribe to the Lord the glory due his name.

Bring an offering and come before him;
  worship the Lord in the splendor of his holiness.
Tremble before him, all the earth!
  The world is firmly established; it cannot be
  moved.
  Let the heavens rejoice, let the earth be glad;
  let them say among the nations, "The Lord
  reigns!"
Let the sea resound, and all that is in it;
  Let the fields be jubilant, and everything in
  them!
Then the trees of the forest will sing,
  they will sing for joy before the Lord,
  for he comes to judge the earth.
Give thanks to the Lord, for he is good;
  his love endures forever (1 Chronicles
  16:23-34 NIV).

As I studied these verses, I began to pick out key action words and phrases that reflected how I should be worshiping God and how I was to model my new Christian walk. Some of these expressions were:

- Sing to the Lord.
  - Proclaim His salvation daily.
    - Share His marvelous deeds.
- God is worthy to be praised.
  - God is to be feared above all else.
    - God is not an idol but the Creator of the
    heavens.
      - God reflects splendor, majesty, strength,
      and joy.
- Ascribe to the Lord His glory.

- Bring an offering to Him.
  - The earth cannot be moved.
    - The heavens and earth are to rejoice and shout, "The Lord Reigns!"
- The sea, fields, and trees will sing joy unto God.
  - We are to give thanks unto the Lord.

Why? Because He is good, and His love endures forever! After reading this passage I realized I had been approaching God from the wrong direction. As my grandson, Chad, says, "We serve an awesome God."

I began to sing, to tell others about Him, and to praise God for His worthiness. I began tithing and I began to hear the sounds of nature as they sing praises to their Creator. Above all, I began to be scripturally thankful because of who God is.

Jesus was continually telling His disciples and those around Him that they could count on His continuing love. When you begin to have joy in the Lord, you get excited about seeing lives changed through the gospel. When you honestly begin serving and thanking God there will be real joy in your life.

Begin to count your blessings one by one. Meditate on all of them. Don't skim over them as you would the food section of your Thursday newspaper!

Father God, thank You for sending people in my life who have helped shape me into who I am today. Without them serving You in their daily lives, I would not have been able to see Your Word in daily application. As a mature lady looking back, I see that You have given me more than I would ever have wanted. Your abundance has been enormous. Thank You for keeping Your covenants to Your people. We are surely blessed. Amen.

Taking Action

- In your journal write down ten things for which you are thankful.

- Write down three things for which you aren't able to give thanks.

- With blind faith give these three items to God, knowing that in time He will reveal His purpose. (There are some events for which we will never know His purpose until we see Him face-to-face).

Reading On

Romans 8:28	Romans 10:17
Luke 17:5	Hebrews 11:1

Let all of us . . . give thanks to God and prayerful contemplation to those eternal truths and universal principles of Holy Scripture which have inspired such measure of true greatness as this nation has achieved.

—*Dwight D. Eisenhower,*
Thanksgiving Day Proclamation, 1956

If I Had It All to Do Over

Scripture Reading: Luke 22:7-20

Key Verse: Luke 22:19b

This is My body which is given for you; do this in remembrance of Me.

———— ❧ ————

Someone asked me the other day if I had my life to live over, would I change anything?

My answer was no, but I thought about it and changed my mind.

If I had my life to do over again I would have waxed less and listened more.

Instead of wishing away nine months of pregnancy and complaining about the shadows over my feet, I'd have cherished every minute of it and realized that the wonderment growing inside me was to be my only chance in life to assist God in a miracle.

I would never have insisted that the car windows be rolled up on a summer day because my hair had just been teased and sprayed.

I would have invited friends over to dinner even if the carpet was stained and the sofa faded.

I would have eaten popcorn in the "good" living room and worried less about the dirt when you lit the fireplace.

I would have taken time to listen to my grandfather ramble about his youth.

I would have burned the pink candle sculptured like a rose before it melted while being stored.

I would have sat cross-legged on the lawn with my children and never worried about grass stains.[2]

Here is a woman looking back on life and remembering all the little phases and events we often overlook the first time around.

Each of us, regardless of what our ages are, look back with regret that we didn't take more time to _____. My Bob gets melancholy when we see our old photo slides of the children when they were young. He remembers when he could have if he would have. But we can't go back and recapture lost opportunities. We need to take advantage of each day and live it to the fullest.

When we take communion at our church, the elements are placed on a table with these words carved on the side facing the congregation: "This Do in Remembrance of Me." The Scriptures state very clearly that we are to look back to the cross and remember what Christ did for us. At the communion table we are to—

- *Break bread:* "This is My body which is given for you; do this in remembrance of Me."
- *Drink from the cup:* "This cup which is poured out for you is the new covenant in My blood."

We are to remember what Christ Jesus did for us in history. Elisabeth Elliot states, "Ultimate hatred and ultimate love met on those two crosspieces of wood. Suffering and love were brought into harmony."

As we look back over our life, let's make sure that we have accepted Jesus as He suffered for us and our sins on the cross and paid the price of His death because of His ultimate love for us. This unselfish act has been the greatest event in human history. As we look back, may we clearly remember Jesus, the bread, and the cup of wine.

Father God, I remember back to when I was 16 years old; it seemed like just yesterday that I accepted Jesus as my personal Savior. Through that very act You assured me that Jesus was my Messiah of the Old Testament. In one instant I had become a completed Jewish girl. As I remember back I have never regretted the decision I made one night on my knees beside my bed. You have been my strength and support over these years. Without You I fear what might have become of my life. You have been the difference between who I am and what I could have been. Reveal Your Son, Jesus Christ, to other women who are searching for meaning in their lives. Amen.

Taking Action

- Write in your journal your recollection of when you became a child of God: date, time, place, and situation.

- If you cannot write this down but would like to, select a pastor, a friend, a neighbor, or someone at work who is already a child of God and ask her to tell you about God's salvation through Jesus.

- When you are able to write this down as your own experience, do so. Also, write the date inside the front cover of your Bible. Then you will always have assurance when you doubt. You can look in your Bible and see written in your own handwriting the specific date when you first accepted Christ.

Reading On

Romans 3:23   Ephesians 2:8,9
Romans 6:23   Romans 10:9,10

He is no fool who gives
what he cannot keep to
gain what he cannot lose.

—*Jim Elliot*

Do Not Lose Heart

Scripture Reading: 2 Corinthians 4:7-18

Key Verse: 2 Corinthians 4:16,17

Therefore we do not lose heart . . . for momentary light affliction is producing for us an eternal weight of glory far beyond all comparison.

———— ❦ ————

If you are having financial troubles, setbacks . . . it's not the end.

If you have been lied to and deceived . . . it's not the end.

If you have lost your job . . . it's not the end.

If you have lost your home . . . it's not the end.

If something has been stolen from you or if you have been robbed of your inheritance . . . it's not the end.

If you have a child who is ensnared in a sin, entangled in a web of wrong relationships, failing according to life's report card, or refusing to communicate with you . . . it's not the end.

If your mate has walked away, chosen someone else instead of you . . . it's not the end.

If you have just lost a loved one to death—sudden death, expected or unexpected—it's not the end. Even if your loved one committed suicide . . . it's not the end.

If you have behaved like an absolute fool and are mortified by what you did . . . it's not the end.

If you are incarcerated for a crime . . . it's not the end.

If you are losing your hearing or your sight . . . it's not the end.

If you are in the depths of depression, if you are battling

depression or a chemical imbalance that has thrown all your emotions and even your way of thinking out of kilter . . . it's not the end.

If you have learned that you have a terminal disease, a crippling disease, a wasting disease . . . it's not the end.

If you have stepped onto the threshold of death . . . it's not the end.

I can tell you all this with the utmost of confidence and know that what I am telling you is truth.

It may seem like the end . . .

you may wish it were the end . . .

but it is not the end because God is God and the end has not yet come.[3]

As I was reading this newsletter from Kay Arthur, thoughts of the past two years zipped through my mind. Often during this time I didn't want any more pain, heartache, or disappointments. I would ask God while walking the canal (my prayer closet), "God, aren't You finished yet? I thought yesterday's revelation was the end, but now You're telling me there is more!"

I so want to get through this situation of the present and move into something more positive in the future. Then God reveals to me that I get through the present day by remembering that it is not the end. I had been looking at the present condition as a negative, but He was telling me that I won't always be here (temporal), that the end (eternal) will be my final destination and that it will bring victory in all areas of my life.

The great women of the past were overcomers, and we too are overcomers. Each of us in our own way have realized victory in our walk with our Lord.

Whatever is born of God overcomes the world; and this is the victory that has overcome the world—our faith (1 John 5:4).

We too have a future and a hope because we belong to a covenant-keeping God. He never breaks His promises.

I am brought back to reality by reconfirming my faith in an almighty God and Father who reigns supreme over all.

I look upward and am reminded that I'm not to look at the things which are seen, but at the things not seen, for these have eternal value.

> *Father God, thank You again for reassuring me that this isn't the end, for the end will be an "eternal weight of glory" far beyond all comparisons. I know that what I'm thinking and feeling are only temporal, and though they really hurt, I trust You for the perfecting that's taking place in my life. I appreciate Your concern for me and my loved ones. Amen.*

Taking Action

- In your journal list several of your temporary afflictions.
- Beside each one write, "This is producing an eternal weight of glory for me."
- Turn these over to the Lord in prayer and reconfirm your commitment to God, knowing that He reigns supreme over all.

Reading On

Jeremiah 29:11   1 John 5:4
1 John 2:17   Romans 8:28

God helps us to do what we can, and endure what we must, even in the darkest hours. But more, He wants to teach us that there are no rainbows without storm clouds and there are no diamonds without heavy pressure and enormous heat.

—W.T. Purkiser

□ ■ □

Who Is the Greatest in the Kingdom of Heaven?

Scripture Reading: Matthew 18:1-6

Key Verse: Matthew 18:4
Whoever then humbles himself as this child, he is the greatest in the kingdom of heaven.

———— ❦ ————

Jesus is saying that unbelievers need to humble themselves before the Lord as little children so they can gain salvation. In fact all of us need to humble ourselves until we become as a little child: exhibiting trust, openness, and eagerness to learn. These are the childlike qualities that constitute greatness.

Jesus used children as an illustration of the faith, trust, loyalty, and submission to God which are required in order to become part of His kingdom. The sharing of the gospel to children must be a priority for home and church. All believers have the assignment to model a godly life before the children in their presence and to love them and tell them about the Lord.

The gospel message is to be given to all, and a response is required by all who are old enough to know the difference between right and wrong (Matthew 28:19,20). Children are very capable of responding to God and can respond to Him in praise, worship, prayer, and thanksgiving.

In this passage Jesus does not tell children to become like adults but tells us adults to become like children. He also gives a very strong warning to those who might bring harm to these little ones. In Matthew 18:6 He states, "Whoever causes one of these little ones who believe in Me to stumble, it is better for him that a heavy millstone be hung around his neck, and that he be drowned in the depth of the sea."

That is a very serious statement of consequences, and therefore I want to do all within my power to take it seriously. We are to be teachers and edifiers with proper instruction for our children. In my latest book, *Fill My Cup, Lord*, I talk about a cup of prayer as found in Colossians 1:9-14. I want the reader to learn how to pray for their children. These little ones (or big ones—they still remain your children even though they are grown adults) need a hedge of prayer daily. A series of books that I find most helpful in praying the Scriptures for my children and grandchildren is done by Lee Roberts and Thomas Nelson Publishers:

Praying God's Will for My Son
Praying God's Will for My Daughter[4]

These resources quote Scripture and let you insert the children's specific names so you can personalize your prayers. I have literally worn out my one book while praying for my daughter these last 2½ years. One of the side effects is that I see changes taking place in my own life. Oh, the Lord is certainly working in Jenny's life because of all my anointed prayers, but He is truly performing a miracle in my own life as well.

My friend Donna Otto has listed in her recent book *The Stay-at-Home Mom* ten ways in which a parent can pray for her children. She states: "Let's face it, without prayer anything else you do to influence your children for Jesus is feeble at best."

1. Pray that your children will fear the Lord and serve Him (Deuteronomy 6:13).

2. Pray that your children will know Christ as Savior early in life (Psalm 63:1).

3. Pray that your children will be caught when they're guilty (Psalm 119:71).

4. Pray that your children will desire the right kind of friends and be protected from the wrong kind (Proverbs 1:10,15).

5. Pray that your children will be kept from the wrong mate and saved for the right one[5] (2 Corinthians 6:14).

6. Pray that your children and their prospective mates will be kept pure until marriage[6] (1 Corinthians 6:18-20).

7. Pray that your children will be teachable and able to take correction (Proverbs 13:1).

8. Pray that your children will learn to submit totally to God and actively resist Satan in all circumstances: "Submit therefore to God" (James 4:7).

9. Pray that your children will be hedged in so they cannot find their way to wrong people or wrong places, and that wrong people cannot find their way to your children (Hosea 2:6,7).

10. Pray that your children will honor their parents so all will go well with them.[7]

The only assurance I have of access to my children's hearts is through prayer and the power of the Holy Spirit.

> *Father God, I have been challenged again today to be in earnest prayer for my children. As I survey the world and its changing attitudes toward children, I want to be a shining beacon supporting them in every way possible. You have inspired me to care for all of their other needs in life. Now You have placed on my heart a burden to pray and instruct them in the ways of the Lord. Amen.*

Taking Action

❦ Write the names of your children (grandchildren) in your prayer journal. Assign several pages for each child.

❦ Go through your recent photos and cut out a picture of each child. Glue it at the top of page 1 for each child.

❦ For each child write down at least one prayer request. Save room at the end of the request to note the date when you see an answer to that prayer. (In some cases be willing to allow weeks, months, and even years before an answer comes.)

❦ As time goes along, jot down other prayer requests for each child.

Reading On

Look up and read each verse of Scripture given earlier in the list of ten ideas on how to pray for your children.

---------- ❦ ----------

The Reverend Moses Browne had 12 children. When someone remarked to him, "Sir, you have just as many children as Jacob," he replied, "Yes, and I have Jacob's God to provide for them."

---------- ❦ ----------

□ □ □

Do You Have Enough to Do?

Scripture Reading: 2 Thessalonians 3:6-15

Key Verse: 2 Thessalonians 3:10
Even when we were with you, we used to give you this order: if anyone will not work, neither let him eat.

———— 🍎 ————

The Camel's hump is an ugly hump
    Which well you may see at the Zoo;
But uglier yet is the hump we get
    From having too little to do.

Kiddies and grown-ups too-oo-oo,
If we haven't enough to do-oo-oo,
    We get the hump—
    Cameelious hump—
The hump that is black and blue!

We climb out of bed with a frowzy head
    And a snarly-yarly voice.
We shiver and scowl and we grunt and we growl
    At our bath and our boots and our toys;

And there ought to be a corner for me
(And I know there is one for you)
    When we get the hump—
    Cameelious hump—
The hump that is black and blue!

The cure for this ill is not to sit still,
Or frowst with a book by the fire;
But to take a large hoe and a shovel also,
And dig till you gently perspire;

And then you will find that the sun and the wind,
And the Djinn of the Garden too,
Have lifted the hump—
The horrible hump—
The hump that is black and blue!

I get it as well as you-oo-oo—
If I haven't enough to do-oo-oo!
We all get hump—
Cameelious hump—
Kiddies and grown-ups too![8]

Life can be boring or exciting, depending on which you choose. Take time to look at your life's purpose and you can soon figure out how life is going. I've found that women who take the time to write out their "mission goals" and look to the future seem to have an excitement for life, but those who have never thought out what life is all about and only live for the moment seem to be bored with life.

My suggestion for living a happy life and not to grow a hump is to live life with a purpose. Give yourself away to a cause. Andrew Murray said it so well: "I have learned to place myself before God every day as a vessel to be filled with His Holy Spirit. He has given me the blessed assurance that He, as the everlasting God, has guaranteed His own work in me."

Some of us are called to labor by plowing or planting or harvesting. But each of us has a special calling to be used as a worker for God.

Often women ask me, "Do you get tired of what you're doing?" To be honest with them I say, "Yes, I do get tired of airports, airplanes, different time zones, the demands of people, and long lines waiting for an autograph, but seldom do I get tired of the ministry of my work." I get so excited when I can give a stressed mother peace, assurance, self-confidence, and a renewed walk with our Lord.

May you grasp the excitement of living life with a purpose. Do what you like to do before the Lord and do it with all the energy and creativity you have, regardless of the social ranking or prestige of the calling.

David the psalmist wrote in Psalm 37:4,5, "Delight yourself in the Lord, and He will give you the desires of your heart. Commit your way to the Lord; trust also in Him, and he will do it."

Two words stand out to me in this passage: *Delight* and *commit*. These are both action words that require us to do thinking and planning. Remember to live life with a purpose, not by accident. You can take control of your own life, so don't wait for others to determine your fate in life. With God's help you can find complete enjoyment and can arise each morning with a song in your heart and a bounce in your walk. In fact, people will stand back and ask you, "What's come over you? There's something different about you!"

> *Father God, You know how exciting life is for me. I have so many wonderful things to accomplish. I truly do have a delight for You and I want to continue committing my ways to You. I can't comprehend people who think life is boring. Give me the strength and health to encourage women to be all that You have for them. Let them want to be women after God's design. Amen.*

Taking Action

❧ In your journal write a mission statement expressing what you want out of life. Find a verse of Scripture that supports this statement.

❧ Write down three desires that you have.

❧ What are you going to do to make these desires

a reality?

🦃 Commit all of these to the Lord.

🦃 Pray for the desires of your heart.

Reading On

Psalm 8:3	Romans 11:6
Psalm 111:3	James 1:25

The law of nature is that a certain quantity of work is necessary to produce a certain quantity of good of any kind whatever. If you want knowledge, you must toil for it; if food, you must toil for it; and if pleasure, you must toil for it."

—*Ruskin*

To Pray Is to Work, To Work Is to Pray

Scripture Reading: Proverbs 31:10-31

Key Verse: Proverbs 31:31
> Give her the product of her hands, and let her works praise her in the gates.

———— ❧ ————

For some reason we think that women going to work started during World War II, when women had to fill the gap while the men were away defending our country. But today's Scripture reading goes back to about 800 years B.C. Long before we even thought of women being in the labor force, this capable woman was an energetic, hard worker who labored far into the night.

We see her virtues by looking at the following verses in Proverbs 31:

- 13: She looks for wool and flax. She works with her hands in delight.

- 14: She is like a merchant ship. She brings her food from afar.

- 15: She rises before sunup. She feeds her household. She gives to her maidens.

- 16: She considers real estate. She has her own money. She plants vineyards.

- 17: She works out and is in good physical shape.

- 18: She analyzes her profits. She plans ahead. She works into the night

- 19,20: She gives to those in need.

- 21: She sews her household's garments.

- 24: She sews to sell for a profit.

- 25-27: She radiates good business practices.

- 28,29: She attracts compliments from her family.

- 31: She exudes excellence from her work and is praised in her neighborhood.

This woman knew all about work even though she didn't have an MBA from Harvard or Stanford. She was a woman who feared (respected) God, and because of her noble efforts in the workplace she was praised.

In today's work climate we find that Monday is the most difficult day of the week—the most absenteeism, the most accidents, the most illnesses. Many of today's workers focus on Fridays—the getaway days. In fact, a popular restaurant is named TGI Friday (Thank God It's Friday). If you go into this restaurant to eat, you sense a party atmosphere. It's a place to forget all your cares. Let's have a party!

This attitude has a lot to say about modern man's approach to work. It's a far cry from the day when the adage was "To pray is to work, to work is to pray." In those days work was a reflection of worship to God. When we worked we worked to the Lord, not the pleasing of man. That's when the artisan was a creator of excellence in art, music, literature, and the professions. Martin Luther once said that a man can milk cows to the glory of God. It is our own attitude toward work that reflects the joy of the Lord.

Oh, if we could recapture this concept of work! We would take the drudgeries of everyday life and give them to God. If we took the routines surrounding our work and began to pray about them, I believe our whole attitude would change for ourselves and those in our family. No longer would we wait for the whistle to blow on Friday so we could let the real life begin. For us every day would be a Friday.

In Genesis we read that in the beginning God *created*. He believed in the honor of work. It was a godly activity. It was not cursed, as it is today. God worked for six days and then rested. How is your rest period? Do you get any?

Jesus, a carpenter, was a worker making goods out of wood. The Scriptures teach that if we aren't willing to work we shouldn't expect to eat.

How do we learn that to pray is to work, and to work is to pray?

- Each morning when we wake up we thank God for a new day and all that is in it.

- We offer to God in worship all of our energies, creativity, time, and skills.

- We recognize that work done in an attitude of prayer brings excellence, which in turn bears testimony to God.

- We realize that we are obedient to God when we provide for our family and their needs.

- We model to our children that work is good, so that they see us give worship to God for the work He has given us.

> *Father God, at times when I face the drudgeries of all that I have to do, when I wipe the sweat from my brow and my back aches from the weight of lifting, I forget that how I do my job is a reflection upon my worship to You. I truly want to wake up each morning with a song in my heart and an eagerness to start a new day. In the evening before I fall asleep*

I want to praise You for another day's work. Let me be in continuous prayer while at work. Let me work for You and forget about the praises of man. Amen.

Taking Action

❦ Assign prayer to your work.

❦ Thank God for the skills He has given you to perform worship to Him.

❦ Does your work reflect excellence? If not, what can you do to change this? Note it in your journal.

❦ Are you remembering to rest one day a week?

Reading On

Ecclesiastes 2:11   Titus 3:8
Matthew 5:16   Psalm 8:3

———————— ❦ ————————

It is our best work that He wants, not the dregs of our exhaustion. I think He must prefer quality to quantity.

—*George MacDonald*

———————— ❦ ————————

Home Rules

Scripture Reading: Deuteronomy 6:1-9

Key Verse: Deuteronomy 6:7a
You shall teach them diligently to your sons.

———— ❦ ————

Home is the one place in all this world where hearts are sure of each other. It is the place of confidence. It is the place where we tear off that mask of guarded and suspicious coldness which the world forces us to wear in self-defense, and where we pour out the unreserved communications of full and confiding hearts. It is the spot where expressions of tenderness gush out without any sensation of awkwardness and without any dread of ridicule.[9]

In our Scripture passage today God outlines the responsibility that we have as parents to teach our children at home and in other venues that are appropriate. So important were the commands of the Lord that Moses directed us to do everything possible to remember these commands and to incorporate them into everyday life.

The spiritual education of the children was the responsibility of the parent. The teaching would take place daily through the example of the parents as well as through the repetition of the law. The importance of this command is seen by the extent to which parents were to go in order to teach their children. This was more than simply teaching the facts of the law; it was to be the demonstration of a lifestyle woven into the tapestry (see verses 8,9) of everyday life. Creativity is essential in teaching the precepts of God while we are involved in mundane chores of the household.

CHARACTER AND CONDUCT

> Conduct is what we do; character is what we are. Conduct is the outward life; character is the life unseen, hidden within, yet evidenced by that which is seen. Conduct is external, seen from without; character is internal—operating within. . . . Character is the state of the heart, conduct is its outward expression. Character is the root of the tree, conduct, the fruit it bears.
>
> —*E.M. Bounds*

Today that becomes our biggest task—to teach Christian values and responsibilities in a creative fashion. How can we compete with TV sound bites, Disney mindset, computers, and laser printers? We live in an age of fast-paced technology that throws fast, colorful, and short concentration bites of information to all of us, including our children.

It takes creative parenting to teach our young ones biblical principles. Often our children pick up on our walk better than on our talk. They have great discernment in observing how Mom and Dad (and other adults) live out these principles.

In verse 7 we find that teaching and learning doesn't always take place in a formal, rigid classroom setting. We are to talk of these principles when we sit in our house, when we walk by the way, when we lie down, and when we rise.

Twenty-four hours a day we can integrate biblical truths in everyday settings.

Ann Landers printed a set of Home Rules from a lady in California:

> If you sleep on it—
> make it up.
>
> If you wear it—
> hang it up.
>
> If you drop it—
> pick it up.
>
> If you eat out of it—
> put it in the sink.
>
> If you spill it—
> wipe it up.
>
> If you empty it —
> fill it up.
>
> If it rings —
> answer it.
>
> If it howls —
> feed it.
>
> If it cries —
> love it.[10]

If your children understood these nine simple rules when they started kindergarten, the teacher would sing praises to your name, for these form the basic foundation for citizenship. It is amazing how many adults can't demonstrate these simple, basic manifestations of responsibility.

> *Father God, being a godly parent is not easy. Sometimes I just want to go back to the simple life without having to face the awesomeness of raising children. I get so tired and weary of being the one to transmit virtue values to the next generation. Restore in my soul*

the desire to keep on keeping on. There are some days when I think it's impossible to continue with what I feel is an endless task of teaching my children. Please reassure my faith in what I've set out to do—to be obedient to Your commands. Amen.

Taking Action

❦ Take a three-by-five card and print one of the home rules on it. Take it to the dinner table and discuss how you as a family can incorporate the rule into this week's schedule.

❦ Do the same for each of the nine rules. After the ninth week, go back and review how you did.

❦ Bring back for another week those rules that need more work done on them.

Reading On

Deuteronomy 11:18-20   Ephesians 6:4
Proverbs 22:6   2 Timothy 3:15

———————— ❦ ————————

The Bible doesn't say very much about homes; it says a great deal about the things that make them. It speaks about life and love and joy and peace and rest. If we get a house and put these into it, we shall have secured a home.

—*John Henry Jowett*

———————— ❦ ————————

Make Breakfast and Lunch for Jesus

Scripture Reading: Genesis 2:8-25

Key Verse: Genesis 2:18

The Lord God said, "It is not good for the man to be alone; I will make him a helper suitable for him."

Several years ago I was teaching a women's Bible study in our home, and one Friday morning we had a lesson on the creation of women and their role in marriage. When we came upon this passage there was a lot of discussion about the role distinction between men and women and what God intended when He created both.

We eventually got around to discussing how we could be helpers to our husbands, and of course this sparked a lot of controversy, especially when I casually mentioned that I got up early in the morning and prepared Bob's breakfast and his lunch for work. One of the young women was having difficulty accepting this concept and said, "I could never do that for my husband!" In a kind fashion I asked her why, and her reply was that he wouldn't appreciate it, and besides, she liked to sleep later in the morning.

In a split instant a brilliant thought came to my mind. I looked this lady in the eye and asked, "Jane, would you be willing to get up and make Jesus breakfast and lunch?"

Without a moment's hesitation she replied, "Yes." So I instructed her, "Then don't make breakfast and lunch for Bill, but make them for Jesus." "I can do that without any problems," responded Jane.

To this day both Jane and Bill credit this idea as the most instrumental turning point in restoring their love for each other, even though for some years Bill wasn't aware that Jane was making breakfast and lunch for Jesus. When Jane saw Bill's response toward this love gift, she soon started making breakfast not just for Jesus but for her husband as well.

Here was a woman who was willing to try something new in life: She trusted God to enable her to be a helper to her husband.

LORD OF ALL POTS AND PANS

Lord of all pots and pans and things,
Since I've no time to be
A saint by doing lovely things
Or watching late with Thee,
Or dreaming in the dawnlight
Or storming heaven's gates,
Make me a saint by getting meals
And washing up the plates.

Thou who didst love to give men food
In room or by the sea,
Accept this service that I do—
I do it unto Thee.

—*Author Unknown*

God in His marvelous plan knew what He was doing when He created marriage. Marriage was perfect in its establishment: one man and one woman in a lifetime commitment.

From the very beginning (Genesis 2:18) God never intended for man to be alone. Woman was taken out of man, then presented to him in order to complete him (Genesis 2:22,23). Ladies, do you look upon your purpose in life as a completion for your husband? If you do, then you and your husband will receive blessings that come from this mindset. As I look around I see many women who don't realize that their husbands aren't functioning properly because their wives aren't willing to be their helper.

In Genesis 2:24 we see that we need to lay aside all our old loyalties and lifestyles of separate goals and plans and instead be joined together as one. This bond produces a much stronger result than either individual had produced separately (Ecclesiastes 4:9-12).

No human relationship is to be stronger than the bond between husband and wife. Marriage is a vow made to God not only to love but also to be faithful and to endure in this life-long togetherness.

Even in the church we have lost the miracle meaning of marriages. We have become conformed to the world (Romans 12:2) and aren't willing to be transformed by the renewing of our minds.

The miracles of marriage are:

- We are joined together socially.

- We become one flesh biologically.

- We reflect the relationship between God and His bride (the church) spiritually.

Oneness is the strength of any marriage. Women, you and I play a tremendous part in marriage when we learn and exhibit the helper role that God has intended us to have. Can you honestly state that your husband is complete because you are his wife? If not, you might want to make Jesus breakfast and lunch. Take a risk and be all that God wants you to be!

Father God, I thank You for letting me learn

many years ago about my role as a helper for my husband. By Your grace I don't have to feel inferior or that I'm going to be taken advantage of. Over the years I know that Your plan works—I have experienced it in my own life and have borne witness to it in the lives of many other women. I know that for some women this is all a new idea to them, but may they be willing to serve Jesus by making His breakfast and lunch. Amen.

Taking Action

- ❦ In your journal list five things you do that make you feel like you are completing your husband.

- ❦ List three areas that you are having difficulty with. What can you do to help yourself in these areas?

- ❦ Ask a friend to support you in prayer concerning what needs to be done.

- ❦ Have her check back with you at least every two weeks to hold you accountable in these areas.

- ❦ Pray specifically that God will help you strengthen these areas.

Reading On

I Corinthians 13:4-8   Hebrews 12:5-11
Proverbs 31   Ephesians 5:23-27

God is our refuge and strength,
a very present help in trouble.

—*Psalm 46:1*

371

Complement, Not Compete

Scripture Reading: Ecclesiastes 4:1-12

Key Verse: Ecclesiastes 4:9,10

> *Two are better than one because they have a good return for their labor. For if either of them falls, the one will lift up his companion. But woe to the one who falls when there is not another to lift him up.*

A couple of years ago my Bob and I were speaking at the Southern California Women's Retreat. I was introducing my new book, *The Spirit of Loveliness*, and he was speaking to the 700 ladies on his new offering, *Your Husband, Your Friend*.

As Bob was finishing up his presentation he had a few minutes before closing, so he opened the floor for questions. The first question was from a middle-aged woman who asked: "Bob, aren't you threatened as a man when your wife has written so many books and is asked to speak all over the country?" With a slight pause Bob replied, "No, because Emilie and I aren't in competition, but we complement each other." Many of the women applauded the response.

When word got back to me about Bob's answer, tears filled my eyes, because I realized the growth that had taken place in my Bob's life.

For 28 years of our married life I had always been "Bob's

wife" because he was the breadwinner. He brought home the checks with his name on them. But when Bob decided to help me in our growing ministry, he all of a sudden became "Emilie's husband," since checks were made out in my name and not his.

For a man this is a most difficult situation, since a man's work is his worth. I'm sure that the all-time low for Bob came when a lady approached him at one of our seminars and wanted to know if he was Mr. Emilie Barnes!

No matter how we may try to do otherwise, we live in a competitive world that rates people by performance. So for my Bob to state that we weren't in competition with each other but that we complemented each other showed remarkable growth in his life.

I can truly say that he lives out that principle in our lives. I continually get told what a valuable asset he is to me and our ministry. I could not do what I'm doing without his input, creativity, energy, love, and support. Where I am weak, he is strong. He encourages me to use the strengths that God has given me and he fills in the gap where he is gifted.

> Your husband will never truly
> be yours until you have first
> given him back to God. He is
> yours only when you are willing
> to let him go wherever God
> calls him and do what God
> wants him to do.
>
> —*Lila Trotman*

The longer I live the more I realize that two are better than one. Our passage for today reinforces this concept, and I can tell you how true it becomes in real life—not only as we get older, but through all the trials and testings of our youth.

As we travel in ministry and in pleasure, we observe other couples who have decided to complement, not compete. What a soothing effect this has in all our relationships! The Scriptures are full of verses that emphasize unity and oneness.

If I had one recommendation for couples who want strong marriages, I would stress this concept of oneness. Women, I challenge you to examine your relationship with your mate (if you are married) and see whether you have a marriage built on oneness or are just going your separate way. If your marriage is one of separation, I encourage you to begin anew and set out to become one. If you reflect oneness, I thank the Lord for that. Continue to model before others what God has given you as a couple. The world is hungry to see proper modeling of His Word.

Suzanne Wesley once stated that there are two things you do with the gospel:

- You believe it.
- You live it.

How do we grow into oneness? We begin to:

- Trust our mate.
- Understand our mate.
- Verbally praise our mate.
- Be mutually accountable to each other.
- Love each other just as Christ loved us.
- Give and accept forgiveness when necessary.

Father God, how I am encouraged to realize that my husband truly wants us to be one. I'm thankful that You have given me such a man. However, I realize that this isn't the case in all homes. May You touch the woman who wants this to be true and give her clear direction to work toward that goal. May she realize the blessings of such unity. Amen.

Taking Action

- In your journal write down your desire to have a marriage that stresses oneness. What are you going to do to make it happen?
- Pray for your mate that he will grasp the same desire.
- Share with your mate how God has challenged you in this direction.
- Ask your husband to support and encourage you in this decision.

Reading On

Genesis 2:23-25	1 Corinthians 12:12,13
Philippians 2:1-4	1 Corinthians 12:26,27

A selfish person works in competition with others. He misses the rewards of cooperation.

❑ ❑ ❑

What Would Jesus Do?

Scripture Reading: 2 Timothy 3:10-17

Key Verse: 2 Timothy 3:15
> From childhood you have known the sacred writings
> which are able to give you the wisdom that leads to
> salvation through faith which is in Christ Jesus.

———— ❧ ————

One evening while sitting around the meal table with our grandchildren, we had a discussion of what to do when Mom and Dad were not around to tell them right from wrong. We love those kinds of discussions because then we can teach moral values without preaching to the grandchildren.

For some reason the thought came to my mind "WWJD?" They all looked funny at me and asked, "What's WWJD?" Without a moment of hesitation I replied, "What would Jesus do?" Christine, our oldest grandchild, replied, "That's good, Grammy, I like that." She went on to express how she often has to decide when she is with friends, "Should I do that or should I not?" Then she added, "WWJD will help me make wise choices." Even as adults, we could ask ourselves when these situations come up, "WWJD?"

Now when something comes up when the grandchildren ask a "What should I do?" question, we just say, "WWJD." Enough has been said. They know just what we mean.

Today's verses teach that from childhood you have known God's Word, which is able to give you wisdom. Who is responsible for this dissemination—the schools, the government, the church? No, the primary responsibility falls upon us as *parents* to teach our children the Scriptures. In Deuteronomy 6:6-9 Moses tells us as parents to:

- teach Scripture diligently to our children;

- talk to our children about Scripture when we sit in our home, when we walk by the way, when we lie down, and when we rise up;

- bind Scripture as a sign on our hands and as frontals on our foreheads (see Exodus 13:9);

- write Scripture on the doorposts of our house and on our gates.

This sounds like serious stuff to me. Children can't achieve good moral values while watching and reading some of the material offered in our society today.

If our children are to stand a chance to survive and be able to escape all the evils around them, they must have spiritual ammunition to ward off the enemy. We are no longer playing for fun. Life must be lived with a purpose, and we as parents are to guide our children into wise choices through proper instruction in the home. This can't be left to the church, the Sunday school teacher, the Awana leader, or the Boy Scout/Girl Scout leaders. Nowhere in Scripture are those mentioned. Yes, they can help, but we as parents are given the commands to teach our children at an early age.

At the end of his life Joshua made a challenging statement: "You may serve whatever god you want, but as for me and my house, we will serve the Lord." Yes, it begins with Dad, then Mom, and then the children. We must choose which god we will serve. We have to stand up and be counted if we are going to live life with a purpose. The road is narrow, and it is the road less traveled.

If we are going to tell our children "WWJD?" they need to know Jesus well enough to have a storehouse of information about who He was and is today.

Father God, today You have made me realize what an awesome job it is to be a parent. As I see my children and grandchildren struggle to keep their heads above water, I want them to have instant maturity. May You come alongside them and put a protective fence around them. Life is such a struggle even when we know Your Word. I can't imagine what it is like without having Your Scripture in my mind. Thank You for being there when I need You. Amen.

Taking Action

- Go to your pastor or a trusted friend for a recommendation on good study materials.
- Set aside time daily to meet with your children to read and discuss God's Word. You might start with the book of John.
- Place a chalkboard somewhere in your home and use it to write down those specific verses that have been meaningful to you and your family. Change the verses at least once a week.
- Each week use three-by-five cards to jot down certain verses of the Bible for you and your children to memorize. Hold each other accountable. Work on these daily.

Reading On

Ephesians 6:4	Joshua 24:15
Deuteronomy 6:6-9	Exodus 20:1-17

The study of God's Word, for the purpose of discovering God's will, is the secret discipline which has formed the greatest characters.

—James W. Alexander

We Have to Burn Our Ships

Scripture Reading: Matthew 19:3-9

Key Verse: Matthew 19:6b
What therefore God has joined together, let no man separate.

———— ❦ ————

Hernando Cortés had a plan.

He wanted to lead an expedition into Mexico to capture its vast treasures. When he told the Spanish governor his strategy, the governor got so excited that he gave him eleven ships and seven hundred men. Little did the governor know that Cortés had failed to tell him the entire plan.

After months of travel, the eleven ships landed in Veracruz in the spring of 1519. As soon as the men unloaded the ships, Cortés instituted the rest of his plan: He burned the ships.

That's what you call commitment. That's what you call no turning back. That's what you call burning your bridges. Cortés didn't have any bridges, so he burned the ships.

By burning the ships, Cortés eliminated the options. He didn't know what he would encounter on his expeditions to the interior. He didn't know the strength of the people he would be fighting. But he did know this: There were now no escape routes for his men. If the fighting got too fierce or the expedition got too exhausting, there would be no talk of going back to Veracruz and sailing home. In one fell swoop he had not only eliminated their options but had created an intensely powerful motivation to succeed. Like it or not, they were now committed.[11]

That's the kind of fervor we must have in our own marriages—both husband and wife. There are no options to be considered. When our children see that Mom and Dad love each other there is a settling effect over the family.

Burning the ships expresses that there is no turning back, no matter what. We are committed to our marriage. I realize that in today's culture there are situations that make this very difficult. Sometimes we may not have a vote, but in most cases we are able to stand and defend our marriage.

Commitment means that no matter what comes into the future we are going to stick it out. We are obligated to follow through on the words of our marriage vows.

The nineties is the "Don't I have a right to feel good decade?" Everyone wants to feel good. If it doesn't feel good, don't do it. Change until it feels good again. Go for awhile with whatever you're doing. When that stops feeling good, change until it feels good again.

There are times in a marriage when the bells and whistles stop making joyful noises. But just because we don't *feel* like we're married doesn't mean we *aren't* married. In today's key verse Jesus commands that if we have been joined together by God, let no one separate us. These are strong words. In essence Jesus is saying, "Burn the ships."

We live in a day when commitment means little. Every day we see a lack of it in politics, sports, business, and marriage. Everyone wants to renegotiate their contracts. In the old days a shake of the hand between two people was as good as a signed contract. But today even signed contracts mean very little. Commitment is a cheap word. We only honor commitment when it is convenient.

The sixties should have taught us that when we are doing our own thing we are being selfish. Selfishness is the number one crime that ultimately destroys a relationship.

When Bob and I were married, our vows to each other stated that we were to be committed in sickness and in health, for richer or for poorer, for better or for worse, until death would part us. These are strong words, but they mean very little if taken lightly. For the words to be meaningful, the ships must be burned in the harbor.

How can you love your mate? By daily *choosing* to love him. Every day, not just when it's convenient. Love is a choice, not a feeling. We have been misled by the "feeling" advocates. We need to get back to the Scriptures and see what God says about commitment and marriage.

We often hear a person stating, "But I just don't have chemistry for him anymore." Our loving pastor states that the only "C" of marriage mentioned in the Bible is *commitment*.

Are you willing to burn your ships in the harbor?

> *Father God, as I read today's words of instruction from Your Word, I'm challenged to examine my own life to see if I've held out on burning the last few ships I've hidden for escape. I need Your help to hold me up when I feel so weak. I need more help in trusting my mate in all of our affairs. Give me today enough faith to destroy those few remaining ships. Today I promise to burn all the ships that remain. Amen.*

Taking Action

❦ Burn any remaining ships that you have in the harbor.

❦ In your journal write the names of these ships you have burned.

- Share with your mate how much you love him and how much you appreciate all he does to make the family united.

- Send your husband a love note at his work. Tell him you can't wait until he gets home this evening.

- If you can do so comfortably, share with him how you've made a new commitment to the success of your marriage.

Reading On

Genesis 1:27   Deuteronomy 24:5

Genesis 2:23,24   Proverbs 31:23

A happy marriage is the union
of two good forgivers.

— *Robert Quillen*

Be a Living Presence

Scripture Reading: Psalm 127:1-5

Key Verse: Psalm 127:3
*Behold, children are a gift of the Lord; the fruit of womb
is a reward.*

———— 🌱 ————

The young mother asked her guide about the path of life.

"Is the way long?" she inquired.

And her guide replied: "Yes. And the way is hard. And you will be old before you reach the end of it. But the end will be better than the beginning."

But the young mother was happy, and she would not believe that anything could be better than these years. So she played with her children, and gathered flowers for them along the way, and basked with them in the clear streams; and the sun shone on them and life was good, and the young mother said, "Nothing will ever be lovelier than this."

Then night came, and storm, and the path was dark, and the children shook with fear and cold, and the mother drew them close and covered them with her mantle, and the children said, "Oh, Mother, we are not afraid, for you are near, and no harm can come." And the mother observed, "This is better than the brightness of day, for I have taught my children courage."

And the morning came, and there was a hill ahead, and the children climbed and grew weary, and the mother was weary too, but she said to the children, "A little patience and we are there." So the children climbed, and when they reached the top they said, "We could not have done it without you, Mother." And the mother, when she lay down that night, looked at the stars and said, "This is a better day than the last, for my children have learned fortitude in the face of hardness. Yesterday I gave them courage, and today I have given them strength."

And the next day came strange clouds which darkened the earth—clouds of war and hate and evil, and the children groped and stumbled, and the mother said, "Look up. Lift your eyes to the Light." And the children looked and saw above the clouds an Everlasting Glory, and it guided them and brought them beyond the darkness. And that night the mother said, "This is the best day of all, for I have shown my children God."

And the days went on, and the weeks and the months and the years, and the mother grew old, and she was little and bent. But her children were tall and strong, and walked with courage. And when the way was hard, they helped their mother, and when the way was rough, they lifted her, for she was as light as a feather; and at last they came to a hill, and beyond the hill they could see a shining road and golden gates flung wide.

And the mother said: "I have reached the end of my journey. And now I know that the end is better than the beginning, for my children can walk alone, and their children after them."

And the children said, "You will always walk with us, Mother, even when you have gone through the gates."

And they stood and watched her as she went on alone, and the gates closed after her. And they said: "We cannot see her, but she is with us still. A mother like ours is more than a memory. She is a living presence."[12]

In our society today the most dangerous place for a child to be is in her mother's womb. Who would ever have thought that to be true? Too many women and parents have never known or have forgotten the promise of the Lord that children are a gift: They are the fruit of the womb.

Does this promise just happen, or are there things that we do to earn this promise? No, it doesn't just happen. For a mother to become a "living presence" she must spend time, time, and more time with her children. "Is the way long?" Yes, it is. In fact at times it seems forever.

Young mothers write letters or talk to me completely frustrated with life because the children take so much time from their day. I tell them they won't always be in that phase of their lives. Enjoy the children while they're young, because as they get older both parents and children will have new sets of difficulties.

Each phase of life has challenges that are new to us. I can vividly remember when Bob and I had five children under the age of five and I was only 21 years old. I thought I would never make it. But was it worth it? Yes, it was. I can truly say that children are a gift from God and that they are a fruit from the mother's womb.

I have found that you develop a living presence with your children if you—

- raise them at an early age to know Christ personally;

- show interest in their friends and activities;

- show them that you really love your spouse (if you are married);

- exercise fairness with them in conversation and discipline;

- let them grow up without overprotection; let them make mistakes, make decisions, and get bumps and scrapes;

- use encouraging words to lift them up;

- let them have and express different opinions from your own;

- be good role models so they will know their gender roles (boys are to become men and girls are to become women);

- be willing to clearly confess and admit your wrong doings and ask for forgiveness;

- establish firm and clear boundaries.

Proverbs 31:10-31 can help you become a capable woman. This passage is an acrostic poem exalting the honor and dignity of womanhood. In verses 30 and 31 we read, "A woman who fears the Lord . . . shall be praised. Give her the product of her hands, and let her works praise her in the gates."

Is the way long? Yes, and the way is hard. And you will be old before you reach the end of it. But the end will be better than the beginning.

Get on board, for the trip will be a blessing for you and for all those fortunate enough to be in your family!

> *Father God, thank You again for the assurance that Your plan works. As I talk to friends, see the news on the TV, and read the newspaper, I get so discouraged about having children. I truly want my children to be a gift from You and the fruit of the womb for me. In turn I also want to be a blessing in their lives. Give me the strength today to set my foot on the path of life. Amen.*

Taking Action

- Recommit your life to Christ and rededicate yourself to become a living presence to your children.

- Give each of your children a hug today and tell them how much you love them.

Be a Living Presence

❧ Tell your spouse (if you have one) of your new challenges and commitment in raising your children.

Reading On

Job 42:12,13	1 Samuel 1:8
Proverbs 22:6	Acts 2:38,39

As a little girl was eating her dinner, the golden rays of the sun fell upon her spoon. She put the spoon to her mouth, exclaiming, "O mother! I have just swallowed a whole spoonful of sunshine!"

— *B.M. Adams*

What Shall I Do with Jesus?

Scripture Reading: Matthew 27:11-26

Key Verse: Matthew 27:22

Pilate said to them, "Then what shall I do with Jesus who is called Christ?"

———— ❧ ————

When I was a young girl, I anxiously waited each week for one of my favorite television shows, "The $64,000 Question." A contestant would answer all kinds of questions in a multitude of categories. If he or she was successful over a period of weeks, he could arrive to the plateau of answering a series of questions which if answered correctly would award them $64,000 dollars.

I couldn't imagine that much money or that anyone could be smart enough to answer those very difficult questions. To my disappointment, a scandal broke which charged the producer of the show with leaking answers to the contestants so they could continue up the scale and build excitement for their viewers. I was really let down because I truly believed that someone was smart enough to answer all the questions of life with surety.

It wasn't until I was dating my Bob that I would be confronted by him with the most basic, fundamental, and important question in my life. After coming home one evening from a wonderful date, we were sitting on the sofa of my living room apartment when he asked me the same question that Pilate asked the crowd in today's Scripture reading: "What shall I do with Jesus who is called Christ?" I had never in my young life been asked that question. I had been raised in a Jewish family and had recently graduated from Hebrew school; Jesus wasn't a personality name to be discussed in my circle of family and friends.

I asked Bob, "What do you mean? Why do I need to answer that question? I'm a good Jewish girl, I'm not a sinner, and I have no need for Him. I believe in God."

I knew that Bob was a Christian and that he believed differently than I did, but what did Jesus have to do with it? In the quietness of that room Bob began to share with me who this Jesus was. He gave me the full gospel of the birth, the life, and the resurrection of this man named Jesus. He very lovingly shared the plan of salvation with me and told me that he would pray for me regarding the answer to the big question he had asked me. In the weeks and months that followed Bob asked my mother if he could take me to church with him. My sweet and darling mother said yes. I couldn't believe she would give me permission to go to a Christian church.

While attending the services I heard teaching from Scripture that really made me ask questions—questions I had never thought about before.

Then one night in the stillness of my bedroom I knew how to answer Bob's question, "What shall I do with Jesus who is called Christ?" At that instant I asked Jesus to come into my life, to forgive me of my sins, to become my Lord and my Messiah.

The rewards that evening were worth far more than the 64,000 dollars offered on my favorite TV show.

Over the years I have realized that this is the greatest question that any person must answer in life. However you answer that question will determine what road your life will take.

How do you answer that question?

Father God, as I look back over the years, I'm
so glad I answered that question with a big yes when

I was 16 years old. That was the foundation for all the other questions that come into my life on a daily basis. You have truly been the stability when life seems so rocky. I daily appreciate what Jesus did on the cross for me. Amen.

Taking Action

- ❦ In your journal list several of your questions. Realize that you will not always know the immediate answer to these questions.
- ❦ Turn these questions over to God in prayer and give them to Him.
- ❦ Thank God for all the questions you have answers for.
- ❦ If you do not have Jesus as your Lord, ask Him into your heart today. Pray a simple prayer asking forgiveness of sins and tell Him that you want to change direction in your life. Share this news with a friend.

Reading On

John 1:49	John 3:16
John 3:3	John 3:36

---❦---

I'm going to heaven and I believe I'm going by the blood of Christ. That's not popular preaching, but I'll tell you it's all the way through the Bible and I may be the last fellow on earth who preaches it, but I'm going to preach it because it's the only way we're going to get there.

—*Billy Graham*

---❦---

There Was Only One

Scripture Reading: Luke 17:11-19

Key Verse: Luke 17:15

One of them, when he saw that he had been healed, turned back, glorifying God with a loud voice.

———— 🍂 ————

As a wife and mother who is dedicated to her family and really does things because of her love for them, there are times when I would like them to take a moment and loudly say, "Mmm, that was really a good dinner! Those peas are my favorite!" Or "Mom, thanks for washing my clothes so I always have something clean to wear to school." Have you ever longed for that token of thanks? All of us, regardless of what we do (bus driver, waitress, gardener, teacher), would like to hear "Thank you!"

I'm sure Jesus was no exception to our own human needs, since He became a man for us. He was hoping that of the ten men He had healed, more than one would come back and say, "Thank You, Jesus!" But only one came back, glorifying God with a loud voice. He was truly appreciative and knew that a miracle had been performed on him. This man also realized that an almighty God had performed this miracle, and He was going to be glorified.

I would love to have been a quiet mouse in the corner listening to the other nine men's excuses for not coming back to Jesus to say thanks. It might go like this:

- Leper number 1: Left to shop at Nordstrom's. He didn't have time.

- Leper number 2: Was late to play a round of golf. He didn't have time.

- Leper number 3: Had to rush home to mow the lawn. He didn't have time.

- Leper number 4: Had a sick grandmother and had to take her for a doctor's appointment. He didn't have time.

- Leper number 5: Had to get a haircut for church the next day. He didn't have time.

- Leper number 6: Had to take his son to a soccer game. He didn't have time.

- Leper number 7: Had to go back to the office to do some paperwork. He didn't have time.

- Leper number 8: Had to pick up a few groceries at the market. He didn't have time.

- Leper number 9: Was too embarrassed because the majority of the men weren't going back. He didn't have time.

But thank God for Leper number 10. He had time to go back and say, "Thank You, Jesus." Notice in verse 19 that Jesus said, "Rise and go your way; your faith has made you well." He was healed both physically and spiritually.

One of God's chief complaints against mankind is that they do not glorify Him as God, nor do they take the time to say "Thank You."

One of the ways we can give thanks to God for all His abundance is to have grace or a blessing at the dinner table. At an early age our children were aware that Mom and Dad took time to bless our food. As they got older they were given an opportunity to thank God in their own unique way. Our fourth grandchild, Bradley Joe, insists that we end our prayer with a catchy tone and words that say, "Amen, Amen, Amen, Amen, Amen."

A quiet time for individual or group devotions helps to instill in our family an awareness of God's blessings on our family. Somehow find your own unique way to show God that you and your family glorify Him and say thanks with a heartfelt enthusiasm.

> *Father God, I want to respond as Leper number 10 did and tell You how much I thank You for all You have done for me. I am so blessed to be one of Your children. May I never stop thanking You. You are my number one priority, and I want my life to reflect that in my daily living. Amen.*

Taking Action

- ❦ Right now take time to thank God for His forgiveness of your sins.
- ❦ Write down the names of five friends to whom you've recently said thank you for something they did for you.
- ❦ Take time to call or write three people who need to hear your thanks toward them.

Reading On

Matthew 11:25	2 Corinthians 9:15
Matthew 26:27,28	Philippians 4:6

Let us . . . give thanks to God for His graciousness and generosity to us—pledge to Him our everlasting devotion—beseech His divine guidance and the wisdom and strength to recognize and follow that guidance.

—*Lyndon B. Johnson,*
Thanksgiving Proclamation, 1964

□ □ □

Be a Friend

Scripture Reading: Proverbs 18:20-24

Key Verse: Proverbs 18:24b
There is a friend who sticks closer than a brother.

A mouse one day happened to run across the paws of a sleeping lion and wakened him. The lion, angry at being disturbed, grabbed the mouse and was about to swallow him, when the mouse cried out, "Please, kind sir, I didn't mean it; if you will let me go, I shall always be grateful, and perhaps I can help you someday."

The idea that such a little thing as a mouse could help him so amused the lion that he let the mouse go. A week later the mouse heard a lion roaring loudly. He went closer to see what the trouble was and found his lion caught in a hunter's net. Remembering his promise, the mouse began to gnaw the ropes of the net and kept it up until the lion could get free. The lion then acknowledged that little friends might prove great friends.

—Aesop

Friends and friendships are unique social happenings. Often I wonder why some people are attracted to others. Is it because of common interest, past experiences, physical attraction, having children that are friends of a potential friend, or going to the same church? What is it that bonds people together? As I consider the many friends I have, I sense it's a little of all of the above. They come from various backgrounds, religions, economic levels, and educational attainment. There does, however, seem to be one common strand that runs through most of these friendships: We have a kindred spirit in the Lord.

The writer of today's Proverb gives a warning in the first part of verse 24: "A man of many friends comes to ruin." When I first read that I was confused. I thought to myself, "I thought we were to have a lot of friends, so why this warning?" But as I thought about this, a thought came to me. He was stressing that too many friends chosen indiscriminately will bring trouble, but a genuine friend sticks with you through thick and thin. When we use this criterion for a friend, we begin to thin the ranks of who are truly our friends.

I know without a doubt that several of my friends would be with me no matter what the circumstances, what day of the week, and what time of the day or night I needed help. I call these my "2 A.M. friends."

As in our Aesop story today, you never know when you will need a friend. I have found that those who have friends are themselves friendly. They go out of their way to be a friend. In order to have friends, one must be a friend.

The skill of friendship-making is a skill that we need to teach our children. We as parents have only a short window of opportunity to teach the value of positive friendships to them. Each year we have less time for our influence on them. The music, dress, dance, and jewelry selections of the world seem to pull our children from our group. While there is still time, we need to steer our youngsters to choosing the right kind of friends.

Father God, I thank You for the many wonderful friends You have given me over the years. I know how each one has been, and continues to be, a support system for me. They cry with me, laugh with me, pray with me, and hold me in all of life's episodes. *Be with the woman reader today who lacks friends; may You reveal to her ways of developing the kind of friends that will stick closer than a brother or sister. Amen.*

Taking Action

- Evaluate your friends. What does each bring to your relationship with her or him.

- Set out today to be a friend with someone.

- Plan a "tea party" and invite some friends for an afternoon gathering.

- Call or write a friend and tell her how much you enjoy her friendship.

Reading On

John 15:13	John 15:15
Proverbs 17:17	James 2:23

If a man does not make new acquaintances as he advances through life, he will soon find himself left alone. A man should keep his friendship in constant repair.

—*Samuel Johnson*

He Began a Good Work in You

Scripture Reading: Philippians 1:1-11

Key Verse: Philippians 1:6

I am confident of this very thing, that He who began a good work in you will perfect it until the day of Christ Jesus.

At one point in my young married career I found my motivations to be all wrong. I really wanted to be a helpmate for Bob, but I was caught up in the pressure of trying to meet everyone's expectations, including my own. The house always had to be perfect and the children spotless. I was frustrated as a wife and mother because I was doing it all myself—100 percent from me and nothing from God. I was trying to be the perfect wife, perfect in every way. I was trying to be—

- loving
  - kind
    - a friend
      - patient
        - well-organized.

In addition to all this—

- I balanced discipline and flexibility;
  - my home was always neat and well-decorated;
    - my children were always well-behaved;

- I was serious, but I could laugh;
  - I was submissive, but not passive;
- I was full of energy and never tired;
  - my dress was proper and suitable for all occasions;
    - I could work in the garden without getting dirt under my fingernails;
  - I was always healthy;
    - and I had a close walk with God.

Needless to say, I wasn't being very effective at anything I did. I had created a superwoman image that I couldn't pull off.

During this time in my life I came across Philippians 1:6: "I am confident of this very thing, that He who began a good work in you will perfect it until the day of Christ Jesus." I realized that I was the product of God working in me and that I had three alternatives for solving my dilemma: First, I could continue trying to be superwife and supermom by doing everything myself; second, I could follow the old adage "Let go and let God," and let God do everything; or third, I could enter a balanced partnership between myself and God.

I selected the last alternative because according to Philippians 2:12,13 God was at work inside me, helping me to obey Him and to do what He wanted. God had made me a wife and a mom on purpose, and He would help me perform my role. Once I accepted this truth, a burden lifted from my life. I experienced less stress and I had a better understanding of what God wanted from me and what resources He was able to provide me. The drudgeries of homemaking became a real joy when I saw myself as a partner with God in developing godly traits in my children and creating a warm, safe nest for our family.

As I searched the Scriptures to discover my role in this partnership, I came up with three areas.

1. *Faithfulness*. According to 1 Corinthians 4:2, if I am to be a good manager of my home, I must remain faithful. Specifically, God wants me to faithfully thank Him that His plans are being fulfilled in my family. I am often impatient and want things to change right now. But God wants me to stop being concerned about His timetable and to just give thanks that He is doing His job. Over the years I have learned that if I am faithful in giving thanks, God is faithful in His part.

2. *Obedience*. It is my responsibility to act upon God's promises for my life. I can't just sit back and do nothing. Nor can I wait until all situations are perfect and safe. I must do a good job of preparation and then move ahead obediently, even if it means risking failure. Some of my best steps of growth have come after failure.

3. *Growth*. When Bob and I attended Bill Gothard's seminar several years ago he was distributing a lapel badge with the following initials: PBPGINFWMY. I was intrigued by the badge, and soon found out that the letters represented the simple message "Please be patient; God is not finished with me yet."

Yes, the Christian walk is a process of growth. I wanted to arrive instantly at the level of being a perfect wife and mother, but God showed me that my focus was to be on the lifelong process, not on arrival. If we focus on perfection we will always be disappointed because we will never achieve it. But if we focus on the process of growth we can always have hope for improvement tomorrow.

> *Father God, thank You for revealing to me that life is a process. I don't have to be superwoman or some phantom wife that society has depicted for me. You know who I am, what strengths and weaknesses I possess, and that my goal is to serve You. Please reveal to me a balance in living out life. Help those women who are in a similar state of life today. Give them the power to overcome the forces of false expectations. Amen.*

Taking Action

- List in your journal several phantoms that exist in your life.

- Beside each one, state how you are going to overcome this false expectation.

- Give your list and solutions over to the Lord in prayer.

- Be willing to believe that God has a better plan for your life.

Reading On

Philippians 2:12,13   Psalm 90:12
1 Corinthians 4:2   Matthew 6:33

When the darkness of dismay comes, endure until it is over, because out of it will come that following of Jesus which is an unspeakable joy.

— *Oswald Chambers*

Oxen and Donkeys Don't Go Together

Scripture Reading: Deuteronomy 22:1-11

Key Verse: Deuteronomy 22:10
You shall not plow with an ox and a donkey together.

———— 🍎 ————

One evening as Bob and I came home from a date and were sitting on the sofa in my small apartment's living room, he held my face between his hands and looked me straight in the eyes. He told me that he loved me very much and that someday he would like to marry me, but he couldn't ask me to marry him. I thought that was strange, because when two people are in love why can't they be married? Then I asked "Why not?" as tears were coming down my cheeks.

Bob, in a very caring and loving way, quoted 2 Corinthians 6:14, which was deeply engraved on his heart and mind: "Do not be bound together with unbelievers; for what partnership have righteousness and lawlessness, or what fellowship has light with darkness?" (Some translations speak of not being unequally yoked together.) Then he gave me three reasons why he couldn't marry me.

First, a Christian cannot marry a non-Christian because of what unequal marriage will do to the non-Christian. There is no fellowship between light and darkness. The marriage will have a divided loyalty. Bob said, "If I promise to marry you, I am choosing to spend my life with someone who is going in a completely different direction from me. We will move farther and farther apart. I have no right to draw you into a relationship which is doomed to disharmony."

Second, a Christian can't marry an unbeliever because of what it will do to him if he disobeys God on this issue. He will compromise his standards later and disobey God again and again. Too much is at stake if he disobeys God's clear command about marriage.

I asked, "But what if I become a Christian after we're married?" Bob responded that marriage is not a mission field. God never called Christians into an unequal marriage in order to convert the unbelieving partner.

Third, an unequal marriage cannot honor God. He did not create us and redeem us so we could live for ourselves. God placed us here to glorify *Him*. And a Christian home is the only home which can truly glorify God. When a husband and wife both belong to Jesus Christ and live in obedience to Him, they provide a vital witness to the society around them.

I SAID A PRAYER FOR YOU TODAY

I said a prayer for you today,
And know God must have
heard, I felt the answer in my
heart, Although He spoke no
word. . . . I asked that He'd be
near you, At the start of each
new day, To grant you health
and blessings. And friends to
share your way. I asked for happiness for you. In all things great
and small, But it was for His loving care I prayed the most of all.

—*Margaret Gould*

In my innocence I asked, "How do I become a Christian?" And from that moment I began to ask myself if Jesus Christ was the Messiah my Jewish people were awaiting. After several months of seeking answers, I prayed one evening at bedtime, "Dear God: If You have a Son, and if Your Son is Jesus, our Messiah, please reveal Him to me!" I expected a voice to answer me immediately. But God did reveal Himself to me within a few weeks.

One Sunday morning I responded to Pastor Sailhammer's challenge to accept Jesus Christ as my personal Savior. That evening I was baptized. I was thrilled.

Because of Bob's farming background he knew experientially that you did not join two unlike animals together to plow a field. They each pull differently and plow at different paces. It creates chaos when a farmer attempts such a teaming together. The Scriptures also state clearly that believers should not be married to unbelievers, because a similar result will take place. Each party marches to a different drumbeat.

I'm so thankful that Bob had such a strong conviction as a young man. Without that I might never have been challenged to examine the claims of Jesus. I know for sure that we would not have had the same quality of marriage that we have today.

God gives certain warnings in Scripture that save His children a lot of pain down the line. If we don't heed the warnings, then we must be willing to endure the consequences of that neglect.

Scripture provides very practical teachings to those who find themselves the wives of unsaved husbands:

- Do not preach to an unsaved husband (2 Corinthians 4:4).
- Salvation is the work of the Holy Spirit (2 Peter 3:9).
- Cultivate a quiet and gentle spirit (1 Peter 3:4).

- Be submissive in your love (2 Timothy 1:7; 1 Peter 3:1).

- Pray for your husband's salvation (Acts 16:31).

Father God, to this very day I appreciate Bob's willingness to stand firm in his convictions of scriptural truths. Because of his willingness to be faithful in this area of his life, I have benefited in other decisions requiring sound biblical interpretation. Amen.

Taking Action

❦ Has this principle been a blessing in your marriage?

❦ How might you have been blessed if you had heeded this warning?

❦ If your husband is a fellow believer, thank God today for that gift.

❦ If your husband is not a fellow believer, ask God to use you in a mighty way so that your husband can see Jesus through your life.

Reading On

2 Corinthians 4:4	1 Peter 3:4
2 Peter 3:9	1 Peter 3:1

In marriage, *being* the right person is as important as *finding* the right person.

—*Wilbert Donald Gough*

Created Differently

Scripture Reading: Psalm 139:13-18

Key Verse: Psalm 139:13
> *Thou didst form my inward parts; Thou didst weave me in my mother's womb.*

A few months ago our local ABC affiliate was promoting a documentary special that reflected the latest research findings. It was going to give the viewer the latest evidence that men and women are made differently. I looked at Bob and he looked at me and we both laughed. Where had these producers been the last 2000 years?

We don't pride ourselves as intellectual geniuses, but we certainly had a grasp on this topic, even though for years the media has tried to tell us that there aren't any differences between men and women. Unfortunately, much of the Christian community has bought into this lie. A woman can't comprehend why her husband doesn't look at situations the same way she does. Why isn't he sensitive, why doesn't he like to go shopping with me, why does work seem more important to him than family?

Men and women are different in many ways: in physiology and anatomy, in thought patterns, in cultural roles and expectations. For the most part these differences are the result of God's design. Genesis 1:27 reads, "And God created man in His own image; in the image of God He created him; male and female He created them." Psalm 139:13,14 states: "Thou didst form my inward parts; Thou didst weave me in my mother's womb. I will give thanks to Thee, for I am fearfully and wonderfully made."

In these two passages we get a glimpse of God's marvelous plan in human creation. Men and women, as different as they are, are made in God's image. God called this creation good, and David said it was wonderful. A Christian husband and wife can move into their marriage relationship with the confidence that God has put each partner on the earth for a special purpose. Our differences are by God's design.

In Matthew 22:37-39 Jesus outlined simply and directly the greatest two commandments in the Scriptures: "You shall love the Lord your God with all your heart, and with all your soul, and with all your mind" and "You shall love your neighbor as yourself." These commands provide the primary guideline for responding to our differences as husband and wife.

- First, we are to love God. This implies that we accept His creation as good and agree that the male/female differences He designed are good.

- Second, when we love ourselves it means that we accept ourselves for what God has made us: a unique man or woman created for a special and different purpose than our mate.

- Third, we are to love others, particularly the mate God gave us, complete with his or her differences. Loving our mate doesn't mean changing him; that's the Holy Spirit's role. Loving our mate means understanding his differences and accepting him as he is. A loving understanding of each other as husband and wife establishes our house. Seeking to understand each other is a continuous process which leads to less anger and frustration in the relationship. We may still have difficulty with each other's actions, but at least we are growing in the understanding of why our mate does what he does.

Another scriptural guideline for dealing with differences in our marriage is Romans 12:2: "Do not be conformed to this world, but be transformed by the renewing of your mind, that you may prove what the will of God is, that which is good and acceptable and perfect." The world teaches us to stand up for our individuality and not to give in to our mate's differences. But Paul directs us not to conform to that standard, but to be transformed by the renewing of our minds. We are to let God's teaching on the blending of differences permeate our thinking and subsequently our actions.

As Christian men and women, we are (and ever will be) different. But as we take God's attitude toward our differences we will enjoy a house "filled with all precious and pleasant riches" (Proverbs 24:4). These rewards include:

- positive attitudes

- good relationships

- pleasant memories

- mutual respect

- depth of character.

We have a choice: We can live in a war zone fueled by our differences as men and women, or we can live in a house filled with the precious and pleasant riches which come from understanding and accepting our differences.

Perhaps the greatest enemy of understanding and accepting differences is pride. God hates pride, yet we seem to struggle against it in everything we do. We must break down the walls of pride which our differences erect in order to enjoy the rewards which *understanding* promises.

*Father God, thank You so much for making
man and woman so differently. Even though I think
that Bob is weird at times and I'm sure he thinks I'm*

strange, I appreciate his differences when we need to solve a problem. He doesn't get tangled up emotionally like I do and he can stand back and objectively look at what needs to be done. Thank You for creating us so differently. Amen.

Taking Action

❧ List three ways your husband is different from you:
    — emotionally
    — physically
    — culturally
    — spiritually

❧ You might ask him the same question regarding how he is different in each area from you.

❧ Involve your children with the same questions. Let them begin to be aware that God has created us differently—male and female.

Reading On

Genesis 1:27   Proverbs 2:1-5
Matthew 22:37-39   Romans 12:2

There is one glory of the sun,
and another glory of the moon,
and another glory of the stars;
for star differs from star in glory.

— 1 Corinthians 15:41

Five O'Clock or Six O'Clock

Scripture Reading: James 1:19-27

Key Verse: James 1:19,20

Let everyone be quick to hear, slow to speak, and slow to anger; for the anger of man does not achieve the righteousness of God.

———— 🌱 ————

Two of my very favorite relatives were Uncle Saul and Auntie Phyllis. For years, before Uncle Saul passed away, they would tell about a certain event and always disagree on how it happened: They didn't go by boat but flew; they didn't see the movie but the play; they served chicken, not beef; it was snowing, not sunny.

After awhile we said, "Five o'clock, six o'clock, what difference does it make?" Yet they would continue to correct each other on the details of the story. Fortunately they would smile and laugh and not take it personally, but we as outsiders knew they would never agree on anything.

Marriage experts tell us that the number one cause for divorce in America today is a lack of communication. Everyone is born with one mouth and two ears—the basic tools for communication. But possessing the physical tools for communication is not enough. Couples must learn how to use their mouths and ears properly for true communication to take place. Since God created marriage for companionship, completeness, and communication, we can be sure that He will also provide us with the resources for fulfilling His design.

There are three partners in a Christian marriage: husband, wife, and Jesus Christ. In order for healthy communication to exist between husband and wife, there must be proper communication between all three partners. If there is a breakdown in dialogue between any two members, the breakdown will automatically affect the third member of the partnership. Dwight Small says: "Lines open to God invariably open to one another, for a person cannot be genuinely open to God and closed to his mate. . . . God fulfills His design for Christian marriage when lines of communication are first opened to Him."[13] If you and your mate are having difficulty communicating, the first area to check is your individual devotional life with God.

Whenever Bob and I suffer a breakdown in relating to each other, it is usually because one of us is not talking with God on a regular basis. When both of us are communicating with God regularly through prayer and the study of His Word, we enjoy excellent communication with each other as well.

In his book *Communication: Key to Your Marriage*, Norm Wright gives an excellent definition of communication: "Communication is a process (either verbal or nonverbal) of sharing information with another person in such a way that he understands what you are saying. *Talking* and *listening* and *understanding* are all involved in the process of communication."

According to Wright, there are three elements in proper communication: talking, listening, and understanding.

Talking

Most of us have little difficulty talking. We are usually willing to give an opinion or offer advice, even when it hasn't been requested. Often our communication problems are not from talking, but from talking *too much*.

James 3:2-10 states that the human tongue can be employed for good purposes or bad. The tongue is like a rudder which can steer us into stormy or peaceful life situations.

Solomon said, "A word aptly spoken is like apples of gold in settings of silver" (Proverbs 25:11 NIV). Teaching on this passage, Florence Littauer says that our words should be like silver boxes tied with bows. I like that description because I can visualize husbands and wives giving lovely gifts like silver boxes to each other in their conversation. We are not to speak ugly words which tear down our mates, but we are to speak uplifting and encouraging words that will bring a blessing.[14]

Listening

Listening is a skill which most people haven't learned. Of Wright's three elements of communication—talking, listening, and understanding—listening is usually the trouble area. Instead of patiently hearing what our mates have to say, most of us can hardly wait until they stop talking so we can put in our two cents' worth. God gave each of us two ears, but only one mouth. Consequently we should be ready to listen at least twice as much as we speak.

Listening is the disciplined ability to savor your partner's words much like you savor and enjoy a fine meal, a thoughtful gift, lovely music, or a great book. To properly listen is to take time to digest the content of the message and to let it get under your skin and into your system. When we openly and patiently listen to our mates, we truly learn from them.

Understanding

We may speak clearly and our mates may listen intently, but if they don't understand our message, we haven't communicated very well. There are two major reasons why we fail to communicate in speaking.

- First, when we speak there is often a difference between what we mean to say and what we really say. The idea may be clear in our head, but the words we choose to express the idea may be inappropriate.

- Second, when we listen there is a difference between what we hear and what we think we hear. Perhaps the words we heard correctly conveyed the speaker's idea to everyone else, but we misunderstood them. And every time we respond to what we think we hear instead of what was actually said, the communication problem is further compounded.

One way to help clarify our communication is to repeat to our mate what we heard, and then ask, "Is that what you said?" Whenever we stop to ask that clarifying question we are helping to keep the channels of understanding open and flowing.

Many of us don't communicate because we don't believe that Jesus accepts us as we are. And since we don't feel accepted by Jesus, we do not accept ourselves and we cannot accept others and communicate with them either. We are too busy trying to shape up for God so that He will love and accept us. Communication between Christian marriage partners is a spiritual exercise. The closer we each get to God, the closer we get to each other.

> *Father God, You know that Bob and I have spent endless hours trying to be good communicators with each other and to others. We know how difficult, stressful, and emotional this skill is, but we also know how valuable it is to our marriage. As we look around, we see a correlation between good marriages and good communication. May we continue to have the desire to lift each other up in word and deed. Amen.*

Taking Action

❧ Agree with your mate that you will say, "Five o'clock, six o'clock, what difference does it make?" when you differ on your version of the story.

❧ Another good verbiage to be used around the family is, "Is it edifying?" (a concept taken from Ephesians 4:29).

❧ Set a date night on the calendar when you and your husband can get away from the family and discuss real issues of life. Don't make it too heavy. Have fun with each other.

Reading On

James 3:2-10   Proverbs 18:13
Ephesians 4:29   Proverbs 25:11

There is a time to say nothing,
and a time to say something,
but there is not time to say
everything.

— *Hugo of Fleury*

☐ ☐ ☐

David's Prayer
of Repentance

Scripture Reading: Psalm 51:1-19

Key Verse: Psalm 51:12

Restore to me the joy of your salvation and grant me a willing spirit, to sustain me (NIV).

——————— ❦ ———————

In this psalm David pleads for forgiveness and cleansing (verses 1,2), confesses his guilt (verses 3-6), prays for pardon and restoration (verses 7-12), resolves to praise God (verses 13-17), and prays for the continued prosperity of Jerusalem (verses 18,19). This psalm elaborates David's confession of his sin with Bathsheba (2 Samuel chapters 11 and 12, with emphasis on 12:3).

This portion of Scripture highlights the highs of victory and the lows of defeat. We as sinners can appreciate how heavy David's heart was and his desire to approach his heavenly Father to ask forgiveness and to be restored in his daily walk of uprightness in the presence of God. The NIV translation of Psalm 51 reads so poetically that I thought you would like to read it with no interruptions.

> Have mercy on me, O God,
>   according to your unfailing love;
> according to your great compassion
>   blot out my transgressions.
> Wash away all my iniquity
>   and cleanse me from my sin.

David's Prayer of Repentance

For I know my transgressions,
   and my sin is always before me.
Against you, you only, have I sinned
   and done what is evil in your sight,
so that you are proved right when you speak
   and justified when you judge.
Surely I was sinful at birth,
   sinful from the time my mother conceived me.
Surely you desire truth in the inner parts;
   you teach me wisdom in the inmost place,
Cleanse me with hyssop, and I will be clean;
   wash me, and I will be whiter than snow.
Let me hear joy and gladness;
   let the bones you have crushed rejoice.
Hide your face from my sins
   and blot out all my iniquity.
Create in me a pure heart, O God,
   and renew a steadfast spirit within me.
Do not cast me from your presence
   or take your Holy Spirit from me.
Restore to me the joy of your salvation
   and grant me a willing spirit, to sustain me.
Then I will teach transgressors your ways,
   and sinners will turn back to you.
Save me from bloodguilt, O God,
   the God who saves me,
   and my tongue will sing of your righteousness.
O Lord, open my lips,
   and my mouth will declare your praise.
You do not delight in sacrifice, or I would bring it;
   you do not take pleasure in burnt offerings.
The sacrifices of God are a broken spirit;
   a broken and contrite heart,
   O God, you will not despise.

In your good pleasure make Zion prosper;
 build up the walls of Jerusalem.
Then there will be righteous sacrifices,
 whole burnt offerings to delight you;
 then bulls will be offered on your altar.

This is a confession to meditate over. Chew it up and digest it. As I go over this confession, certain words and phrases touch my inner soul. Some of them include:

- Have mercy on me
- Blot out my transgressions (sins)
- I have sinned against You
- I have a sin nature since birth
- Cleanse me and make me whiter than snow
- Let me again hear joy and gladness
- Blot out my iniquity
- Create in me a pure heart
- Renew a steadfast spirit within me
- Don't cast me away
- Restore my joy of Your salvation
- Give me a willing spirit
- I will teach others of Your ways
- Save me from bloodguilt
- My tongue will sing of Your righteousness
- Open my lips and mouth for praise
- Give me a broken and contrite heart.

As you examine this confession you see a man who has been broken and begs for restoration. I have never been to the depths of David's despair, but my sins have brought me to the place where I cry out to God, "Please forgive me, a helpless sinner."

First John 1:9 has been a great restoration promise for me. It reads, "If we confess our sins, He is faithful and righteous to forgive us our sins and to cleanse us from all unrighteousness."

Don't let the sun set on any unconfessed sin. Don't delay to confess because it will build up a callus around your heart and make repentance harder to deal with.

As I see and hear news stories that deal with crime, I see few people who confess and ask for forgiveness. They are always looking to find excuses:

- My father died when I was young
- My home was very dysfunctional
- My mother took drugs
- My father drank a lot
- I had a bad neighborhood
- My schools were underfunded.

Excuse after excuse, but few people want to say as David did, "Against you, you only, have I sinned; please forgive me of my transgressions."

David realized that after confession there would be joy again. If you are burdened down today with a heavy heart because of unconfessed sin in your life, claim 1 John 1:9 and be restored to the joy of your salvation. God will create a pure heart within you.

Father God, I want to give You all of my known and unknown sins today. I don't want to leave Your presence with any unconfessed sin in my life. I want to go away with a clean heart and have Your joy of forgiveness in me. Only by Your grace have You protected me from the ugliness of sin. Please be with the ladies who read today's psalm, so that they too will know of Your grace, love, and forgiveness. Amen.

Taking Action

- Meditate on Psalm 51.
- Study this passage and jot down in your journal the observations you make.
- Say a prayer to God confessing all of your sins.
- Go away with a song in your heart.

Reading On

Luke 18:13   Ephesians 2:8,9
John 3:16   Romans 3:23

It is the duty of nations as well
as of men to confess their sins
and transgressions in humble
sorrow, yet with assured hope
that genuine repentance will
lead to mercy and pardon.

—*Abraham Lincoln*

Keep Your Nest Warm

Scripture Reading: Genesis 2:18-25

Key Verse: Genesis 2:21
> *The Lord God caused a deep sleep to fall upon the man, and he slept; then He took one of his ribs and closed up the flesh at that place.*

———— 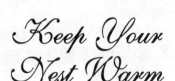 ————

When God created Eve out of Adam's rib, He equipped her with unique characteristics which complemented her husband. Apparently one of the characteristics God invested in Eve and her female descendants was the nesting instinct. Bob and I have noticed that most of the women we meet in seminars have a desire to create and maintain a warm, attractive home for themselves, their husbands, and their children. Though we express it in many different ways, we women seem to be more home-oriented than our husbands.

The changing role of women in our society has tended to submerge the nesting instinct, and today's female doesn't operate much like Grandma did. Women today don't cook, clean, iron, or mother like previous generations. *Careers* are more popular with women, and many are forced to work to support an affluent lifestyle. In many cases a couple cannot even buy a home unless both partners are working full-time.

Children are often the neglected victims of the woman's misplaced nesting instinct. Childcare centers and extended day schools are almost a necessity in our society. One preschool teacher I met said the children she cares for are with her an average of 11 hours a day!

Today's mothers are trusting other people to raise their children. Mom picks up her kids after a hard day's work, races through the fast-food restaurant on the way home, and then kicks off her shoes and passes out. There is no time for nesting and mothering. Older latchkey kids come home to an empty house where potato chips and television are their best friends. Whatever happened to homemade cookies and milk and warm comments like "Tell me about your day" and "May I help you with your homework?"

Today a homemaker committed to nesting and mothering is often seen as inferior to a career-oriented woman. If she teaches someone else's children she is given the title of teacher; if she teaches her own children she is just a mother. If she chooses paint, wallpaper, and fabric for others she is an interior decorator; if she decorates her own home she's just a homemaker. If she professionally cares for the bumps and bruises of other people she's a nurse; if she cares for her own children's physical needs she is only a mom doing her job. Mothers employ the skills of many professions but usually receive much less recognition than professional women.

I loved my role as a wife and mother and grandmother, and I continually endeavored to keep our nest warm. I worked at organizing my time to care for the children so I had time for other activities. It was important to me to exchange recipes, be involved in church, and be available for Bob's needs. Caring for my family was exciting to me, but I didn't depend on them for all my strokes. Reaching out to other activities brought a balance to my life. As the children got older I taught a Bible study and built a thriving business in my home. But my activities were always subject to my priorities of seeking the Lord first, being a helpmate to Bob, guiding our children, and keeping our nest clean.

My friend Barbara is a master at making her family's nest a joyful and comfortable place. When her family goes on vacation, Barbara takes her nest with her. Upon arrival at the hotel or motel she pulls out a checkered tablecloth, candles, crackers, and cheese. She brings flowers to place by the bed and a perfumed candle or spray to enhance the bathroom. When her children were small Barbara brought games, popcorn, crayons, and each child's favorite pillow, toy, or "blankie" on each trip. Barbara keeps building her nest wherever the family goes. The effort required isn't great—throwing a few extra things in a suitcase or backpack—but the effort expended is sure worth the positive results.

The apostle Paul wrote: "Older women likewise are to be reverent in their behavior, not malicious gossips, nor enslaved to much wine, teaching what is good, that they may encourage the young women to love their husbands, to love their children" (Titus 2:3,4). As a young wife and mother my heart's desire was to be the kind of younger woman that Paul described in these verses. I was a new Christian and I knew I needed the positive influence and teaching of older, more mature women. I began to search out this type of older woman who could teach me all about being a maker of a home. Over the years I have had many mentors help me grow into where I am today. And God has now given me that role to encourage women all over this country to be a role model in keeping their nest warm.

Father God, thank You for all the women You have given me to help light my path. Without them I know I would not be the woman I am today. As You give me the opportunity to be a Titus woman, may the women who come to my seminars see Your Son, Jesus, in a real, true-to-life experience. I'm so appreciative for all You do for me and my family. I really do love my nest and all those who are part of it. Amen.

Taking Action

❦ List in your journal three to five women who have been Titus women for you. After each name write what they have contributed to your life.

❦ If they are still alive, take a moment to call them on the phone or to write a note and say, "Thank you for what you have done for me." This will do wonders for you and they will be greatly encouraged as well.

❦ Buy some fresh flowers and have them in the nest when your family arrives home this evening.

Reading On

Proverbs 31:27,28   Titus 2:3-5
Psalm 139:23   Psalm 73:26

The Christian home is the Master's workshop, where the processes of character-molding are silently, lovingly, faithfully, and successfully carried on.

— *Richard Monckton Milnes*

Living by God's Surprises

Scripture Reading: James 1:2-12

Key Verse: James 1:2

Consider it all joy, my brethren, when you encounter various trials.

———— ❧ ————

Throughout Scripture we read of victory through troubles and suffering. Helmut Thielicke, the great German pastor and theologian, testified to this kind of victory during the horrors of World War II.

When Thielicke said, "We live by God's surprises," he had personally suffered under the Nazis. As a pastor he wrote to young soldiers about to die; he comforted mothers and fathers and children after the bombs killed their loved ones. He preached magnificent sermons week after week as bombs blew apart his church and the lives and dreams of his parishioners. He spoke of God not only looking in love at His suffering people, weeping with them as they were surrounded by flames, but of God's hand reaching into the flames to help them, His own hand scorched by the fires.

From the depths of suffering and the wanton destruction during the Nazi regime, Thielicke held out a powerful Christian hope. To Germans disillusioned by the easily manipulated faith of their fathers, he quoted

Peter Wust: "The great things happen to those who pray. But we learn to pray best in suffering."

Prayer, suffering, joy, and the surprises of God...they are all tightly enmeshed. But most shrink from the above statement, seeing suffering as the surest killer of both joy and "great things."

When we are rightly related to God, life is full of joyful uncertainty and expectancy...we do not know what God is going to do next; He packs our lives with surprises all the time.

What a strange idea: "joyful uncertainty." Most of us view uncertainty as cause for anxiety, not joy. Yet this call to expectancy rings true. The idea of standing on tiptoe to see what God is going to do next can transform our way of seeing. Prayers go maddeningly unanswered as well as marvelously fulfilled. Prayer becomes the lens through which we begin to see from God's perspective.[15]

When I read of men or women with such courage, I feel so insignificant when I approach God each day in prayer. It's hard for me to grasp the height of joy that these personalities of God must have experienced during this time in history. When James writes, "Consider it all joy, my brethren, when you encounter various trials, knowing that the testing of your faith produces endurance; and let endurance have its perfect result, that you may be perfect and complete, lacking in nothing" (James 1:2-4), I realize that life will be a challenge.

Who said that the Christian walk will be easy? These passages and events make me realize that there will be surprises when we live for God. We in America have it pretty easy compared to the rest of the world. Throughout Jesus' ministry He shared with His followers that there would be a cost if they followed Him.

Thielicke, along with the other historical pillars of the church, give testimony that prayer becomes the lens through which we begin to see life from God's perspective.

I hear many people ask in a harsh tone, "Well, I'm going to ask God when I get to heaven why He did. . . . !" But I think we will stand in such awe in His presence that such questions will be meaningless, because then we will see history from God's point of view.

Wouldn't it be wonderful if when we got out of bed each morning we stood on our tiptoes to see what God is going to do today? We would joyfully look forward to see what God is going to do next. When we see life like that, our cup will surely "run over" and life will be joyful. Our cup will always be full, and as we pour out its contents God will give us new refreshment to fill it full again. Lord, I want to experience that joy!

Father God, I want to live life so that I truly live expectantly for Your surprises. I want to tiptoe to see Your mysteries unveiled for me. May I learn to see life from Your end, and forget about all of man's wonderful knowledge, even though it is magnificent. Give me depth in my prayer life to match that of Helmut Thielicke. Here is a man who undoubtedly saw Jesus face-to-face with a true joy of assurance. Amen.

Taking Action

- Evaluate the quality and quantity of your prayer life. How can it be strengthened?

- Be willing to stand on your tiptoes to see what God is going to do next in your life. What do you think you might see?

- How will you react to it? What will you do for support?

Reading On

Romans 8:28	James 1:2-12
Matthew 6:33	1 Corinthians 10:13

There are three ways that prepare us for life's trials. One is the Spartan way that says, "I have strength within me to do it, I am the captain of my soul. With the courage and will that is mine, I will be master when the struggle comes." Another way is the spirit of Socrates, who affirmed that we have minds, reason, and judgment to evaluate and help us cope with the enigmas and struggles of life. The Christian way is the third approach. It doesn't exclude the other two, but adds, "You don't begin with yourself, your will, or your reason. You begin with God, who is the beginning and the end."

— *Lowell R. Ditzen*

I'm Too Sick

Scripture Reading: Romans 8:18-30

Key Verse: Romans 8:28

We know that God causes all things to work together for good to those who love God, to those who are called according to His purpose.

———— ❧ ————

It was a women's retreat I was looking forward to in February, to be held at a retreat center in Fall City, Washington. We arrived safely and on time; it was a drizzly day but it felt good to be away from dry Southern California.

As usual, the women were excited and arrived anxious for a fun-filled spiritual weekend. After two sessions on Friday evening, by 10:30 P.M. I was tired. I was in our cabin, which also housed the summer camp nurses (and looked like they needed a little nursing themselves), I anxiously fell into bed for a much-needed rest.

Two hours later I was sick with what I think was a good dose of food poisoning, although no one got sick but me. All night I spent time in the small, musty bathroom. By morning my Bob was very concerned about my strength to speak at three more sessions on Saturday. "I'll be fine," I kept reassuring him. But by 9:30 A.M. I knew there was no way I could pull myself up to speak.

"Maybe I could do it for you," my Bob suggested. "Of course you can, what a great idea!" I responded. Bob met with the retreat leaders and they were thrilled that he could fill in for me. During that morning session Bob spoke on his book

427

Your Husband, Your Friend. The session lasted almost two hours, and the women were hanging on his every word. What a treat to get a man's perspective on women, marriage, and relationships!

But the best was yet to come. By noon I was able to clean up pretty well and down a bit of soup and crackers. The afternoon sessions went well as I sat on a stool and finished the retreat with the Lord's strength.

Many of the women came up to me and shared how Bob's message touched them and answered questions they had always had about marriage and men.

As Janet approached me she said, "Emilie, I'm so sorry you were sick today, but if that's what it took for your Bob to speak, I'm so thankful because his message just saved my marriage. I came this weekend to get away and had decided I was leaving my husband as soon as I got back home. But today gave me understanding and hope. I'm going home to try harder and put my heart into a commitment we made years ago." Was it worth getting sick? You bet! Did God work all things together as our Scripture for today states? You bet!

In over 20 years of speaking that was the only time I ever missed a speaking engagement. God knew what Janet needed to hear and He brought it about to save a marriage.

Father God, how we thank You that when situations seem so difficult You are able to give us strength in our weakness, to change the impossible to the possible. Help us to keep on keeping on when our marriage relationship seems to be off the track; help us to get back on track and do our part to love our mate through You. Amen.

Taking Action

❦ List two things you can do to help build your relationship with the one you love.

❧ Say a prayer today for your husband's needs in his awesome responsibility as the head of the family.

❧ Praise the one you love for one of his good qualities.

Reading On

Genesis 50:20   Proverbs 15:11
Romans 8:31-39   Matthew 10:29-31

He who does not believe that
God is above all is either a fool
or has no experience of life.

— *Statius Caecilius*

□ □ □

I Will Be with Your Mouth

Scripture Reading: Exodus 4:10-12

Key Verse: Exodus 4:12

Now then go, and I, even I, will be with your mouth, and teach you what you are to say.

———— ❦ ————

Because of the turmoil in my home as a child, I decided I would not speak, in fear that I would say the wrong thing. I became quiet and would grasp my mother's leg in order to hide from people. I didn't want to be around people; I was afraid of my own family members and certainly strangers.

My father had a major drinking problem that put everyone on pins and needles. Everyone watched what he or she would say, because Daddy would get mad very easily and make life miserable to the messenger who said the wrong thing or in the wrong way.

I was this way until I got into high school and found myself being liked by my fellow students. As a junior I had the female lead in our senior play, "Best Foot Forward." My success in this performance began to instill in me some self-confidence.

It was also at this time that I met my Bob, who made me feel safe to be around him and his loving family. But I was very quiet and reserved, for fear that I might say the wrong thing. Bob would always say, "Emilie, speak up—you've got to tell me your thoughts on this," but I was very hesitant to express myself, fearing that I would say the wrong thing.

It wasn't until I was in my late twenties, when I signed up for a Christian women's retreat in Palm Springs, that I realized God had a speaking program for my life. Since the women of my church knew that I came from a Jewish faith, they asked me if I would give a three-minute testimony at the retreat. I felt like Moses in Exodus 4:10: "Please, Lord, I have never been eloquent, neither recently nor in time past, nor since Thou has spoken to thy servant; for I am slow of speech and slow of tongue." Then the Lord said to me as to Moses: "Who do you think made your mouth? Is it not I the Lord?"

So I reluctantly said, "Yes, I'll do it." I wasn't sure what I would say or how I would say it, but I had confidence that my Lord and God would be by my side.

Our key verse for today gave me great strength. God said to Moses: "Now then go, and I, even I, will be with your mouth, and teach you what you are to say." That was over 35 years ago, and He still goes before me, giving me the words to say and teaching me from His Word.

I can honestly say that God will be with your mouth. I travel all over this continent sharing with women of all denominations the words He has given me to say. Along with the spoken word, He has also entrusted me with writing over 22 books, with well over a million books in print.

As a little girl who was afraid to speak I didn't have the faintest idea that God would use me to touch the lives of thousands through the spoken and written word. It only happened when God saw a willingness in my spirit to be used by Him.

My testimony was so well-received by those in the audience that I received many invitations to go to their local clubs to share my story. Of course, I had to expand it beyond the original three minutes to at least a 30-minute presentation, but God richly provided the words to say.

Am I still nervous when I get up to speak? Yes—every time. I still have to rely upon Him each time I speak to give me a peace and calm before I begin. I often wonder as I look out on the faces of my audience, "Why me, Lord? There are many better speakers and writers than I am." But He always answers back, "Now then go, and I will be with your mouth and teach you what to say."

> *Father God, I am amazed that You have been able to use me—an ordinary wife, mother, and grandmother. You continue to amaze me in how You take the ordinary and make it extraordinary. May I always be willing to share my story as long as there are people who want to hear it. The "bouquet of flowers" is laid at Your feet each night. You are to receive all the glory. Amen.*

Taking Action

- ❦ Are you holding back saying yes to God because of fear?
- ❦ In what ways?
- ❦ How can you turn your "no" answers into "yes" answers?
- ❦ Start with one "yes" answer, then watch how God will use your willingness to be used.

Reading On

Psalm 8:2	Matthew 15:11
Proverbs 26:28	Romans 10:10

❦

He who indulges in liberty of speech will hear things in return which he will not like.

—*Terrence*

❦

Tea at Nordstrom's

Scripture Reading: Colossians 4:1-6

Key Verse: Colossians 4:2
Devote yourselves to prayer, keeping alert in it with an attitude of thanksgiving.

I met some of my dearest friends while we lived in Newport Beach, California. Although we were there for only four years, it was a time of major spiritual growth in my life. The Tuesday morning prayer group taught me to pray without thee's and thou's and to communicate with my Lord as though He were sitting in the room having tea with us. I loved my Newport Beach years and the closeness I had with those Titus women.

Leaving to move to Riverside was a difficult change for me. Two weeks in our new town brought a phone call from a young mom who said she heard I was lonely and said she wanted to meet me. That meeting became a friendship that has lasted over 25 years. Her name is Vonis Waugh, and although she moved to Oregon we still maintain a very special friendship.

Recently, upon hearing that Vonis was coming to town to visit family, four of us friends decided to meet Vonis for a quick teatime at the courtyard of our local Nordstrom's department store. Two people brought candles and we ordered latte, tea, or coffee. Since it was just before Christmas none of us had much time, but it was a reconnecting of friendships, if only for 90 minutes.

Vonis complained of a pain in her stomach that had been a source of irritation for several weeks. We all gave her our own diagnoses, which ranged from ulcers to a parasite. Two weeks later Vonis called to tell us she had cancer in the form of a tumor the size of a football on her aorta artery.

Now we had to deal with this devastating news. No one knew what the next several months held in store for Vonis: tests, chemotherapy, hair loss, weight loss, depression, fear, and much more. But the treatment was working and Vonis was responding as she was surrounded with love, prayers, hope, and positive input.

Then came her next visit to Riverside, and six of us joined together at Julie's home for afternoon tea with the one we loved so dearly. The time was fun as we laughed over her bald head, long surgery scar, and cute wig. We all tried it on and laughed some more. Stories were told of old times, family, and even household pets.

But my spirit was heavy as I thought why we were here. Was it just to have meaningful conversation? I don't think so. Laughing and loving, yes, but what about our friend, who inside was worried about her life, her children, and her grandchildren that she may never see grow up? We needed to pray for a miracle for Vonis, her doctors, her health, her family, her future, and her difficult decisions.

Gathering all together, we had a circle of prayer—not too long, just enough to cover and surround her with our loving prayers. Tears flowed, hugs followed, and peace came to all of us. At this writing Vonis is doing well. The tumor has shrunk to the size of a golf ball, but still the unknown lies ahead.

Women, today we must be in touch with the needs of our friends and those we hold close to our hearts. We need to listen as they talk and to pray as we listen.

I have Vonis and her family's photo on the door of our refrigerator. Each time I open that door I pray for her. It could be 20 times a day. Our verse today says to devote ourselves to prayer. Although we are all busy women, we can devote our hearts to prayer with an attitude of thanksgiving as we come and go in our daily business. How faithful God is!

> *Father God, help me to be reminded daily to bring before You those who hurt, are ill, and are spiritually weak. Bring to my mind today that friend who needs a special touch from You, our Heavenly Father. Thank You. Amen.*

Taking Action

- Place a photo, handprint, or note on your refrigerator as a reminder to pray for a friend.
- Take time to drop a note to someone who needs a special encouragement.
- Remember to thank God for His goodness.
- Have a cup of tea with a friend.

Reading On

Luke 6:12	Romans 12:12
Acts 6:4	Philippians 4:6

> Prayer is for the religious life what original research is for science—by it we get direct contact with reality. . . . We pray because we were made for prayer, and God draws us out by breathing Himself in.
>
> — *P.T. Forsyth*

□ □ □

Seek His Thoughts

Scripture Reading: Isaiah 55:6-13

Key Verse: Isaiah 55:8

"My thoughts are not your thoughts, neither are your ways My ways," declares the Lord.

———— ❧ ————

Suppose a man should find a great basket by the wayside, carefully packed, and upon opening it he should find it filled with human thoughts—all the thoughts which had passed through one single brain in one year or five years. What a medley they would make! How many thoughts would be wild and foolish, how many weak and contemptible, how many mean and vile, how many so contradictory and crooked that they could hardly lie still in the basket. And suppose he should be told that these were all his *own* thoughts, children of his own brain; how amazed he would be, and how little prepared to see himself as revealed in those thoughts! How he would want to run away and hide, if all the world were to see the basket opened and see his thoughts![16]

Compared to the thoughts of God, we humans seem so frail. I can't imagine being exposed for the lowliness of my thoughts. I'm sometimes amazed that I could even think of such things. At times I think, "God, why did You permit that plane to crash, or why was it necessary for that murder to take place?" At times I want to crawl inside God's mind and see how it functions and how He thinks. Then I realize that He is the potter and I am the clay. His thoughts are so much higher than mine.

It must really be frustrating for a genius with a 200-plus IQ not to be able to outthink God. (I don't have that problem, since I'm nowhere near that level of thought!) But still I wonder about God's thought power.

In Philippians 4:8 Paul gives us some idea of God's level of thought process. He tells us to think on these things:

- Whatever is true
- Whatever is honorable
- Whatever is right
- Whatever is pure
- Whatever is lovely
- Whatever is of good report.

If there is any excellence and if anything worthy of praise, let your mind dwell on these things. Then in verse 9 he gives us some action:

- What you have learned, received, heard, and seen in me—
- Practice these things.
- Then the God of peace will be with you.

As Christians we are all models that people watch to see what God is like. They are watching and hearing what we have to say about life. Either they accept our level of thought or they reject it by what they have learned, received, heard, and seen in us.

We want to be a reflection of God: As people see us in action, do they see what this Christian walk is all about? Do our children and those around us ask, "Have I ever seen a Christian?" Or do they know absolutely that they have seen a Christian when they look at us?

If people were to find our "thought basket" on the wayside, what kind of flowers would they pull out?

> *Father God, thank You for challenging me in*
> *this area of thoughts. Let me focus on pure thoughts*
> *that will stimulate me to be more Christlike. When*
> *I have a choice between two levels of thought, give*
> *me the strength and courage to take the higher road.*
> *Help women who read today's thoughts to be chal-*
> *lenged to think upon the good things of life. May we*
> *all raise our level of thought. Amen.*

Taking Action

❦ Evaluate your thought life. What do you see?

❦ What do others see?

❦ What do you like?

❦ What do you want to change?

❦ How will you change?

Reading On

Galatians 5:19-21   Psalm 94:11
Galatians 5:22,23   Matthew 15:16-20

❦

If you would voyage Godward,
you must see to it that the rudder of thought is right.

—W.J. Dawson

❦

Blessed Assurance

Scripture Reading: Psalm 37:1-40

Key Verse: Psalm 37:1-40
Read and meditate on each verse today.

I don't know if you're anything like I am, but when I look at the local news events on television and in the newspaper, I see very little hope for the future. I get concerned for my children and grandchildren, and even for my great-grandchildren. I see a moral decay from what I cherished by being raised in the fifties. When I go by a high school, visit a mall, listen to the music of the youth, see the art of the masses, or witness the violence of the movies, I scream in my soul, STOP!

Then the Lord brings before me Psalm 37. In this passage David exhorts the righteous to trust in the Lord. Even when it looks like evil will overpower righteousness, God never abandons His children (verse 25). Though they may experience the heartaches of a sinful, fallen world, God's children are never forsaken. In fact, His blessings will extend to the next generation (verse 26).

During my quiet time with the Lord in this particular psalm, certain key phrases comfort my soul:

- *Do not fret*, be not envious (verse 1).

- *Trust* in the Lord, cultivate faithfulness (verse 3).

- *Delight* yourself in the Lord, He will give you abundantly (verse 4).

- *Commit* your way to Him, trust also in Him (verse 5).
- *Rest* in the Lord, wait patiently (verse 7).
- *Cease* from anger, do not fret (verse 8).
- The *humble* will inherit the land (verse 11).
- *Depart* from evil (verse 27).
- *Wait* for the Lord (verse 34).

Then in verses 39 and 40 we read of the great blessings we receive as children of God: "The salvation of the righteous is from the Lord; He is our strength in time of trouble. And the Lord helps them and delivers them; He delivers them from the wicked and saves them, because they take refuge in Him."

I'M DRINKING FROM
THE SAUCER

. . . If God gives me strength
and courage, When the way
grows steep and rough, I'll not
ask for other blessings—I'm already blessed enough. May I
never be too busy, To help bear
another's load. I'm drinking
from the saucer, 'Cause my cup
has overflowed!

—*Author Unknown*

As I leave my prayer closet I am again able to face the negative issues of the day because David took time centuries ago to write this poetic psalm of comfort.

Father God, again You come to comfort me in to-
day's psalm. You give me assurance that righteousness

does deflect evil, and that Your promises are as true today as they were centuries ago. Let me dwell on these significant words from this passage: TRUST, DELIGHT, COMMIT, REST, BE HUMBLE, WAIT. I ask that You give comfort to the ladies today as they bring their cares to You. Amen.

Taking Action

❦ Underline in your Bible those action words that give you direction. For example: TRUST, DELIGHT, COMMIT, etc.

❦ Write one of these key verses on a three-by-five card. Put it in a special place where you will see it several times a day.

❦ Memorize this verse.

Reading On

Proverbs 3:31   Proverbs 24:19,20
Proverbs 23:17   Psalm 62:8

———————— ❦ ————————

For God to explain a trial would
be to destroy its object, which is
that of calling forth simple faith
and implicit obedience.

— *Alfred Edersheim*

———————— ❦ ————————

The Work of Our Hands

Scripture Reading: Psalm 90:12-17

Key Verse: Psalm 90:17b

> *Confirm for us the work of our hands; yes, confirm the work of our hands.*

For many years I struggled with the idea of worth in my work. I didn't have an advanced college degree and I was a homemaker with five children. I was always tired, with little energy for anything else—including romancing my husband. I didn't have a good handle on who I was as a person. I found myself saying to myself:

- You aren't worth much.

- You didn't have a career.

- Your job is so mundane.

- Anyone can do what you do.

- I don't have enough energy to do anything else.

- I'm stuck in a rat race with no place to go.

Over and over these thoughts went through my head. As you can suspect, I wasn't too exciting to be around!

I'm sure many readers of today's passage feel they have little worth in their hands. They have been browbeaten into thinking that life is fleeting by and they are being left behind. During this period in my life I was involved in a small Bible study with a few godly women who shared with us young ladies two passages of Scripture that changed my life.

One was Proverbs 31, which talked about the virtuous woman, and the other was Titus 2:4,5, which describes a wife's core role as "husband lover" and "child lover." These two sections of Scripture gave me the tools I needed to establish priorities and roles in making lifestyle decisions. I soon realized that this whole concept of work and worth was very complex and that there was no right answer to fit all situations. I realized that each woman and each family has to determine what is best for them, using biblical guidelines.

As I looked at Titus 2:4,5 I realized that God wanted me to be a lover of my husband and children. This was refreshing to me because I had looked at all these drudgeries as an end unto themselves, not as a means to fulfilling one of my primary roles as a woman. But now I found my attitude toward this work changing. I was beginning to do it out of love rather than obligation.

Once you see, you appreciate
and then you become inspired.
—*Alexandria Stoddard*

I also realized that I did more than fulfill this role, but the role gave me some structure and direction. Up to this point in our marriage I had been experiencing frustration and disappointment because I had no direction in marriage.

The Proverbs 31 passage also made me realize that the ideal Hebrew woman handled many activities outside the home. But even while these extra activities were going on she remained focused on her husband, children, and home. Her husband can trust her, the passage says, because "she does him good and not evil all the days of her life" (verse 12).

With this new information I began to shift my focus from simply doing tasks to becoming a lover of my husband and children. To this day my core focus remains in this area of my life. Even though I have gone way beyond those early beginnings, I come across countless women who don't know about or aren't willing to perform the basic focus for a married woman: being a lover of their husband and children.

When I began to change my focus, I began to realize what today's key verse, Psalm 90:17b, was addressing: "Confirm for us the work of our hands; yes, confirm the work of our hands."

What's in it for me as a woman? Proverbs 31:28,29 gives me my blessing: "Her children rise up and bless her; her husband also, and he praises her, saying, 'Many daughters have done nobly, but you excel them all.'"

When my children and husband rise up and call me blessed, then I truly know that many years ago I made the right choice when I decided to be a lover of my husband and children. Without a doubt I know that God has confirmed the work of my hands.

> *Father God, thank You again for sending me Titus women at a young age to help me focus my role as a wife and mother. As I stand before You today I'm assured that I made the right decision. I know that many women are confused about their role as a woman. May they somehow grasp this lifesaving concept of being a lover of their husband and children first, and then other opportunities will be opened to them. Amen.*

Taking Action

❦ How has God confirmed the worth of your works? Write in your journal.

❦ If you're not sure, think about this thought: "Are you a lover of your husband and children?" Yes or no?

❧ If yes, how do you manifest this love in your home? If no, how can you manifest it in your home? What changes will be necessary?

Reading On

Proverbs 31:28,29   Psalm 8:3
Titus 2:4,5   Psalm 111:3

❧

I am beginning to see that the things that really matter take place not in the boardrooms but in the kitchens of the world.

—*Gary Sledge*

❧

□ □ □

The Heart
of the Home

Scripture Reading: Proverbs 19:1-8

Key Verse: Proverbs 19:8
He who gets wisdom loves his own soul; he who keeps understanding will find good.

———— ❦ ————

In another translation we read, "Do yourself a favor and learn all you can; then remember what you've learned and you will prosper" (TEV).

Today we are returning to a new traditionalism. We are looking at our past mistakes and beginning to see what we can do to correct them in order to become the women that God uniquely created us to be. Yes, we're going back to tradition, but we will do it in a new way. We'll take on the mystique of the feminine woman, being a lady for whom men will open doors—not the "too-tired-for-sex" woman, but the woman who is beautiful inside and has charm that a man desires.

How are we going to do this? By changing our values from straw and sticks to gold and silver and by building a strong foundation of faith in God's Word (1 Corinthians 3:12).

Women, we are the mortar that holds together our homes and families. We set the thermostat in our homes. Proverbs 14:1 says that homes are made by the wisdom of women but are destroyed by foolishness. Yes, we've been foolish in some areas; we've grown and learned from that, and now we're ready to commit ourselves to making positive changes.

My mother was a beautiful example of how the woman is the heartbeat of her home. When I was six years old my mother made me a green-and-white gingham dress with puffy sleeves, a full gathered skirt with pockets, and white heart buttons. She had a treadle Singer sewing machine. I loved to watch the rhythm of Mama's touch with her feet to make it sew. I also loved that dress. It fit so perfectly, the skirt twirled just right, and it had a nice big hem in it so I could wear it for a long time.

My mother was quite a seamstress; her father had been a tailor in Brooklyn, New York, and he had to have perfection in his garments. So my dress was well-made. At first I could only wear it on special occasions, and absolutely could not play in it.

One of my favorite times as a little girl was when my aunt and uncle came to visit us, and I got to wear my green gingham dress. One Sunday they were late in arriving and I got tired of waiting, so I went out to play—only to slip and fall into a pile of dog toot.

My dress was all I could think of as I ran home smelling very bad. But Mama was great. She pulled off my dress, washed me and the dress, and assured me the dress would be fine. But the episode took the newness out of that dress, and soon the green gingham dress became a school dress.

I grew and the hem had to be let down. Mama sewed a band of rickrack over the hemline so it wouldn't look as if it had been altered. And I was to change my dress after school. I always wanted to wear that dress, so Mama made me a new one for a best dress in the same style as my green gingham dress, but with a different fabric. Yet it just wasn't the same as my original green gingham dress.

I was growing, and my favorite dress, now with three rows of rickrack, became too short to wear. Mama said it would make a fine play dress with slacks underneath. So I wore it on Saturdays to ride my bike down to the beach. When I was eight years old I finally had to give up my green gingham dress to the rag box.

But my mother taught me how to sew, and one of my first projects was to make an apron. Out came the green gingham dress from the rag box. We cut off the gathered skirt, added a waistband and ties (pockets were already there), and presto! The dress became an apron. There was still some fabric left over, and with this Mama and I made pot holders.

I loved that apron, and Mama and I both wore it proudly as she taught me how to cook and clean. The pockets were big and handy to hold tidbits of trash as I cleaned each little room. What with cooking and cleaning, however, the apron began to get stained and a bit tattered. Unfortunately, even aprons are outgrown after a time, so back into the rag box it went.

It reappeared later, however, torn into pieces. The soft fabric made fine cloths for dusting and wiping up. One day I saw my gingham dress swishing across the floor in a rag mop. Mama made our mops out of old rags, and they worked very well. The white heart buttons popped up on several dresses after that, and also on flannel nighties. After years of continued use, I still have two of those heart buttons, 46 years later!

Heart in the home is created by teaching, delegating, and being there. We need to be there for our families. When Jenny got a splinter, had a fever, tried out for the swim team, was rejected by friends, had hair that didn't fall right, broke up with a boyfriend, and planned her wedding—I was there.

My mother became a single parent after my father died. She worked far into the night, and during all her years until she died at age 78, she remained the heart of our home. Through all the abuse, alcohol-related problems, low finances, and anger in our home, Mama remained the soft, gentle-spirited woman. During her later years she lived in a senior-citizen building in a tiny efficiency apartment. Yet she had a wreath of flowers on her front door and a few fresh daisies or pansies on the table, and she always had a cup of tea ready for anyone who knocked.

What can we do to repair the brokenness of our homes, hearts, health, marriage, relationships, and children? We can begin by looking at the 8760 hours we have each year and reducing the 70 percent of stress in our lives that is caused by disorganization. If we sleep an average of eight hours per day, that equals 2920 hours a year. We then work about 2000 hours, which gives us 3840 hours to wash, iron, plan and prepare food, clean, attend Little League or soccer games or music recitals, keep doctor appointments, help with homework, and watch television. About 37 hours a week is what it takes to accomplish our domestic chores. If we work outside our homes, how can we be there to do all that? There is no time left for us or for any interaction with our family.

Our survival lies in three areas.

- *Delegation.* Women, we can't do it alone. Super Mom must go out the window. Call a family meeting and share with them your need for help and how they can help you. I know your family will come through. Prepare ahead of time a list of areas in which they can help to relieve the stress from your life.

- *Dialogue.* Continue to share your stress feelings and allow your family to share with you. As busy as we all are, it is important to communicate back and forth about our feelings concerning teachers, schoolwork, friends, and (especially) God.

- *Interaction.* There is much we can teach our children as we work side by side with them. When the children bake cookies with me, or as we make a salad, mow the lawn, wash a car, clean the bathroom, change the linens, rake leaves, and shovel snow together, we are a team. It is amazing what I found out about my children and their feelings as we worked together. I was there—the available one for them to dump on. In turn they learned how to work, and many times our conversations were turned in spiritual directions.

Women, we are the remodelers, the harmonizers of our homes. We are a country of broken homes, broken hearts, and broken health. Staying married today is more of a challenge than getting married. To keep the flame of love alive takes creative work. Several things need to happen.

- We need to surrender our egos to the needs of the other person. Ephesians 5:21 NIV says, "Submit to one another out of reverence for Christ."

- We need to pay attention to the other person. Make your husband feel special and unique, honoring and treating him as you would want to be treated.

- We need to see our man as our leader and hero. When you married him you saw his many fine qualities. Now be willing to follow his leadership in spite of the fact that you may be smarter, stronger, greater, prettier, wiser, and even more organized.

- We need to make our husband feel good about himself: to build him up in his eyes, our eyes, and the eyes of the world. We have the opportunity to make our husband look and feel good. Building up our hero's masculinity in his eyes and in the eyes of other people is very important.

- We need to shower our man with love. Let's not waste time arguing day and night. A smart woman will love, love, love. It takes years to learn patience, to bite your tongue and overlook faults. My Bob may not always be easy to love, but he is sure worth it. So who is the winner? We women are! We keep the harmony for us and for our children, and we preserve our love. We are the women who make or break the home.

The brokenness of our lives and homes can be repaired if we are willing. Great women are willing to make positive changes, and those changes first come in our relationship with God.

- *Submit to Him.* Give God your family, yourself, and your failures. We will never change our mate or other people, but God can, and He does.

- *Commit to Him.* Give God your attitudes, your behavior, your stresses, your work, your career, and all the areas in which you feel the need for peace.

Receive or rededicate yourself to Christ. Be an active part of the family of God, and then wait to allow God to work in your family.

> *Father God, thank You for choosing me to be the heart of our home. By nature that is my love. I get so excited when I see how my family responds to all that I do. Yes, there are times when I have to ask for a thank you, but thank You for giving me a husband, children, and grandchildren who respond in such a positive fashion when I do my mother things. I know I have made a positive impact when I see my children, Jenny and Brad, do some of the same things in their homes. May those reading today's thoughts step out in a new way. Amen.*

Taking Action

- ❦ Submit to God in this area of your life.
- ❦ Commit to God your attitudes and behavior in this area.
- ❦ Set the thermostat in your home by having a candle and flowers on tonight's dinner table (do it even if only you show up).

❦ Have soft music playing while eating (no television or loud noises allowed).

❦ Write your husband and children love notes and put them on their pillows.

Reading On

Proverbs 14:1   Deuteronomy 6:5
1 Corinthians 3:12,13   John 13:35

WE ARE LIBERATED

• Liberated in our homes because we've built a strong foundation.

• Liberated in our lives as we live a life built with strong bricks.

• Liberated in our professions because we are creative women and can have a balance between home, work, family, and church.

• Liberated in traditionalism as we learn from the mistakes of the past and move toward the future with excitement and less stress.

• Liberated in Jesus Christ because He is our source of strength, love, forgiveness, peace, and joy.

A God of Order

Scripture Reading: Colossians 4:1-6

Key Verse: Colossians 4:5
Conduct yourselves with wisdom toward outsiders, making the most of the opportunity.

In Scripture we find that the concept of organization and order deals far more with our *relationships with people* than with our *handling of things*. When we do things in order, we find ourselves moving through life with purpose and meaning. God delights in turning weaknesses into strengths and in bringing order from confusion (1 Corinthians 14:10). He redeems our time as well as our toils (Colossians 4:5).

When we are in order, we find that we have smoother communication, more effective problem-solving, better task management, better interpersonal relationships, and better direction of what needs to be done.

There are several places in Scripture where God directed order.

- Moses was to establish a multitiered judicial system (Exodus 18:13-26).

- Jesus directed the hungry masses to be seated on the grass so they could be fed (Mark 6:39,40).

- Jesus sent His disciples out two by two and gave them specific guidelines (Mark 6:7).

Scripture wants us to be organized so that our lives will be lived without chaos and confusion and that we will have maximum freedom for achieving His goals in our lives.

Over the years I have received countless letters from women who want to know how to get organized. Perhaps through coaxing from their husbands, children, friends, or clergy, they have begun to realize that they could be more effective if they could somehow get organized.

The word organized means many things to many people. For some it might mean putting their papers in colored file folders, for some it means putting all their seasonings in ABC order, for some it means a clean house, and for others it means being able to retrieve papers that have been stored away.

Even after writing books with a combined total of over 4600 pages and over a million copies in print dealing with the single topic of organization, I'm not sure I have covered all bases for all women. However, I have found the following to be basic requirements when a person wants to become organized.

- *Start with you.* What is it about you that causes you to be disorganized? I find that organized people have a calmness and serenity about them that disorganized people don't have. Search your own self to see what is causing all that confusion. See if you can't get rid of that clutter before you move on. In some cases you may need to meet with your clergy or even a professional counselor who can help you unravel the causes of this disorganization. (I didn't say it was going to be easy to get organized!)

- *Keep it simple.* There are many programs available, but choose one that's simple. You don't want to spend all your time keeping up charts and graphs.

- *Make sure everything has a designated place.* One of our sayings is "Don't put it down, put it away."

Another is "Don't pile it, file it." If there is no place for stuff to go, it's going to get piled. That's one thing you want to prevent—piles.

- *Store like items together.* Bob has his gardening supplies and tools together. I have my laundry items in one place, my bill-paying tools in one area, my prayer basket and its tools together, my cups/saucers, my drinking glasses, and my dinnerware all in their general area. You don't want to spend time going from here to there getting ready for your tasks. Put like things in one place.

- *Even though you are neat, you may not be organized.* I tell my women to use notebook organizers and that there are two things they need to remember: One, write it down; and two, read it. It doesn't do you much good if you write down that birthday date or that appointment on your calendar and yet you forget both because you didn't read it on the calendar. Remember to write and read.

- *Get rid of all items you don't use.* See my *More Hours in My Day* book to help you in this area. It will give you great help in getting rid of all the unused stuff.

- *Invest in the proper tools.* In order to be organized you need proper tools: bins, hooks, racks, containers, lazy Susans, etc.

- *Involve the whole family.* Learn to delegate jobs and responsibilities to other members of the family. My Bob takes care of all the repairs. When something is broken, he is Mr. Fix-It. Depending upon the ages of the children, you will need to tailor-make their chores. Also, change off frequently so they don't get bored. Don't do something yourself that another member of the family can do.

- *Keep master lists.* I've learned to use my three-ring organizer, my three-by-five file cards, and my journals to keep track of all our stuff. Many of these techniques are woven throughout my various books. You may think you'll never forget that you loaned that CD to Brad or that video to Christine, but you will. Write it down and keep the list in a place where you cannot overlook it. (In *Survival for Busy Women* I have some charts on how to do this.)

- *Continually reevaluate your system.* Nothing is written in concrete; it can be changed. See how other people do things, read a book to gather ideas, and evaluate your own system. Change it when it's not working.

- *Use a lot of labels and signs.* If containers, bins, drawers, and shelves aren't labeled, the family won't be able to spot where things go. I have also used color coding to help identify items belonging to various members of the family: blue for Bevan, red for Chad, and purple for Christine. I use a finepoint paint pen very effectively to label clothes, glass and plastic jars, and wooden items. (Don't use water-base pens—they will not last very long.) You can also purchase a label maker for around six dollars at a variety store.

Where to start? Start with these suggestions. Get them under control, and then you can move into more specific areas.

Remember that the end result is to give you more available time to do God's will for your life. People always matter more to the Lord than rules.

> Father God, I thank You for being a God of order. Your examples have been a great inspiration for my life. I appreciate how you take confusion and chaos and make it meaningful. My life has certainly been a living example of that. May my readers see Your model and know that order can be learned and is not just something we are born with.
>
> I certainly like the extra time You give me so I can give You more time doing the ministry You have for me. Amen.

Taking Action

❦ Think on these thoughts: Why are you disorganized? Is there something about your life that is causing chaos? Examine yourself and see what needs to be done internally first.

❦ Go to your hall closet, if you have one, and clean it out. Reorganize the contents, and discard or give away what you are no longer using.

Reading On

Ephesians 5:15,16 Matthew 15:35
Exodus 18:13-26   Mark 6:7

❦

People before things; people before projects; family before friends; husband before children; husband before parents; tithe before wants; Bible before opinions; Jesus before all.

❦

Mary, Martha, Me

Scripture Reading: Luke 10:38-42

Key Verse: Luke 10:42

Mary has chosen the good part, which shall not be taken away from her.

———— ❧ ————

This truly is the dilemma of today's woman. I've been more like Martha than like Mary. I desire to be like Mary, but my Martha side keeps getting in the way. Is Mary the better woman? For the moment she probably had more focus on the priorities that needed immediate attention. As Jesus entered Bethany from a hectic teaching schedule He just wanted to kick back and do the real basics. He didn't want a big party with a lot of people continuing to draw His energy. He had just had a big day and He only wanted a basic meal with the opportunity to get to bed early and have a good night's rest.

I can really relate to that situation. Often after I have given a Friday evening and Saturday seminar a very gracious person on the sponsoring committee wants to have a party in my honor. I deeply appreciate that and will go and be upbeat, courteous, and cheerful, but often I would just as soon take off my dress clothes and shoes, throw myself on the bed of the hotel, and REST. I'm sure that's how Jesus felt on this occasion.

My *Martha* side says I've been waiting for this special guest in my home and I want it to be clean and in order. I'm sure she swept, mopped, scoured, dusted, and cleaned all day. She probably did the dishes, the laundry, the ironing, the dusting, and the cooking. Of course there was the mending and the feeding of the children too. She had worked so hard to make every-thing just right, but now she felt abandoned because Mary, who was to help her, left her side and just sat at Jesus' feet. Martha needed help to carry this party off, but Mary was giving her no help. So Martha became a little impatient.

My *Mary side* says housework can wait; Jesus is more im-portant. He doesn't come this way very often, and I need to spend my time with His needs. I can always tidy up after He journeys on His way.

Martha/Mary/me says I need a balance in my tidiness and in my passion for other people's needs. Discernment is very im-portant as we try to prioritize our activities. In fact Martha got so upset with Mary that she went to Jesus for help. She asked, "Lord, do You not care that my sister has left me to do all the serving alone? Then tell her to help me." I'm sure Martha was disappointed with Jesus' reply: "Martha, Martha, you are wor-ried and bothered about so many things; but only a few things are necessary, really only one, for Mary has chosen the good part, which shall not be taken away from her."

Jesus said that Mary was pleasing Him by paying attention to Him and His situation. It wasn't that Martha's activity wasn't useful, but for the moment the "being" of Mary was bet-ter than the "doing" of Martha. The Martha of me nags to keep my house in order each day, but my Mary side says gen-tly, "I need time to pray." Martha is concerned with what neighbors might think if they drop in and find dishes stacked in the kitchen sink. But Mary answers, "Selfish! I think it's a crime if you don't share with others your talents and time."

Both issues must be addressed in our lives. For us to move effectively as wife, mom, and maybe outside employee, we must learn to say no to good things and save our yes for the very best. We have to balance out the Martha and Mary sides of our lives so that our Lord is pleased with what we do. If we don't take charge of our own lives, someone else will.

Father God, again Scripture has put before me the options of life. Let me be so discerning that I will know when to act properly. I don't want to clean when I need to take care of personal needs around me. On the other hand I don't want to be so casual in ministry that I don't recognize the basic needs of my home and family. Let me balance these out in my life so I can be more effective in serving You. Amen.

Taking Action

❧ When do you need to be more like Martha?

❧ When do you need to be more like Mary?

❧ How will you balance out the two?

❧ Send a card to a needy friend today.

❧ Clean out the silverware drawer.

Reading On

Matthew 20:28   John 12:26
Galatians 5:13   Romans 12:11

❧

A man should be encouraged
to do what the Maker of him
has intended by the making of
him, according as the gifts have
been bestowed on him for that
purpose.

—*Thomas Carlyle*

❧

A Yarmelke Christmas

Scripture Reading: John 8:12-20

Key Verse: John 8:12

I am the light of the world; he who follows Me shall not walk in the darkness, but shall have the light of life.

———— ❧ ————

Finding a happy way to celebrate Christmas with my side of the family has always been difficult. Trying to bond the Jewish side with the Christian beliefs just didn't happen easily. So over the years when the families came to our homes, we would have a country Christmas with a decorated tree, garlands, twinkly lights, angels, and lots of packages. As the years went on, I became braver and braver in incorporating some Christian traditions: tucking Scripture verses under the coffee and tea cups, reading a Christmas story, and even singing Christmas carols. My Jewish family endured these Christian Christmas events over the years.

In 1982 I began to give holiday seminars, which included organizing for Thanksgiving and Christmas, gift giving, gift wrapping, building memories, Christ-centered traditions, and ending the three hours with a "festival of lights." This part is where I tell the story of Hanukkah and describe how it is celebrated in Jewish homes all over the world. I light the menorah candles as the story is told. When all my candles are lit, the room sparkles with the beauty of the candles shining. The lights look like twinkling stars.

But it doesn't end there. As I continue, everyone is still looking at the menorah and its beauty. If we look and watch long enough, the candles eventually burn down, blow out, or spark out. But when we have the light of the Messiah in our hearts the light never goes out.

After eight years of 23 seminars in 45 days, my own light went on as to our own personal family Christmas. Why hadn't I thought of it sooner? So my new plan went into action. I couldn't wait for December to come that year. I sent invitations to all the family as usual, and as usual they all showed up, even my Uncle Hyman's cousin from New York. That year Hanukkah came during our family event date, which was perfect for my new plan. The menorah was on the table and the candles were ready to be lit. As usual, I had the Scripture verses tucked under the cups, with a story ready to be read and songs ready to be sung.

My family, right off, saw the menorah displayed, much to their surprise. We then asked my Uncle Hy to be the acting rabbi for the family and to tell the Hanukkah story and light the candles. A serious smile came over his face and a twinkle lit up his eyes. Yarmelkes were passed out to all the men and even the small young boys. (A yarmelke is a small black cap that is worn only on the crown part of a male's head as a sign of reverence to God.) It was a special sight. My uncle took his job seriously and the short service began. We all stood around him, and the menorah candles began to sparkle their lights throughout the living room. It was wonderful. We then proceeded into the living room for a great traditional turkey meal.

That event totally changed the attitude of my family, and we were praised for a beautiful party and a yarmelke Christmas, tying the two faiths together.

It was the best Christmas ever, and thus began a new tradition in our family.

In our key verse today, Jesus draws an analogy between the sun as the physical light of the world and Himself as the spiritual light of the world. This theme is also mentioned in the ninth chapter of John.

In my own Christian walk, I have found that the light that permeates from Jesus and His Scriptures has given me direction when the way seems dark. Often darkness gives dark advice, so we have to go to a light source to illuminate the truth.

Light is always a threat to darkness. If we go into a gathering where there is darkness and turn on a light, the people gathered there will shout, "Please turn down the lights!" Darkness doesn't like light because it exposes evil deeds.

Father God, help me to remember the needs of those in my family who come from other faiths. May Your spirit be present in times together and open the hearts of those who do not know You personally. It is because of You, Lord, that we can love one another, for Your light gives truth. Amen.

Taking Action

❦ Write a note to a family member and tell him or her one reason why you love him.

❦ Plan ways you can let the light of the Lord shine in your life. What will you specifically do?

❦ Smile and laugh more.

Reading On

John 9:5	Genesis 1:3
John 11:9,10	Psalm 27:1

❦

In darkness there is no choice. It is light that enables us to see the difference between things; and it is Christ who gives us light.

—C.T. Whitmell

❦

What Is Love?

Scripture Reading: 1 Corinthians 13:4-8

Key Verse: 1 Corinthians 13:4-8
Read the complete passage.

———— ❦ ————

One of the most searching questions we have to answer as adults is, "What is love?" We see people who search so hard yet seem to miss the mark and aren't able to grasp love in either their heads or their hearts.

The people of the nineties seem so dysfunctional when it comes to this topic of love. In our reading, hearing, and expounding we seem to miss the mark of what is truly love. As young babies we enter the world with all kinds of love bestowed on us by our parents and grandparents. They make such a fuss over us and give us so much attention, but then we seem to lose grasp of this concept. In most cases they have decided to love us no matter what. Yet, somehow through the years we go from a *decision* to love to a *feeling* of love.

Our modern culture has gone from decision to feeling in a matter of just a few years. From looking around we see that loving and being loved are not as easy as we would like to think.

What started out as mother's love has declined to the point of dysfunction in the current family. We have lost our focus on true love. Some of the confusing signals we get when thinking about love include:

- Falling in and out of love
- A feeling too deep for words

- Never having to say you're sorry
- We'll give it a trial run
- A sickness full of woes
- A warm puppy.

No wonder we're confused when we get serious about true love!

The Greeks understood three levels of love:

- Agape: love for an adorable object
- Eros : physical love between husband and wife
- Phileo: brotherly love for others.

The Western culture tries to describe these relationships by one encompassing word "love." We use a confusing word that doesn't let us define degrees or types of love.

This agape love that is found today in our readings characterizes God (1 John 4:8) and what He manifested in the gift of His Son (John 3:16). It is more than mutual affection; it expresses unselfish esteem of the object loved. Christ's love for us is undeserved and without thought of return. It was and is a decision, not a fuzzy feeling.

> Deeper love . . . down to our
> very soul. It's there we have an
> anchor who will not let us go;
> the Lord who calmed the sea is
> the One who sees us through;
> He's given us a deeper love.
>
> —*Diane Machen*

Our son Brad and his wife, Maria, used this passage in 1 Corinthians at their wedding. This portion of Scripture is used more than any other when two people want to consummate their love in marriage. Unfortunately, many times it is used as good verse and literature, but only lip service is given to the message.

As Paul wrote to the church in Corinth he told them to come together in love rather than chaos and disharmony. He contrasted the present with what Christ would be like in heaven as he showed the supremacy of love over the conflicts of gifts. He began:

> Love is patient, love is kind and is not jealous;
> Love does not brag and is not arrogant,
> Love does not act unbecomingly;
> It does not seek its own, is not provoked,
> Does not take into account a wrong suffered,
> Does not rejoice in unrighteousness,
> But rejoices with the truth;
> Bears all things, hopes all things, endures all things.
> Love never fails.

If we could only recapture this agape love that Paul spoke about, we could become healthy, wholesome, and functional families again. My cry is that love is much more than a warm puppy. It is an act of an unselfish decision to love and honor your commitment made at the altar between husband, wife, and God.

> *Father God, I appreciate Your sharing with me again what love is all about. I sometimes get so confused between decision and feeling. I'm continually bombarded with this concept of feeling good. Truly every day I must willfully decide again to love my mate. Don't ever let me get distracted and become conformed to the world. I want to be transformed by the renewing of my mind. Thank You for giving me a good marriage with a love that encompasses agape, eros, and phileo. Amen.*

Taking Action

- ❦ In your journal list from today's passage what true love is.

- ❦ In what areas of your life has feeling taken over decision?

- ❦ What are you going to do about it?
- ❦ Tell your mate these words today:

    "I believe in you."

    "I want you."

    "You're the greatest."

Reading On

Romans 12:2	1 John 4:8
John 3:16	Deuteronomy 6:5

When iron is rubbed against a
magnet it becomes magnetic.
Just so, love is caught, not
taught. One heart burning with
love sets another on fire. The
church was built on love; it
proves what love can do.

—*Frank C. Laubach*

*If You Are
Only Kind*

Scripture Reading: Ephesians 4:25-32

Key Verse: Ephesians 4:32

> *Be kind to one another, tenderhearted, forgiving each
> other, just as God in Christ also has forgiven you.*

———— ❧ ————

As a society we have forgotten to teach this very important element of character called kindness. Of course our media
doesn't see kindness because that doesn't spark reader and
advertising interest. People have become almost immune to
the truly good things of life. If a movie doesn't have the most
thrilling special effects it won't have people flocking to the
box office to pay for the tremendous budgets of producing
films today.

Even our literature and songs must have violence and
exposé in order to attract attention. Even our schools have
left out the teaching of character. Our students have a very
difficult time learning about values, and when they do, the
question arises, "Whose and what?" Going to biblical principles is prohibited because of confusion on the subject of
"church and state." Therefore it is up to our homes and
churches to teach about kindness. As parents we have to
have a specific desire to teach such values.

We can go to our Christian bookstore and ask for referrals on
books, videos, and music that have a message of values. The modern Christian bookstore is a tremendous resource on such topics.

Ways that Bob and I have found to be effective in teaching good values include:

- reading good literature to the children on a regular basis;
- modeling good character traits in the home;
- listening to wholesome music;
- not watching television very often and restricting certain sitcoms that are downers;
- making sure the children are involved in good youth organizations that teach values;
- having the children be involved around strong models who exhibit like values;
- encouraging strong, outside-the-immediate-family support from Sunday school teachers, coaches, aunts, uncles, and grandparents;
- having family conference times where values can be discussed.

Throughout the life of Christ He exhibited various acts of kindness in how He responded to situations, people, and things.

In our key verse today we see commands that deal with this subject:

- Be kind to one another.
- Be tenderhearted.
- Be forgiving to each other.

Why? Because "God in Christ also has forgiven you." The basis for us as believers forgiving others lies in the fact that we ourselves have been graciously forgiven by God and released from any obligation to make restitution. This concept of understanding what Jesus did for us on the cross is the basis of our kindness to others. We as humans can't forgive unless we understand forgiveness as modeled by God in Christ.

As parents we often spend more time in teaching our children how to be dancers, actors, musicians, athletes, and scholars than in teaching them character values. As a country we need young people who have true strength of character. I challenge you today to think of how you are going to teach your children kindness.

> *Father God, I thank You for forgiving me of my sins. Only by Your grace can I be freed from the imprisonment of unforgiven sin. On the cross Christ paid for all my past, present, and future sins. Because You have forgiven me I am able now to forgive others. Because of this forgiveness, I am able to relate to others with kindness, tenderheartedness, and forgiveness. May I always be true to Your will for my life, and may others see Christ in me. Amen.*

Taking Action

❦ Thank God for your forgiveness as a believer.

❦ If you aren't a believer you may want to investigate the life of Christ and see if you can accept who He was and is.

❦ Develop a plan with your spouse (if you have one) on how you are going to teach values to your children.

Reading On

Proverbs 19:22   2 Corinthians 6:6
Galatians 5:22,23   2 Peter 1:7

MARY'S LAMB

Mary had a little lamb,
Its fleece was white as snow;
And everywhere that Mary went,
The lamb was sure to go.

He followed her to school one day,
Which was against the rule;
It made the children laugh and play,
To see a lamb at school.

And so the teacher turned him out,
But still he lingered near,
And waited patiently about,
Till Mary did appear.

Then he ran to her, and laid
His head upon her arm,
As if he said, "I'm not afraid—
You'll keep me from all harm."

"What makes the lamb love Mary so?"
The eager children cried.
"Oh, Mary loves the lamb, you know,"
The teacher quick replied.

And you each gentle animal
In confidence may bind,
And make them follow at your will,
If you are only kind.

—*Sarah Josepha Hale*

Planning Your Days

Scripture Reading: Matthew 6:25-34

Key Verse: Matthew 6:33

Seek first His kingdom and His righteousness, and all these things shall be added to you.

We live in a very anxious society. Many of us are more worried about tomorrow than today. We bypass all of today's contentment because of our worry about what might happen tomorrow. In our passage today we read that the early Christians asked the same basic questions (verse 31):

- What shall we eat?
- What shall we drink?
- With what shall we clothe ourselves?

Jesus tells them in verse 34, "Do not be anxious for tomorrow, for tomorrow will care for itself. Each day has enough trouble of its own." Then He gives them a formula for establishing the right priorities of life in verse 33: "Seek first His kingdom and His righteousness, and all these things shall be added to you." My Bob and I have used this verse as our mission verse for the last 35 years. Each day we claim these two instructions:

- Seek His kingdom.
- Seek His righteousness.

When we seek these two things we find that our day takes shape and we can say "yes" we will do that or "no" we will not do that. Often we are overwhelmed by having too many things to do. Life offers many good choices on how to schedule our time. But we all have only 24 hours a day. How are we to use those hours effectively?

When we begin to set priorities, we determine what is important and what isn't, and how much time we are willing to give each activity.

The Bible gives us guidelines for the godly ordering of our lives:

- Our personal relationship to Him (Matthew 6:33; Philippians 3:8).

- Our time for home and family (Genesis 2:24; Psalm 127:3; 1 Timothy 3:2-5).

- Our time for work (1 Thessalonians 4:11,12).

- Our time for ministry and community activities (Colossians 3:17).

We cannot do all the things that come our way. My Bob and I have a saying that helps us when we have too many choices: "Say no to the good things and save each yes for the best."

Don't be afraid to say no. If you have established Matthew 6:33 as one of the key verses in your life you can very quickly decide whether a particular opportunity will help you to—

- seek God's kingdom;

- seek God's righteousness.

After learning to say no easily, you can begin to major on the big things of life and not get bogged down with issues that don't really matter.

Father God, since You are a God of order I also want to have order in my life. Thank You for sharing this verse with our family many years ago. It has certainly helped us to major on the major and minor on the minor issues of life. May other women get excited about not being anxious for tomorrow and realize that You take care of our daily needs. Amen.

Taking Action

❦ Look in the mirror and say no 10 times. Do this every day for a week.

❦ Memorize Matthew 6:33 and write it in your journal.

❦ Each morning write out a "to-do list." After each activity write yes or no. Then disregard each no.

❦ Rank each yes in order of importance. (Let the most important one be number 1.)

❦ Cross off each activity as you get it accomplished.

Reading On

Psalm 119:105   1 Corinthians 14:40
Psalm 32:8   Luke 5:15,16

Do all the good you can, By all
the means you can, In all the
ways you can, In all the places
you can, At all the times you
can, To all the people you can,
As long as ever you can.

—*John Wesley*

The Blankie

Scripture Reading: John 14:27-31

Key Verse: John 14:27

> *Peace I leave with you; My peace I give to you. Not as the world gives do I give to you. Let not your heart be troubled, nor let it be fearful.*

When our first grandchild was born, her parents named her Christine Marie. Christine from her mother's middle name and Marie from my middle name. As a namesake I'm very proud of Christine Marie. At this writing she is our only granddaughter, along with four grandsons. We love them too!

From flannel fabric I made her a piece of pink-printed blanket with some small roses. The blanket was edged with a pink satin binding. It was only about 8 inches square. Well, as you might guess, it became her security blankie while she sucked her thumb. The blankie got twisted, wadded up, and smoothed by little Christine. She was finally able to pull loose an end and twist the threads around her fingers.

Christine loved her pink rosebud blankie. It gave her comfort when she was hurt, softness when she was afraid, and security when she felt alone. Then one day five years later the blankie got folded one last time and was put in an envelope that she tucked away in her dresser drawer.

Christine was 13 recently, and from time to time she still pulls out that envelope to look at the rosebud flannel security blanket.

Jesus is like the security blanket that Christine once held close to her—only today she has almighty God our Heavenly Father, God the Son, and God the Holy Spirit to hold tight to.

As our Scripture states, Jesus is who gives us peace in the midst of the storms of life: when we are going through that difficult tornado of a broken marriage, the death of a dream, financial troubles, childless pain, ill health, or all the other trials we encounter in just living out our daily lives.

Christ is our security blanket when we are afraid and feel fearful of tomorrow. My mama used to tell me in the middle of the night when I needed to go to the bathroom but was afraid of the dark, "Be afraid, but go." Today I know I can go because I have my Lord, who is with me wherever I go. When I'm weak and upset, He holds me and comforts my heart.

Jesus is much more than a security blanket. He is our Comforter, our Savior, the Messiah, the Alpha and Omega, the Almighty, our bright and morning star, our counselor, our strength, our redeemer, our peace, our high priest, our foundation, and our master builder.

First Corinthians 3:11 says, "No man can lay a foundation other than the one which is laid, which is Jesus Christ."

It's time to give our blanket over to Jesus and allow Him to be our Master Comforter.

Christine's blankie is now in a beautiful frame, hanging on the wall in her bedroom as a treasured memory of her babyhood. She will carry this along her lifetime from babyhood into her golden years. But best of all, she will carry Jesus in her heart for eternity.

> *Father God, thank You for letting me put away my old childhood security blanket and giving me the faith to trust You in all situations. May I never go back to my blankie. You have been so faithful to me during these adult years. You are all I need—nothing else. Amen.*

The Blankie

Taking Action

- List all the security blankets in your life.
- Recall a childhood memory and write it in your journal.
- Write down a time when God comforted you in difficult times. Thank Him again for that comfort.
- Praise God today for who He is, the Almighty God.

Reading On

Psalm 4:5	Isaiah 26:4
Proverbs 3:5	Hebrews 2:13

When I was a child, I used to speak as a child, think as a child, reason as a child. When I became a man, I did away with childish things.

—1 Corinthians 13:11

□ □ □

You Are Not Alone

Scripture Reading: Matthew 6:1-13

Key Verse: Matthew 6:9-13 (The Lord's Prayer)
Read the Lord's Prayer.

———— ❦ ————

Some of you may not have a prayer life at all. Others of you may have a very vital prayer life. Some of you want to have a prayer life but are fumbling with it because you don't know how to incorporate it into your life or how to organize it. I was once in that position. I was fumbling in my prayer life because I didn't know the steps to take. One of my first learnings was to trust God for my every care. Often in life I had been disappointed by those I trusted, but the following helped me realize I was never alone.

ONE SET OF FOOTPRINTS

One night a man had a dream. In his dream he was walking along the beach with the Lord, when across the sky flashed all the events of his life. However, for each scene he noticed two sets of footprints in the sand, one belonging to him and the other to the Lord. When the last scene had flashed before him, he looked back at the footprints and noticed that many times along the path there was only one set of footprints in the sand. He also noticed that this happened during the lowest and saddest times of his life.

This really bothered him, so he said to the Lord, "You promised that once I decided to follow You, You would walk with me all the way, but I noticed that during the roughest times of my life there was only one set of footprints. I don't understand why You deserted me when I needed You the most."

The Lord replied, "My precious child, I love you and I would never leave you. During those times of trial and suffering when you saw only one set of footprints, it was then that I carried you."

—Author Unknown

You see, God is always with us. When the times are the lowest, that's when He picks us up and carries us. Isn't that wonderful! Some of us right now are in a position where we're being carried through a rough situation or problem in our life. It's wonderful to know that we have our Lord there to carry us when times get low and things get rough.

Often we don't take the necessary time with our Lord in prayer and communication. But do you know what? He loves us anyway. He loves us unconditionally. Prayer doesn't have to be long, either. Sometimes we get turned off because we feel it takes so much time, but it doesn't have to be long.

In several of my books I have given you a way in which you can organize your daily prayer life so you aren't overwhelmed with this phase of your spiritual life. Please refer to those chapters which give you a step-by-step plan for an organized prayer life. As I introduce ladies to prayer who aren't accustomed to a disciplined life of prayer, I want them first to be exposed to the model prayer as found in today's readings. The Lord's Prayer—

- begins with adoration of God (verse 9);

- acknowledges subjection to His will (verse 10);

- asks petitions of Him (verses 11-13a);

- ends with praise (verse 13b).

To better understand this prayer, we break it down into small phrases with their meanings. This gives us a model for all our prayers.

- "Our Father who art in heaven" (verse 9a). Recognize who He is—the Person of God.

- "Hallowed be Thy name" (verse 9b). Worship God because of who He is.

- "Thy kingdom come. Thy will be done" (verse 10). Seek and do God's will. His Word is the way to find His will.

- "Give us this day our daily bread" (verse 11). Ask God to meet your everyday needs in order to perform your godly work.

- "And forgive us our debts" (verse 12). Ask God for pardon and forgiveness in your daily failures.

- "And do not lead us into temptation" (verse 13). Ask for protection from the evils of temptation.

- "For Thine is the kingdom and the power and the glory" (verse 13). Praise God for who He is.

Father God, I so appreciate the Lord's Prayer. So many times in life I am able to recite it in moments of need and praise. I thank You for being my heavenly Father. Since my earthly father lacked some parenting skills that a young daughter needed, I find You a great support and encouragement for me in time of need. With You I find I am never alone. Amen.

Taking Action

- ❦ Memorize this model prayer.
- ❦ Recite it every night for a week before going to sleep.
- ❦ Write it down in your journal.
- ❦ Thank God for being your Father.

Reading On

Romans 8:15	1 John 5:14
Psalm 18:3	Philippians 4:9

--- ❦ ---

The true test of walking in the
Spirit will not be the way we
act but the way we react to the
daily frustrations of life.

—*Beverly LaHaye*

--- ❦ ---

The Mitt

Scripture Reading: Isaiah 58:1-11

Key Verse: Isaiah 58:11a
The Lord will continually guide you.

———— ❧ ————

It was our son Brad's first real leather baseball mitt. His dad taught him how to break it in with special break-in oil. The oil was rubbed into the pocket of the glove, then Brad tossed his baseball from hand to hand to form a pocket just right for him. Brad loved his mitt and worked for hours each day to make a comfortable mitt just for him. He was so happy to have such a special glove at his baseball practices and games.

One afternoon after practice one of the older boys asked to see Brad's mitt. He looked it over and then threw it into the grassy field. Brad ran to find his special possession, but he couldn't find it. Nowhere was his mitt to be found. With a frightened and hurt heart, Brad came home in tears with no mitt.

After he told me the story I encouraged him that it had to be there somewhere. "I'll go with you, Brad, and we'll search the lot until we find it." "But, Mom, I did search the lot and it's not there," replied Brad tearfully. So I said, "Brad, let's pray and ask God to help us." By now it was beginning to get dark and we needed to hurry, so into the car we jumped. As I drove Brad to the baseball field we asked God to guide our steps directly to the glove. Parking quickly, we both headed for the field. As I held Brad's hand we asked God to put us in the right direction.

Immediately Brad released my hand and ran into the tall grass of the field—and there about 20 feet away was Brad's glove.

Brad is a grown man today, with sons of his own. May he never forget that God always answers our prayers. Sometimes the answer is wait, yes, or later. For Brad and me, that day it was yes: "I'll direct you to find the mitt of a young boy whose heart is broken because of a bully kid and a lost glove."

> I know Christ dwells wihin me
> all the time, guiding me and in-
> spiring me whenever I do or say
> anything. A light of which I
> caught no glimmer before
> comes to me at the very mo-
> ment when it is needed.
>
> —*Saint Therese of Lisieux*

Do you have a "lost glove" today? Go before God and pray Isaiah 58:11a. If God says it, we need to believe it. He *will* direct you and guide you. Open your heart to hear His direction, and then press ahead. The grass may seem too tall for you to see very far, but trust the Lord and keep walking until you feel the peace that the found mitt will give you. God may lead in a direction that we least expect, but if we don't step forward in His direction, how will we ever know if the lost mitt will be there?

Father God, help me today to trust Your Word. Help me to walk in the field of grass as You continually guide me. Most of all, help me to trust You even when I don't feel like trusting because I just can't seem to find the mitt. Thank You, Lord, that You do care for a little boy's lost glove. Thank You for the peace in my heart as I hold Your hand of direction. Amen.

Taking Action

- Thank God today for five things in your life.

- Call a friend in need and pray with her by phone.

- Thank God that He is in control and that He will lead you to the answer of your prayers.

Reading On

Proverbs 15:8	Matthew 18:19,20
1 Thessalonians 5:17	Romans 8:35

I have been driven many times to my knees by the overwhelming conviction that I had nowhere else to go.

—*Abraham Lincoln*

A Mark of Distinction

Scripture Reading: 2 Samuel 14:25,26

Key Verse: 2 Samuel 14:26

When he cut the hair of his head . . . he weighed the hair of his head at 200 shekels.

———— ❧ ————

All throughout history, hair has been a mark of distinction. The length, color, and style have been focal points in all societies. When our children were in junior high and high school our heated discussions were related to hair fashion.

Even today as I read popular magazines I see striking advertising relating to hair care. My Bob always tells me that I and most women friends of ours think the next new hairstylist will be the one who recaptures our youth with the perfect hairstyle. It is true that most of us are looking for the hair designer who will cut, tone, and color our hair the best. Shampoos and rinses are also popular searches for us. We realize that hair and its proper care mean a lot to the American culture.

In the Old Testament, Absalom had beautiful hair that was admired by many. Today's verse states that he weighed his hair and found it to be 200 shekels, or about three or four pounds in our measurement. That's a lot of hair!

Length of hair in the New Testament was considered a mark of distinction between men and women (1 Corinthians 11:14,15). A woman's long hair is given to her for a covering. Hair represents the proper covering in the natural realm, even as the veil is the proper covering in the religious realm.

The veil of the temple was the heavily woven curtain that hung between the Holy Place and the Most Holy Place (Luke 23:45; Hebrews 9:3). Its presence was a continual reminder of the separation between mankind and God. The writer of Hebrews states that the veil represented Jesus' body (Hebrews 10:19,20). The tearing of the veil at Jesus' death on the cross signified the removal of the barrier between God and anyone who would accept Jesus' sacrifice (Hebrews 4:16; 6:19).

Scripture addresses several areas relating to hair:

- Excessive adornment of hair (1 Timothy 2:9; 1 Peter 3:3).

- Wisdom and experience of those with gray hair (1 Samuel 12:2; Job 15:10).

- Ointment for hair as a mark of hospitality (Luke 7:46).

We have also worked hair-related phrases from Scripture into our culture:

- "Not one hair of his head [shall] fall to the ground" (1 Samuel 14:45).

- "More numerous than the hairs of my head" (Psalm 40:12).

- "The very hairs of your head are all numbered" (Matthew 10:30).

What we take as everyday fashion sometimes has tremendous religious significance and origination. Our hair truly is a mark of distinction that needs to be respected as God's gift to us. First Peter 3:3,4 says, "Let not your adornment be merely external—braiding the hair; and wearing gold jewelry, or putting on dresses; but let it be the hidden person of the heart, with the imperishable quality of a gentle and quiet spirit, which is precious in the sight of God."

Father God, I truly want to have the heart that reflects the quality of a gentle and quiet spirit. Each day I yearn to be acceptable in Your sight by my speech, attitude, selection of clothes, and outward adornment. I want to be sensitive in these areas so I'm not offensive to another brother or sister in Christ. Don't let me get mired down in worldly fashions that send out the wrong signals to those around me. Amen.

Taking Action

❧ Evaluate your external adornment. Would it be precious in the sight of God?

❧ List the areas that wouldn't glorify God. What changes need to be made?

❧ How is your gentle and quiet spirit doing?

❧ What changes need to be made in this area?

Reading On

1 Corinthians 11:14,15   Hebrews 10:19,20
1 Peter 3:3,4   1 Timothy 2:9

❧

God's fingers can touch nothing
but to mold it into loveliness.
—*George MacDonald*

❧

□ □ □

Like a Counterfeit
$100 Bill

Scripture Reading: 1 Samuel 2:11-30

Key Verse: 1 Samuel 2:30b
*Far be it from Me—for those who honor Me I will honor,
and those who despise Me will be lightly esteemed.*

———— ❦ ————

A young man had just graduated from law school and
had set up an office, proudly displaying his shingle out
front. On his first day at work, as he sat at his desk with his
door open, he wondered how to get his first client. Then
he heard footsteps coming down the long corridor toward
his office.

Not wanting this potential client to think he would be
his first, he quickly picked up the telephone and began to
talk loudly to a make-believe caller.

"Oh, yes sir," the young lawyer exclaimed into the
phone, "I'm very experienced in corporate law. . . . Court-
room experience? Why, yes, I've had several cases."

The sound of steps drew closer to his open door.

"I have broad experience in almost every category of
legal work," he continued, loud enough for his impending
visitor to hear.

Finally, with the steps right at his door, he replied,
"Expensive? Oh, no sir, I'm very reasonable. I'm told my
rates are among the lowest in town."

The young lawyer then excused himself from his "conversation" and covered the phone to respond to the prospective client who was now standing in the doorway. With his most confident voice he said, "Yes, sir, may I help you?"

"Well, yes, you can," the man said with a smirk. "I'm the telephone repairman, and I've come to hook up your phone!"[17]

We sometimes fake the Christian life in this same way. Preoccupied with self and wanting our own way, we ignore God and pretend to be spiritual. Instead of having Christ's character imprinted on our lives, we go our own way, and our Christianity becomes a forgery. Like a counterfeit $100 bill, we may look real, but we lack genuine value.

Do we fake the Christian life ourselves? On Sunday, do we act and talk Christian, but come Monday or when we are away from church, do we forget all about our Christianity? If so, we are just like the young lawyer. We look good, we talk good, and we act good, but our communication to God isn't right.

We feel best when our heart is in good relationship to God. On the other hand, when we are disobedient to God we place a terrible yoke of guilt upon ourselves. On these occasions we feel like the counterfeit $100 bill—worthless.

Each day as we awake from our sleep we have two basic decisions to make:

- Not to obey God today.
- To obey God today.

What we choose each day will determine our course for that day and eventually for our entire life. For us to live by faith in God we have to be active in choosing what is right. True faith is not passive; it is an active process. Does this mean that if we choose to disobey God we will have a bad day and if we choose to obey God we will have a good day? I wish it were that easy, but sometimes the opposite is true.

In our Scripture for today we see how Eli's sons fell under God's disapproval because of their wrong choices in disobeying God. Eli's two sons were in the priesthood of the nation of Israel, but they were not interested in serving their father's God. First Samuel 2:12 says they were worthless men and didn't know the Lord. They were willfully disobedient and scorned God's commands. So in verse 30b God says, "Far be it from me—for those who honor me I will honor, and those who despise me will be lightly esteemed."

The one who obeys will be honored by God, but the one who disobeys will be lightly esteemed by God. As we look at those who live a life of disobedience toward God, we see dysfunctional people in today's society. Eli's family would also have been a good example of such dysfunction.

"Dysfunctional families have common patterns:

- They do not talk (keeping family secrets);
- They do not see (ignoring inappropriate behavior as well as altered perception of reality);
- They do not feel (disregarding legitimate emotions);
- They do not trust (living in isolation and fearing more broken promises).

The children strive desperately to be perfect, trying to meet all parental expectations."[18]

What our hurting country needs today is a great spiritual revival that will touch people's hearts to want to obey God. The end result will be a nation that is honored for obeying God.

You as a parent can start that revival by announcing to the world that you and your family will serve the Lord God, and that you are no longer willing to live the life of a counterfeit $100 bill. You want to be an authentic Christian.

Father God, I don't want to be a fake Christian. I want to be real in all aspects of my life. When my family sees me, I want them to know what a real Christian looks like. Help me to train my children to be believers of Your commandments. Thank You, Lord, for letting me hold my head up high because I know I am special in Your sight. Amen.

Taking Action

❦ List three to five new goals to become a better model as a Christian woman.

❦ How are you going to teach your child(ren) to be lovers of God?

❦ What changes will you implement in your relationship with your husband?

❦ Complete this thought in your journal: "I know God loves me because _____."

Reading On

1 Corinthians 3:16	1 Corinthians 12:1-31
Ephesians 2:10	Ruth 1:16,17

Self-discipline never means giving up anything, for giving up is a loss. Our Lord did not ask us to give up things of earth, but to exchange them for better things.

—*Fulton J. Sheen*

☐ ☐ ☐

Hurting Hearts

Scripture Reading: Matthew 19:3-12

Key Verse: Matthew 19:6
What therefore God has joined together, let no man separate.

Over 41 years ago my Bob and I made a commitment to God that we would live together for better or for worse, in sickness and in health. At the time it was a piece of cake to make that promise to God. We were young, naive, and very much in love. All we could think of was getting married, making a cozy home, and living happily ever after.

I wish it were as easy as that, but life brings many turns, curves, mountains, and valleys. We've experienced all the above and we've not ended the journey yet. There will be more to come as we continue on our road of marriage.

The one reason Bob and I are still celebrating anniversaries is because we both believe in commitment and the Word of God. Yes, there were times we could have bailed out when our marriage was cold or lukewarm, but we kept lighting the fire, mending the rips and tears in our relationship, and working on new and creative ways to build our marriage. We've gone to workshops, seminars, retreats, and whatever we could to build a strong wall around us to protect us from the enemy's attack. We wanted this so both our children could feel secure in a home where Mom and Dad honored and respected each other.

But formulas don't always work: The walls can crumble in spite of them. Today over 50 percent of first marriages end in divorce, and 60 percent of second marriages. The children are the ones who suffer the most; they are the true victims.

So what is the answer? It begins at the start of the marriage: the commitment made followed by a lot of hard work. Premarital counseling for six months is not too much anymore. Building a strong foundation and cleaning up the trash and baggage in our lives is critical before the "I do's" are said.

When parents of friends of ours divorced after 32 years of marriage, with five grown children and several grandchildren, they brought distress to the whole family. Yes, they had had a lot of valleys, but they also had had a lot of joys. But when a mate decides not to be married any longer, the walls fall as if hit by a major earthquake. For an adult, it seems like it wouldn't hurt when Mom and Dad divorce, but as our friends said, it's even harder because you're old enough to know all the garbage that goes with divorce.

Our typist's parents divorced when she was in her late twenties, and her world fell apart. Is it easy to be loyal to both parents in such a case? I don't think so. Usually there is a struggle to avoid taking sides. The Word of God states strongly that God hates divorce (Malachi 2:16). Yes, hearts can change, wounds can heal, God forgives, and life goes forward. But we always live with the consequences of a broken marriage, a broken home, and broken children.

God's purpose in creating man and woman (husband and wife) is for them to become "one flesh." It is a oneness of kinship or fellowship, with the physical body as the medium causing marriage to reach the deepest physical and spiritual unity. (See Genesis 2:24.)

The binding commitment of marriage does not depend upon human wills or upon what any individual does or does not do, but rather upon God's original design and purpose for marriage (Hosea 3:1-3).

God rejects divorce for several reasons:

- Marriage is a divine institution (Genesis 1:27; 2:18, 20-25).

- Marriage is by the command of the Creator (Matthew 19:4-6).

- Marriage brings two people together as one (Genesis 2:24; Matthew 19:6).

- Jesus points to the first couple (Matthew 19:8).

- Bad consequences comes with separation (Matthew 19:9).

God does hate divorce, but He also desires to work redemptively when the person who has experienced this tragedy is repentant and desires reconciliation to God.

From my own heart I know the pain. I'm watching the consequences at the time of this writing. Our daughter is in divorce proceedings after 2½ years of separation from her husband.

I've learned much through this experience. God is teaching me to trust Him, forgive others, and thank Him in all things through the name of Jesus.

I still believe in commitment and reconciliation, and I believe we have an awesome God. Today is the first day of the rest of our lives. Let's move ahead and take action.

Father God, help me today to take action to forgive and forget. Especially help me to look at the positive and to thank You for that. I don't want to dwell on the negative, for every day with Jesus is sweeter than the day before. Be with those who are considering breaking their marital commitment. Give them the faith and strength to live out the Scriptures. Amen.

Taking Action

- ❦ Recommit to your original marriage commitment.
- ❦ If forgiveness is needed, go to God and ask Him to help you forgive the one who may have hurt you.
- ❦ Put the past to rest. Don't look back, but move ahead with the power of the Lord in your life.

Reading On

John 15:5	Genesis 2:24
Psalm 37:5,6	Matthew 5:32

God can do wonders with a
broken heart if you give Him all
the pieces.

—*Victor Alfsen*

The Bed and Breakfast

Scripture Reading: 1 Peter 4:1-9

Key Verse: 1 Peter 4:9
Cheerfully share your home with those who need a meal or a place to stay for the night (TLB).

———— 🌱 ————

Over the past few years we have had the opportunity to stay in many "bed and breakfasts" as well as some lovely inns. Our friends Rich and Sue Gregg are continually opening their home to missionaries, students, and anyone else who needs a room for a short period of time (although some have stayed longer than initially intended).

Those who come to visit and stay in our one guest room, which we have named the "Princess Room," have commented that we should open it as a bed and breakfast. We named our room after our daughter, who we called "Princess" when she was a young girl at home. We hope to give our guests the feeling of being treated as a prince or princess when they sleep in the high bed with the down mattress and cozy bedding.

With their wake-up call is presented a tray of hot fresh coffee, tea, a candle, flowers, toast, and a scone or some other type of early morning beginning, all at no charge. This is all fun and easy for me to do with a cheerful heart. However, the Scripture for today says we should share our home "with those who need a meal." Would I readily bring home the person standing in the park or by the street corner who has no home?

—————— ❦ ——————

In today's social climate one should use some discretion when hosting strangers.

Every week our church cooks a meal for the homeless in Fairmont Park. Our grandchildren have gone several times to help serve some of these meals. In downtown Los Angeles, as well as in many cities all over the country, bed and breakfasts are provided for the street people. They're not as fancy and beautiful as the ones we've stayed in, but they provide an opportunity for the homeless to shower, eat, sleep, and hear the Word of God.

All of this reminds me to be thankful for what we have. I say often in my seminars that we can always find someone who has less than we have, as well as those who have more. Let's be thankful for what we have, and make the best of that to glorify God in it.

Let's open our doors to the helpless. Let's share a meal and provide a respite in the life of a busy, stressed-out friend or even one who is just in need of some stillness in his or her life.

God says we are to have a cheerful heart in our hospitality. Let us also give another person a cheerful heart today. Regardless of how large or small a home we may have, we can share it with someone else and break bread together. Your church can help you find someone in need, or perhaps you could simply invite someone home from church for soup and bread.

"Hospitality is the practice of welcoming, sheltering, and feeding—with no thought of personal gain—those who come to our door. Much more than elegant menus, elaborate table settings, or lavish entertainment—hospitality is sharing what we have and who we are with whomever God sends. Hospitality includes setting aside time for fellowship and being flexible in order to accommodate impromptu gatherings."[19]

You can share your heart and your life with others, even if the meal is simple and the setting is humble. The most important gift of welcome simply says, "I care, I love you, and I have prepared a place for you."

> *Father God, please give me a cheerful heart for others. Help me to meet a need in someone's life who has less than I do. Thank You for those who share a ministry to the homeless. May I also be a light in the time of darkness to those who need to hear about You and Your Word. Amen.*

Taking Action

❧ Plan to help serve a meal to someone in need. Perhaps this could be during the Thanksgiving or Christmas seasons.

❧ Involve your children and family in taking a meal to a needy family.

❧ Make today a day to have a cheerful spirit for Jesus.

Reading On

Proverbs 15:17   Matthew 10:42
Titus 1:8   Matthew 6:1-4

You can make more friends in two months by becoming interested in other people than you can in two years by trying to get other people interested in you.

—*Dale Carnegie*

Making Time for Stillness

Scripture Reading: Ecclesiastes 3:1-8

Key Verse: Ecclesiastes 3:1

> *There is an appointed time for everything. And there is a time for every event under heaven.*

———— ❧ ————

I know the objection that is already bubbling up in your mind: Who has time?

It's a common complaint—and a valid one.

It's true that the battle is on between Satan and the spirit of stillness. (The father of lies absolutely thrives on chaos and misery!) And it really isn't easy to eliminate all the distractions—the dust, the dirty clothes, the orders that need filing; timers buzzing, phones ringing, children needing us.

But here's what I've discovered: The people who find time for stillness are the people who have the energy and perspective to stay on top of their hectic "outer" lives.

And we're not alone as we struggle to find time for stillness. I truly believe that if we just recognize our daily need, God will help us discover ways to implement our needed quiet times.

Anne Ortlund, whose books on the godly life have influenced a generation of Christian women, tells of a time when she had three children under three and not a spare moment in her day. Longing for a time of quiet with the Lord, she tried desperate measures.

Normally I sleep like a rock, but I said, "Lord, if you'll help me, I'll meet you from two to three a.m." I kept my time with him until the schedule lightened; I didn't die, and I'm not sorry I did it. Everybody has 24 hours. We can soak ourselves in prayer, in his Word, in himself, if we really want to.

With God's help we can do whatever we really want to do and make time for whatever we feel is a priority in our lives. Could you watch TV 25 percent less? Could you get up 15 minutes earlier or half an hour later to take advantage of a quiet house? Could you trade off meal preparation in return for babysitting? With creativity and God's help, you can make space for stillness.

Perhaps the most important means of making time for stillness is the most obvious: Schedule it! Most of us have a tendency to schedule time for work, chores, errands, and family, but leave our quiet time to happenstance. What happens? We manage to take care of work, chores, errands, and family, but somehow the quiet time falls by the wayside!

One friend of mine attended a one-day professional seminar at a cost of 250 dollars. I was eager to find out what was the one most important thing she had learned. She reported that this high-level course had taught her two important things: 1) Make a "to do" list, and 2) on that list, schedule quality time alone each day!

No one else can do it for you; you are the one who must make it and take it for yourself. Purposefully make yourself unavailable to the rest of the world each day and be available to God, yourself, and ultimately to others.

It doesn't have to be a large block of time. Fifteen minutes here and there can save you. Try getting up 15 minutes earlier so you can be utterly alone—or, if you're a night owl, stay up after everyone else is in bed. Ask a neighbor to watch the kids for just half an hour while you lock the bathroom door, sprinkle a few bath crystals in the tub, and enjoy a time of solitude and relaxation. Stake out a table in a quiet coffee shop in between car pool expeditions—or park your car under a quiet tree and enjoy a time of quiet communion with God.

Whenever possible, try to schedule longer quiet time, too. Author and speaker Florence Littauer travels all over the world, yet she will schedule an extra day here and there just to be alone. She orders room service and just enjoys her time reading, thinking, journaling . . . and just spending time with God. I've learned this from Florence and on occasion will do the same thing. I call it my "catch-up" day—time alone to journal, read magazines and newspaper articles, and do other things that refresh my mind and relieve tension. My favorite thing to do for myself is to listen to classical or praise strings, put on a beauty mask, crawl up on our bed, and read *Virtue or Victoria* magazines.

If you have small children, such a "day off for stillness" may seem like an impossible dream. Even 15 minutes of solitude may seem out of reach. And I will admit that those years when little ones have first rights on your time can be a challenge. I know that you can't schedule preschoolers, and help is often hard to find. And yet . . . there really are ways to nuture the spirit of stillness even in the midst of the loveable chaos.[20]

I have to giggle every time I think of what my daughter Jenny used to do to give herself some quiet time. With three children aged two, four, and six, it was pretty difficult to find time for herself. So she put a beauty mask on her face and the faces of all three children. She used a green mud-type mask, since they loved to have green faces with white eyes and rosy lips. Then all three lay face-up on one bed. They knew their mask would crack if they talked or smiled or wiggled, so they lay very still. Jenny then got on the bed with a magazine and put on soft music, and they all relaxed. Often the children would go to sleep. I was amazed that it really worked.

Another day when the children were driving Jenny crazy about 4:30 in the afternoon (the disaster hour), Jenny stripped off their clothes and put all three in a bubble bath. Then she darkened the bathroom, lit a candle, sprayed some cologne, and sat down on the floor to read her Bible. I know it was God who calmed these cute monkeys down and gave Jenny a few moments of stillness. Now the children often ask Mom for a bubble bath with candlelight!

After all, children benefit from the spirit of stillness too. Small ones may seem to generate chaos, but immature nervous systems and bodies weary from the work of growing get the rest they need in an environment of order and peace. We do our children a favor when we teach them to find the spirit of stillness within themselves and make it a part of their lives.

My Bob and I purposely set aside chunks of our yearly schedule just to be alone with each other and rethink our lives. We work hard all year, fulfilling over a hundred speaking engagements all over the country. Schedules, interviews, and travel keep us on the move. We have to make space for the spirit of stillness, or we would quickly lose track of each other . . . and grow out of touch with God.

The door to stillness really is there waiting for any of us to open it and go through, but it won't open itself. We have to choose to make the spirit of stillness a part of our lives.

I have not always appreciated the value of stillness the way I do now. In fact, I have always been the active, on-the-go type. But I am 50-plus in years now and a grandmother. Finally I am understanding the full importance of quiet time. And it's part of my privilege as a teacher of young women (see Titus 2:4) to share my growing appreciation of the spirit of stillness to show how stillness can enrich our lives and replenish our spirit.

I've come to realize that all people need to get away from everything and everybody on a regular basis for thought, prayer, and just rest. For me this includes both daily quiet times and more extended periods of relaxation and replenishment. And it includes both times spent with my husband and periods of true solitude, spent with just me and God. These times of stillness offer me the chance to look within and nurture the real me. They keep me from becoming frazzled and depleted by the world around me.

I would say the ideal balance between outward and inward pursuit should be about 50-50. By "outward" I mean working toward goals and deadlines, negotiating needs and privileges, coping with stress, taking care of daily chores, striving toward retirement—in other words, getting things done. "Inward" things include tuning in to my spiritual self, talking to God, exploring the sorrows, hopes, and dreams that make up the inner me, and just relaxing in God's eternal presence.

When I was younger, my life was tilted more outward and less inward. As I grow and mature (and perhaps reach another stage of my life), I find I'm leaning more toward the inward. I want my life to be geared more toward heaven. I want to lift my life, my hands, my head, and my body toward God, to spend more time alone with him—talking, listening, and just being. I want to experience the fragrance of His love and let that love permeate my life, to let the calmness of His Spirit replenish the empty well of my heart, which gets depleted in the busyness and rush of the everyday demands and pressures.

I want those things for you, too. That's why I urge you: *Do whatever is necessary to nurture the spirit of stillness in your life.* Don't let the enemy wear you so thin that you lose your balance and perspective. Regular time for stillness is as important and necessary as sleep, exercise, and nutritional food.

Father God, You rested on the seventh day, and I sense a need for more stillness in my life. My nerves and patience wear thin throughout all the demands on my life. When I stop and take time for You, a quietness falls upon me and I can regenerate my battery. I have observed that people do what they want to do, and I want to be STILL. Help me to keep this as a desire of my heart. Amen.

Taking Action

❧ Dejunk your junkiest room. Clutter wearies the spirit and fights against stillness.

❧ Keep a Bible, writing paper, and a pen on your bedside table for spiritual food during still moments.

❧ Make a list of sounds, smells, and places that tend to trigger a spirit of stillness in you.

❧ Try setting aside a "quiet corner" at home with inspirational books, comfortable cushions, and a warm light.

Reading On

Psalm 37:7	Hebrews 9:28
Isaiah 40:31	Psalm 139:8

—— ❧ ——

Don't pray when you feel like it. Have an appointment with the Lord and keep it. A man is powerful on his knees.

—*Corrie ten Boom*

—— ❧ ——

Make Time for You

Scripture Reading: Matthew 22:34-40

Key Verse: Matthew 22:37,39

> *You shall love the Lord your God with all your heart, and with all your soul, and with all your mind. . . . You shall love your neighbor as yourself.*

God originally gave the above verses of Scripture in Deuteronomy 6:4-9 to the Jewish nation as part of their Shema, which became Judaism's basic confession of faith. According to rabbinic law, this passage was to be recited every morning and night. The passage stresses the uniqueness of God, precludes the worship of other gods, and demands a total love commitment.

In Matthew 22 Jesus was asked, "Teacher, which is the great commandment in the Law?" He gave two commandments which stress three loves: the love of God, the love of self, and the love of your neighbor. In our churches we are taught to love God and to love our neighbors, but we are also taught that we are not to dwell too long on our personal selves. I have found many women who do not know how to care for themselves. As women we always seem to be giving so much to others in our family that there is no time left for us.

As a young woman and a new bride, and then as a new mother, I was always tired. I had no energy left over for me, and we most certainly didn't have enough money left over from our budget to give me anything. So what did I do for myself? Not very much. But after studying this passage of

Scripture, I was challenged to study the subject of personal value in the sight of God—not an overemphasis on self, but a balanced and moderate approach that would let me grow as an individual. I knew that if God was going to make me a complete and functioning person in the body of Christ I had to develop a wholesome approach to this area of caring for myself.

As I began to look about me, I found women who had a mistrust of themselves and had begun to withhold acceptance of themselves—women who had no idea that God had a plan for their lives, so those lives instead reflected fear, guilt, and mistrust of other people.

In the 1990's, awareness of the whole topic of the dysfunctional family let us realize that many of us come from a family with some sort of abnormality. We begin to manifest those early childhood fears, guilt, and mistrust of others because we don't want to be hurt, scared, or disappointed again. Along with these manifestations, Satan makes us believe that we are totally worthless as persons, and certainly not worthy to spend any extra time or money on.

As I looked around in my association with women at church, support groups, and home Bible studies, I found many women who did not understand that God had given them a certain divine dignity at birth. The women would relate to their friends either positively or negatively depending on how well they understood this principle.

One Friday morning while we were studying a marriage book, Amy spoke up and said that she didn't take care of her personal self because her father had told her when she was young that pretty girls with good clothes and a nice figure stood a better chance of being molested by older boys and men as they grew up.

At that time Amy decided she would not let herself be molested by an older man, so she began to gain weight, wear sloppy clothes, and certainly not look good in a bathing suit. She even remarked that her husband liked her this way because then other men didn't try to flirt with her. He was safe from any competition, and he liked that.

Over the next several months in our weekly study I began to share how this fear was put there by Satan and not by God. I took extra time encouraging her to be all that God had for her. We looked at her eating habits and why she chose certain foods. (She also sought special counseling to understand what she was hiding behind.) Today Amy is a fine young lady who has a totally new image and who shares with other women her confidence in caring for herself. Because of Amy's self-appraisal, her husband has also joined a support group at church and has lessened his fears from his own insecurities.

Paul teaches in Philippians 4:13, "I can do all things through Him who strengthens me." In using this principle we realize that Christ gives us the inner strength to care for ourselves. Time for ourselves gives us time to reflect on the renewal of our mind, body, and spirit. Not only will we be rewarded personally, but so will all who come in contact with us daily.

> *Father God, I am special because of You and Your grace. You have taught me who I am, and out of my thanksgiving to You daily, You have given me a thankful heart. Through this I realize who I am in Your eyes: a person created in Your likeness. You have showed me how to take time for myself, and it is so meaningful. I know I enjoy life more than I used to. Amen.*

Taking Action

- ❧ Next time you take a walk, pick a few flowers. Tuck them in a vase by your bed.
- ❧ Dust the sheets with baby powder or sweet perfume before crawling into bed. You'll enjoy a welcome sense of relaxation as well as a feeling that is absolutely beautiful.

❦ Hang a tuneful wind chime out on the patio and enjoy its music on breezy days.

❦ Enjoy a bubble bath by candlelight while sipping ice tea or a pleasing beverage.

Reading On

Psalm 40:1-3	Deuteronomy 6:4-9
Psalm 42:1,2	Matthew 19:19

If you want to be respected by others, the great thing is to respect yourself.

—*Fyodor Dostoevsky*

Your Days Are Written in God's Book

Scripture Reading: Psalm 139:16-18

Key Verse: Psalm 139:16

*Thine eyes have seen my unformed substance [embryo];
and in Thy book they were all written, the days that were
ordained for me, when as yet there was not one of them.*

———— 🌑 ————

It was the day our daughter was leaving for college, and we
both looked forward to it with anticipation. Excitement wasn't
quite the word for how we both felt, because Jenny was leaving
home to a new adventure, while for me it meant an empty nest
with a quiet household.

Her blue Volkswagen bug was all packed now, so down the
hill she drove, tooting her horn as she went into the sunset. I
walked slowly up the porch steps into the house. It was quiet at
last—no loud stereo, no popcorn on the floor, no pizza on the
counter, no teenagers around the house, no telephones ringing.
My parenting years were over, now that both our children were
in college. I made a quick swing through the house to put it in
order, only to discover that it was already in order. My organizational skills had been in full swing, and somehow the children
had learned them also. My Bob was building a mobile home
manufacturing company at the time, which was consuming
much of his time. It didn't seem like he needed me.

All at once I realized I wasn't needed anymore. My children didn't need me, my Bob didn't need me, and my house

509

didn't need me. So now what? All that I loved was now ending. I loved my mothering, my organizing, my cleaning, and my cooking. But now it was just me and a part-time Bob.

Little did I know that God's plan was already in progress, as our Scripture for today states. My days were ordained to me before they even began. My homemaking and domestic engineering days were all a part of the training that God had poured into my life, for this was to be our future ministry to families.

I'm grateful that I was an at-home mom, for now with an empty nest I had time to move ahead with the rest of God's plan for me. Because of my friend and mentor Florence Littauer, I was encouraged to write my first book. Then came more books. In 1982 Bob closed his mobile home company to work with me and build God's ministry of "More Hours in My Day."

> Whatever the degree of involvement and however the relationship works itself out, the command is clear: Older women [are] to live for God's glory.
>
> —*Susan Hunt*

I say all this to encourage you today. Whatever you may be experiencing at the present time is all a part of what God has for you in the future, as long as you are willing to allow Him to teach your heart and guide your steps. I would never have thought that a shy and fearful little Jewish girl with just a high school education could write over 22 books and speak on platforms in conferences all over the country. In my own power I still can't do it, but in the power of the Lord we can all do the impossible.

*Father God, encourage that woman today who has
read this devotion. Give her Your love, strength, and
power. And give her the allotted days to develop, learn,*

and achieve what You would have her to do and become. You have certainly given me far more than I ever expected. Amen.

Taking Action

- Write in your journal your goals for the next six months of your personal future.
- Thank God today for what He is teaching you. You will need these things for the future.
- Submit yourself to God today, and ask Him to create in you the woman He wants you to be.

Reading On

Romans 8:29	Acts 2:23
Romans 11:2	1 Peter 1:20

Man's highest reward for his dedication to the pursuit of excellence is not what he gets from it, but what he becomes through it.

—*Author Unknown*

□ □ □

Who, Me Change?

Scripture Reading: John 8:28-36

Key Verse: John 8:32

You shall know the truth, and the truth shall make you free.

———— ❦ ————

One foggy night the captain of a large ship saw what appeared to be another ship's lights approaching in the distance. This other ship was on a course that would mean a head-on crash. Quickly the captain signaled to the approaching ship, "Please change your course 10 degrees west." The reply came blinking back through the thick fog, "You change your course 10 degrees east."

Indignantly the captain pulled rank and shot a message back to the other ship, "I'm a sea captain with 35 years of experience. You change your course 10 degrees west!" Without hesitation the signal flashed back, "I'm a seaman fourth-class. You change your course 10 degrees east!"

Enraged and incensed, the captain realized that within minutes they would crash head-on, so he blazed his final warning back to the fast-approaching ship: "I'm a 50,000-ton freighter. You change your course 10 degrees west!" The simple message winked back, "I'm a lighthouse. You change. . . ."[21]

As a young bride of 17, I wasn't aware of the differences between a man and a woman even though I had been raised in a home with an older brother. I just figured that my Bob would think just like I did. After all, wasn't I raised with everything being right? If there were differences, it must be because Bob did things strangely. Just to show what contrasts we brought to the marriage, I will list a few.

Emilie

1. Raised Jewish
2. Did whatever we wanted on Sundays
3. Ate leg of lamb, rice, rye bread, cream cheese
4. Father passed away when I was eleven
5. Father was alcoholic
6. Lived in an apartment all my life
7. Commuted on a public bus
8. Older brother was in trouble
9. Enjoyed sleeping in until 10 or 11 o'clock on Saturday mornings

Bob

1. Raised Baptist
2. Went to church on Sundays and observed Christian holidays
3. Ate fried chicken, mashed potatoes, gravy and biscuits
4. Had an encouraging and supportive father
5. Father abstained from alcohol
6. Lived in a residential home
7. Had a family car
8. Two brothers were achievers
9. Was an early riser regardless of day of week

These are just a few of our differences. Needless to say, we needed to make some compromises and adjustments! If either of us had demanded that our marriage reflect only our own values, we would certainly have crashed into the lighthouse and our ship would have been smashed on the rocks of the shore.

Even before we were married, we had to settle our differences regarding our spiritual beliefs. Bob had asked my mother if I could go to church with him, and surprisingly she said yes. That started me on my search for truth.

After many months of reading, listening, and praying I had a real peace that Jesus was who He said He was. Our key verse for today stood out so clearly that the truth did set me free. Verse 36 states, "If therefore the Son shall make you free, you shall be free indeed." From that very moment, at 16 years of age, I responded to the Master's call, corrected my course in life, and was amazingly free for every other change in life.

You too may be at a fork in the road of your life. Because of past experiences, you and your husband may not want to budge from your respective positions. I petition both of you today to come to grips with what is holding you a prisoner and to be set free by Christ's atonement for your sins on the cross.

Once you have come to grips with this issue, all other changes seem minor. With some things in life it makes no difference how you do them, but this spiritual change is a pivotal point around which all other changes take place.

Satan would like to destroy our marriage relationships because of differences in the way we like to do things. But we must be willing to serve one another. One of our guiding principles when it comes to change is found in Ephesians 5:21: "Be subject to one another." We each want to serve rather than be served. Each day our prayer is "How can we serve each other today?" With that daily attitude we are free to serve each other in a mature, godly fashion. Anything less than this allows selfishness and pride to enter our lives and ultimately creates an unwillingness to make changes.

Yes, I now like fried chicken and Bob loves a good leg of lamb. Be willing to change your course rather than have your own way by ramming into the lighthouse!

Father God, thank You for a heart that is willing to be flexible and to make changes in life. I don't want to always be right; I want to be free. I cry when I see couples who are so rigid in their ways, for I know what the end will be for them and their family. The consequences of stubbornness will be felt for many generations. I pray for a pliable heart. Continue to give me a serving heart. Amen.

Taking Action

❦ In your journal, make a chart listing your differences with your mate.

❦ Beside each difference state briefly how it is being resolved.

❦ For each one not resolved, set a time to meet with your mate to see if there are any changes to be made.

❦ Resolve those differences that can be, and continue to pray for those that aren't.

Reading On

Genesis 24:48   John 16:13
Psalm 91:4   2 Timothy 2:25

❦

When I came to believe in Christ's teachings, I ceased desiring what I had wished for before. The direction of my life, my desires, became different. What was good and bad changed places.

—Leo Tolstoy

❦

If Talking the Talk, Walk the Walk

Scripture Reading: Matthew 7:1-5

Key Verse: Matthew 7:3
Why do you look at the speck that is in your brother's eye, but do not notice the log that is in your own eye?

———— 🍂 ————

Hypocrisy is a dangerous character trait. Hypocrites are those who say one thing and do another. This is so dangerous because after a while of acting this way they become immune to the whole enterprise. It becomes, for them, just a natural way to live.

However, they do not allow others to live that way. This type of person is the first one to protest when they themselves are hurt by the actions of others who hypocritically approach life. This does not make much sense, does it?

Many years ago, grocers bought their supplies from the local townspeople. They then sold them to those who shopped in their stores. The suppliers, meanwhile, bartered for the things that they needed exchanged for the supplies.

Once there was a woman named Mary who bartered butter with one of the local grocers. Mary had the best butter in the area. She dealt almost all of the time with George down at the market. He bought her butter and traded with her for other things that she needed.

Their arrangement was based on Mary weighing out the butter and bringing it to George. Each pound of butter was worth so much in money or other things from George's store. It was a mutually satisfying arrangement that lasted for quite some time.

After a number of months of dealing with each other, George called the town sheriff and made a complaint. He charged Mary with cheating him in the weight of her butter. The grocer seemed to be sincerely shocked that Mary would do such a thing. The sheriff called Mary to George's store, where George confronted her with his charge.

"For the past four weeks Mary has cheated me two ounces in every pound of butter that she traded with me. I waited this long to say anything to see if she had simply made a mistake once or twice. But now I see that each pound of butter that she brings me is short these two ounces. I cannot believe that someone, especially Mary, would do such a thing!"

Mary responded, "That sure is curious. Four weeks ago I lost my pound weight that I used to weigh the butter. I started using the pound of soap that I bought from you as the weight measure for the butter." George said no more about the butter. He was caught red-handed.

There is an old statement that fits well here: "Clean your own backyard before you try to clean someone else's."[22]

Life without a standard has a tendency to be tossed and turned. It becomes confused because it has faith in an object that can't be relied upon. When Mary lost her benchmark, the pound weight, instead of purchasing an absolute pound weight she substituted George's soap weight. She thought this was a true measurement, not realizing that George had underweighed his soap in order to cheat those who traded with him.

In this story and with today's Scripture reading, I find two lessons to be learned.

First, our actions need to be consistent with our talk. If we are going to take a stand on moral issues, we must be sure that our stand is consistent with our life. I often wonder if all the various activists in life really walk their talk. Jesus used the term "hypocrite" when He described the insincerity of the Pharisees and scribes.

When we are bold and take a basic position on the moral issues of life, we need to have a clean slate regarding our own character record. Our country is currently debating the issue of a person's character. Is it important for a person to have good character in order to be a leader of people? Many people in this country are willing to let character slide as long as the person is able to make good choices outside the moral arena.

The Scriptures are quite clear on the issue of consistency in our lives. As parents we realize that our young ones are watching Mommy and Daddy to make sure we walk our talk. If we don't, the children will recognize that we are frauds, and will want no part of our hypocrisy.

The second lesson I see is taken from the story of George and Mary. Mary lost her object of faith, the pound weight, and substituted another standard of measurement, the soap bar. Without investigating or checking out the new standard, she put her faith in this new object. Even though she was totally sincere in relying on this new standard, she was 100 percent wrong in her blind faith.

Today in our Western culture there are many claims that seem to be right: They "feel good," the people seem sincere, they are well-dressed, etc. But their object of faith is wrong. They have lost sight of Jesus and His Word and have been led astray by thinking they are okay.

If we stray away from the real Jesus, we become a victim of hypocrisy. We need to keep our eyes on Jesus and accept no substitute.

Mother, if you are going to talk the talk, make sure you walk the walk. Don't worry about the speck in other people's eyes, but be willing to remove the log out of your own eye first. If you don't, others around you will point out the log for you.

> *Father God, as You bring before me today the importance of having a pure heart before You and my family, I want You to remove the log out of my own eye. Bring before me those parts of my life that aren't consistent with your Word. I really want to be a good and faithful servant. I want to stand before You with a life that is consistent with my talk. I don't want just hot air coming from my lips. Amen.*

Taking Action

- Look in a mirror and study yourself. What do you see? Write in your journal what you see.
- Look beyond your face and into your heart. Now what do you see? Jot those thoughts down too.
- Is what you see consistent with what you say you are? If not, where are the differences?
- What are you going to do to narrow this conflict?

Reading On

Job 20:4,5	Romans 12:9
Luke 12:1	1 Peter 2:1

No man, for any considerable period, can wear one face to himself and another to the multitude, without finally getting bewildered as to which may be true.

—*Nathaniel Hawthorne*

How to Raise Delinquent Children

Scripture Reading: Proverbs 22:1-6

Key Verse: Proverbs 22:6
Train up a child in the way he should go, [and] even when he is old he will not depart from it.

———— ❧ ————

"Strict parent" is not a very good phrase to use at social gatherings today. From my observations of some children raised in the church, it isn't even politically correct within the confines of *that* institution! One can easily observe in a child's behavior if his or her parents have limitations within the confines of their home.

One of the easiest tip-offs on this topic is to see with what respect the child speaks to his or her parents. Many children today show little respect when addressing the adults in their lives, whether teacher, coach, policeman, pastor, or parent. When we see such behavior, we know that these children come from a home that is not strict.

In all types of situations we read or hear about the sad results when a child is allowed to roam without any boundaries. One of the saddest results is when we hear of a child losing his or her life because he was never required to heed the warning of a parent.

A family had taken shelter in the basement as a severe storm passed over their town. The radio warned that a tornado had been spotted. When the storm had passed by, the father opened the front door to look at the damage. A downed power line was whipping dangerously on the street in front of their house. Before the father realized what was happening, his five-year-old daughter ran right by him, headed for that sparkling wire in the street.

"Laurie, stop!" he yelled.

Laurie just kept going.

"Laurie, STOP!"

Laurie ran right for the enticing cable.

"STOP NOW, Laurie!"

Little Laurie reached down to pick up the wicked power line and was instantly killed.

What a heartbreaking tragedy! But the real tragedy is that this happened because a little girl had never been taught that when her father said no, he really meant no. It cost him the life of his daughter.[23]

What a tragedy when a senseless death occurs because a child has never learned to obey! No is such a simple word, but so difficult to obey.

The world has painted the word "strict" as child abuse, as robbing a child of his free spirit so he won't become himself. But in reality, "strict" is a word that develops focus, discipline, achievement, peace, balance, and success in life.

As our children, Brad and Jennifer, have become older, they thank us for giving them boundaries when they were in their formative years. They knew that Mom and Dad loved them, were affectionate to them, verbally praised them, and emotionally supported them. In fact, in many areas of child-rearing our children are stricter with their own children than we were with them.

Several years ago the Houston, Texas, Police Department sponsored a large public-relations campaign to combat the rising tide in juvenile crime. Chuck Swindoll in his book *You and Your Child* relates one of the most effective messages in this campaign, "Twelve Rules for Raising Delinquent Children":

1. Begin with infancy to give the child everything he wants. In this way he will grow up to believe the world owes him a living.

2. When he picks up bad words, laugh at him. This will make him think he's cute.

3. Never give him any spiritual training. Wait until he is 21 and then let him "decide for himself."

4. Avoid the use of "wrong." He may develop a guilt complex. This will condition him to believe later, when he is arrested for stealing a car, that society is against him and he is being persecuted.

5. Pick up everything he leaves lying around. Do everything for him so that he will be experienced in throwing all responsibility on others.

6. Let him read any printed matter he can get his hands on. Be careful that the silverware and drinking glasses are sterilized, but let his mind feast on garbage.

7. Quarrel frequently in the presence of your children. In this way they won't be so shocked when the home is broken up later.

8. Give a child all the spending money he wants. Never let him earn his own.

9. Satisfy his every craving for food, drink, and comfort. See that his every sensual desire is gratified.

10. Take his part against neighbors, teachers, and policemen. They are all prejudiced against your child.

11. When he gets into real trouble, apologize for yourself by saying, "I could never do anything with him."

12. Prepare for a life of grief. You will be likely to have it.[24]

You and your spouse need to decide today what effects you want to have on your children. Also remember that how they live today is more than likely how their next three generations will live. It is up to us as parents to stand in the gap and hang tough. This is not an easy battle, for the evil one would like you to give in to the path of least resistance, but you must be willing to travel the "road less traveled."

Father God, thanks for encouraging me today that being strict is okay and that the pressure I receive from others means I'm doing a good job in establishing the boundaries in our home. I wish there were an easier way to raise well-behaved children, but I see that there aren't any. I appreciate my caring attitude so that I'm motivated to endure all the backlash. I ask that You put into the hearts of my children a sense of obedience to authority. I so very much want them to care. Please put a protective hedge around their little lives. Amen.

Taking Action

❦ Each day for the next two weeks meet with your spouse and review one of the 12 rules to see how you're doing in each area.

❦ After studying number 12, rank in order the three rules that need the most work in your household.

❦ After each of the three rules, jot down what you are going to do that will turn the negative into a positive.

Reading On

Hebrews 12:9-11   Ephesians 6:4
Proverbs 29:1   Proverbs 22:15

———————— ❦ ————————

My father was a Methodist and believed in the laying on of hands, and believe me, he really laid them on!

—A.W. Tozer

———————— ❦ ————————

□ □ □

Being an Older Woman Is Exciting

Scripture Reading: Titus 2:3-10

Key Verse: Titus 2:4

Encourage the young women to love their husbands, to love their children.

——— ❦ ———

As a young woman and mother, I would read today's Scripture passage and totally disregard the part about the older women teaching the younger women. I just never thought I would be older! However, 35-plus years later, I'm very pleased today to be the older woman teaching younger women. In fact, we are all older to someone. Even our 13-year-old granddaughter teaches the ones she babysits.

I am the person I am today because of the many godly women in my life. I have been taught by older women who didn't even know they were teaching me. I would (and still do) watch others in the ways they dealt with problems, organized their homes, and entertained, and especially in the way they walked with God. I hope I never get to the point where I stop learning.

I remember one older woman who sat in the front row of the church when I was teaching a "More Hours in My Day" seminar. She took notes the whole time. I later found out she was 92 years old! I thought, "At 92, who cares about organization?" But she truly had a teachable spirit, and I'm sure she went out to teach them to someone else. I later found out that

she also had had a goal in her life to water ski, so at 90 years
of age she did so and lived to tell about it!

Passing on ways to love our husbands is so exciting. I have
learned from many women in my life some creative ways to
show love to my Bob: a note of appreciation in a lunchbag or
on the computer; a phone call just to say "I care," "I'm praying," "I'm making your favorite dessert," or just "I love you"; a
thank you for working so long and hard for our family, for being a great dad, for stepping in the gap when I'm at work to
make dinner or water the flowerpots or vacuum.

I've learned that a man needs to be admired and appreciated even for the small things. Even if your husband doesn't do
any of the above, find something (and you can) that you admire him for. The more he knows you appreciate him, the
more he'll do for you. The old saying still holds true, "Treat
him as a king and he'll treat you as a queen." Side by side you
can complete each other and not compete with each other.

As an older woman, I'm thankful for a mother who taught
me meal-planning, shopping, cooking, cleaning, sewing, hospitality, and much more. Today I'm passing this on to the seminar women and those who read my books, as well as to my
children and my children's children.

Yes, being an older woman is rewarding. The younger
women are excited and eager to learn from us. What a joyful
privilege God has given us!

Training younger women in the church is an important part
of the responsibility of spiritually mature women. The mentor-
ing relationship should not be formal, rigid, or overly structured,
but should be a warm, indirect, motherly approach. Our main
goal is to show these younger women how to live out the gospel
in a lifestyle that is pleasing and truthful to God's Word.

Our balanced lifestyle that endures the test of time is what
is caught by the young women around us. Even though we may
not feel skilled in this area, we need to be risk-takers in sharing what God has entrusted to us.

Father God, thank You for older women who are willing to teach what You have taught them through life's experiences. May we always be open to the hearts of those who have teachable spirits. Help those of us who have husbands to show them how much we love and appreciate them. Most of all, Lord, help us to become friends with Your Word, the Bible, and to step out and teach what we have learned. Amen.

Taking Action

❦ List in your journal the women you know whom you can mentor.

❦ List in your journal three things you appreciate about your husband, father, son, or brother.

❦ List 10 things you can teach your children which someday they can pass on to someone else.

Reading On

Ruth 2:20-22   Luke 1:56
Luke 1:41-45   Acts 18:24-28

❦

Having sought for so long the
real meaning and key to life,
and having found it in Jesus,
I couldn't keep quiet about
this discovery. Everybody had
to know!

—*Geoffrey Shaw*

❦

The Spirit of Creativity

Scripture Reading: 2 Corinthians 5:14-21

Key Verse: 2 Corinthians 5:17

If any man is in Christ, he is a new creature; the old things passed away; behold, new things have come.

—————— ❦ ——————

I've heard it a million times, expressed with admiration and usually a little envy: "Oh, she's so creative."

Usually it describes an "artsy" type of person—someone who paints or writes or makes pottery. Such creative pursuits can bring great joy to those who do them and to those who enjoy the results. But you really don't have to be an artist to infuse your home and life with the spirit of creativity.

Creativity is a God-given ability to take something ordinary and make it into something special. It is an openness to doing old things in new ways and a willingness to adapt other people's good ideas to suit our personal needs. And creativity is an ability we all possess, although many of us keep it hidden in the deep corners of our lives.

Every human being is creative. The creative spirit is part of our heritage as children of the One who created all things. And nurturing our creativity is part of our responsibility as stewards of God's good gifts.

Creativity is so much more than just "arts and crafts." It is a way of seeing, a willingness to see wonderful possibilities in something unformed or ordinary or even ugly.

The first year Bob and I moved to Riverside, California, where we now live, we went to our first auction in an old building near Mount Rubidoux. It was fun to see the various "treasures" that were up for sale—everything from armoires to yarn caddies—and to listen as the auctioneer shouted the calls. Then an old, greasy market scale went up, and Bob shouted a bid. I nearly died on the spot. Whatever did he think we would do with that?

He won the bid and paid 32 dollars for that ugly old scale. We went to pick it up, and I looked at it doubtfully, but Bob was sure he had bought a treasure. And he was right! He stripped the old scale clean, shined and polished it until it looked almost new, and then put it on a table. That was over 20 years ago, and we are still enjoying Bob's imaginative purchase. It graces the narrow table behind our sofa and carries fruit in its tray, or sometimes a pot of flowers, a bowl of pot-pourri, or a Boston fern. Over the years, as we continue to shop for antiques, we often see scales not nearly as nice as ours that cost hundreds of dollars. I'm so grateful to Bob for his creative input into our home.

One day Bob brought me another treasure from one of his antique sprees. It was a large, wooden, hand-carved rectangular bowl—another of those "What will I ever do with that thing?" items. But how I enjoy that bowl as it sits on our butcher block island in the center of our kitchen! I keep it full of potatoes, onions, avocados, oranges, lemons, apples, and a variety of other fruits. It's not only beautiful, but very practical—another example of Bob's "creative seeing."

The kind of vision that brings the special out of the ordinary has long been part of the American tradition. Even in the tiniest frontier cabin, pioneer women found ways to express their creative urges and to add touches of loveliness to their environment.

In great-grandma's day, quilting was a wonderfully creative pursuit for women in many areas of the country. When women married or had a baby, friends and families gathered together to make the quilts the new family needed to keep warm. They used old, discarded clothing which was cut up and patched together into colorful designs and then carefully padded and stitched to make warm coverings. The women worked, talked, and exchanged recipes; they solved garden, food, husband, and children problems—all while their hard-working fingers sewed. These quilts were truly labors of love—living testaments to the spirit of loveliness that transforms simple materials and a basic household need into a work of art and an occasion for celebration.

Our human ability to create differs from that of God's in that

- He created the world out of nothing;
- His creativity is unlimited (Genesis 1:1-2:3).

We are limited to doing what is in our existing natural world. Our creativity has to be expressed by thought and experience. Our manifestations are shown in our creative forms of music, art, literature, language, or problem-solving; in creating a new idea, adapting a recipe, or stretching a monthly budget. There are many ways for us humans to express ourselves with our creativity.

We tend to think we need to be original in order to be creative. But I'm continually getting ideas from magazines, decorator shops, programs on the Discovery channel, interviewing friends, and just keeping my eyes open to life. I must be willing to make changes in the way things have always been done. I can't be satisfied with status quo.

I have found that creative people are focused, committed, and disciplined in their lives. In short, they have a plan for their lives. They know where they want to go, and most of them take control of their lives and live it out God's way.

Each of us is to look inward to see what gifts God has given us. The Scriptures teach us to realize that we have divinely appointed abilities.

Don't be afraid of failure because failure is often a stepping-stone to future successes. Failure can give us new direction in solving a particular problem.

Our home can be a wonderful laboratory in which to express our God-given talent. We can open this window in many ways:

- Landscaping
- Cooking
- Decorating
- Home business
- Parenting
- Marriage
- Designing and sewing clothes
- Arts and crafts
- Painting
- Composing
- Writing

One of the most valuable ways we can share the spirit of creativity is by modeling it for our children. We give them a legacy of joy when we teach them to use their God-given creativity to instill the spirit of loveliness into their own lives and homes.

Exercising our creativity is one way for us to be responsible stewards of the gifts and talents God has given us, and to rejoice in our identity as God's children, made in His image. As images of the Creator, we have the opportunity to fashion our lives and our homes into works of art. We can choose to be creative today and every day!

Father God, thank You for giving me my talents and for letting me have a spirit of loveliness. I can't paint, sing, draw, sculpture, design, or play an instrument, but I can dare to experiment with other talents. As such, people look at me and think I'm creative. So if my friends mirror back to me that I'm creative, I must be. Thanks for giving me friends who help me put my best foot forward. My desire is to encourage other women to step out and dare to be creative.

Nothing is more exciting to see than someone trying to fly when You have encouraged her to extend her wings and flap. Amen.

Taking Action

❦ Use your imagination in displaying your collection of cups and saucers, bells, dolls, thimbles, or salt-and-pepper shakers. A side table, shelf, or armoire can serve beautifully, but so might a printer's tray, a special basket, or a windowsill. One friend of mine displayed her collection of teddy bears in a clean but nonfunctioning fireplace.

❦ If you don't have a collection, start one! You'll have fun, and your family and friends will never lack for gift-giving ideas. Some more ideas: pitchers, cookie jars, music boxes. One academically minded gentleman collects university T-shirts. (He displays his collection on himself!)

❦ Throw a pretty tablecloth over your coffee table and serve hors d'oeuvres, tea, coffee, or dessert in the living room or den instead of the dining room or kitchen. Or try setting up a card table for dinner in the garden. Your family or your guests will love the change of pace.

Reading On

1 Peter 4:19	Romans 12:6-8
Romans 1:25	Proverbs 24

Since there is nothing new under the sun, creativity means simply putting old things together in a fresh way.

—*Author Unknown*

She Became My Mirror

Scripture Reading: Ephesians 3:13-21

Key Verse: Ephesians 3:20

*To Him who is able to do exceeding abundantly beyond
all that we ask or think, according to the power that
works within us.*

———— ❧ ————

Peter Foster was a Royal Air Force pilot. These men
(pilots) were the cream of the crop of England—the
brightest, healthiest, most confident and dedicated, and
often the most handsome men in the country. When
they walked the streets in their decorated uniforms, the
population treated them as gods. All eyes turned their
way. Girls envied those who were fortunate enough to
walk beside a man in Air Force blue.

However, the scene in London was far from romantic, for the Germans were attacking relentlessly. Fifty-
seven consecutive nights they bombed London. In waves
of 250, some 1500 bombers would come each evening
and pound the city.

The RAF Hurricanes and Spitfires that pilots like
Foster flew looked like mosquitoes pestering the huge
German bombers. The Hurricane was agile and effective,
yet it had one fatal design flaw: The single-propeller
engine was mounted in front, a scant foot or so from the
cockpit, and the fuel lines snaked alongside the cockpit

toward the engine. In a direct hit, the cockpit would erupt into an inferno of flames. The pilot could eject, but in the one or two seconds it took him to find the lever, heat would melt off every feature of his face: his nose, his eyelids, his lips, often his cheeks.

These RAF heroes many times would undergo a series of 20 to 40 surgeries to refashion what was once their face. Plastic surgeons worked miracles, yet what remained of the face was essentially a scar.

Peter Foster became one of these "downed pilots." After numerous surgical procedures, what remained of his face was indescribable. The mirror he peered into daily couldn't hide the facts. As the day for his release from the hospital grew closer, so did Peter's anxiety about being accepted by his family and friends.

He knew that one group of airmen with similar injuries had returned home only to be rejected by their wives and girlfriends. Some of the men were divorced by wives who were unable to accept this new outer image of their husbands. Some men became recluses, refusing to leave their houses.

In contrast, there was another group who returned home to families who gave loving assurance of acceptance and continued worth. Many became executives and professionals, leaders in their communities.

Peter Foster was in that second group. His girlfriend assured him that nothing had changed except a few millimeters' thickness of skin. She loved him, not his facial membrane, she assured him. The two were married just before Peter left the hospital.

"She became my mirror," Peter said of his wife. "She gave me a new image of myself. Even now, regardless of how I feel, when I look at her she gives me a warm, loving smile that tells me I am O.K." he tells confidently.[25]

We as women reflect to our mates and children acceptance or rejection by our verbal and nonverbal communications. They pick up from us what they are in life. In order for our family to feel worthy within themselves they need people around them that reflect acceptance.

It takes so little to make us glad,
Just a cheering clasp of a friendly
hand, Just a word from one who
can understand; And we finish
the task we long had planned,
And we lose the doubt and the
fear we had—So little it takes to
make us glad.

—*Ida Goldsmith Morris*

Negative reflection builds fear in one's self. We see a nation built on fear. As we observe teenagers at school or at our local mall, we see many of them who radiate the dullness of fear. Your husband, too, will not be able to make good leadership decisions if he lacks confidence in his decision-making ability. But if you give him encouraging words that build him up, then you as his mirror tell him he's okay. (See Ephesians 4:29.)

Our families will exhibit changed personalities when they are no longer captured by the fear of rejection. In 1 John 4:18 we read that "perfect love casts out fear."

People will reflect back to you with what they live:

• People who live with praise reflect confidence.

• People who live with challenges and responsibilities grow up making proper goals and decisions.

• People who live with optimism aren't afraid to try.

- People who live with love learn to give their love away.
- People are glad to be alive when they realize they are a valuable member of a team.

As your husband and children look at you, may they be freed from fear because they are assured they have a valuable place in the family structure. Reassure them each day through your words and deeds that you love them more than anything else.

Recently our daughter, Jenny, sent this birthday card to my Bob. In part it said:

> All my life you've always been there,
> Helping, advising, and showing you care,
> And all my life I'll always be glad
> To have someone as special as you for my Dad!
> Thank you for the unconditional love you show me.
> I love you—#1 daughter,
>
> Jenny

Here was a father who was blessed for having mirrored back to his daughter that she was accepted, even though many times there was pain in Bob's life because of some of her decisions.

I challenge you today to clean off the smudges and fingerprints on your mirror and to start a fresh image with sharp, clean reflections on your mirror of life. Be a builder, not a destroyer.

> *Father God, I want to be the kind of woman that reflects Your love in all that I do. Sometimes my eyes see what I don't like to see, the action breaks my heart, and I fall asleep with tears in my eyes. I know You are in control and I will prayfully trust You in all things. I want to believe in the goodness even when I can't physically see it. May my family see You reflected back when they see my life lived out before them. Amen.*

Taking Action

- Take each member of your family aside this week and tell them how much they mean to you.

- Make a favorite dessert for family appreciation night.

- In your journal, write down three things that you are going to do in the next three months to mirror your acceptance of each of your family members in your life.

Reading On

Ephesians 4:29   James 3:7,8

---- ----

The best things are nearest:
breath in the nostrils, light in
your eyes, flowers at your feet,
duties at your hand, the part of
God just before you.

—*Robert Louis Stevenson*

God Is in Control

Scripture Reading: Philippians 1:1-6

Key Verse: Philippians 1:6

I am confident of this very thing, that He who began a good work in you will perfect it until the day of Christ Jesus.

At a recent seminar we attended, the speaker was giving illustrations on control within a family. Some participants thought various members and acts of the family showed who had control. Comments included:

- The breadwinner of the family has control.
- Mom does because she makes more money.
- The one who signs the checks has control.
- The one who pays the bill at the restaurant when we go out to eat has control.
- The husband has control because he is responsible for the family.

After several more comments were written on the board, a strong male voice in the middle of the audience shouted out, "The one who controls the TV clicker has control!" Everyone laughed, knowing that he was on the right path in most families. Who would ever have thought this statement might really have some validity in our homes? If it is really true, then we have lost sight of God's intent on family leadership.

God Is in Control

In today's study Paul is teaching believers some basic principles on partnership in ministry. He wants us to see the power of God and how He truly is the One in control. Yet so many homes are wracked with a power struggle in deciding who is in control at 1001 West Maple Street.

If we can grasp today's lesson from God's perspective, we can get a better handle on this awesome question, "Who is in control?" If our family is truly a partnership, we will be enacting several components of that partnership taken from today's reading:

- Thank God for all your remembrance of each family member (verse 3).

- Offer prayers with joy (verse 4).

- Each member is an active participant in the gospel (verse 5).

- There is a perspective of confidence for the future (verse 6).

- He who began a good work in you will perfect it until Jesus returns (verse 6).

Such teamwork leads to confidence in the future. The glue that makes all this happen is the One who will perfect your good work when Jesus returns—the Almighty God. It's so refreshing to know that the possessor of the TV clicker is not ultimately in control. (If it *were* true, I couldn't have much confidence in what God is capable of doing in my life!)

God is the potter and I am the clay, and He can do with me whatever He wishes in my life. In all of life's ups and downs, I don't really need the answer to the question "Why, God? Why me?" Instead, I will be more inclined to say, "Why *not* me, God?"

Yes, God is in control and He has done a wonderful job over the centuries. If we are part of His team, we know that we are in good hands. He knows the beginning from the end, and He is more capable of making the right decision than we are.

Father God, over the years I have learned to trust You more. Each time I'm tempted to take control of the events of my life I have to reflect back over all the things You have decided for me, and they were good. May I always be willing to be the clay and for You to design me in Your own way. I gladly give my life to You. Thank You for being so dependable. Amen.

Taking Action

- ❦ List in your journal five things in your life that you have given over to God.
- ❦ List three things that you are still controlling.
- ❦ Today give those three things to God and do not grab them back.
- ❦ Share your decision with a friend and ask her to hold you accountable for it.

Reading On

Proverbs 16:4	1 Corinthians 1:8
Romans 9:21	Romans 8:28

❦

We cooperate with God through obedience, believing that the moment we step out in that obedience the Holy Spirit will meet us with the necessary power.

—*Sandy Smith*

❦

□ □ □

A Moment of Grace

Scripture Reading: Ephesians 2:1-9

Key Verse: Ephesians 2:8,9

By grace you have been saved, through faith; and that not of yourselves, it is the gift of God; not as a result of works, that no one should boast.

In the following story we can see the power of grace at work . . .

During my senior year in high school I had been sick with bronchitis and missed two weeks of school. When I returned I had to make up nine tests in one week. By the last one I was really out of it. I remember looking at this test paper and not knowing any of the answers. I was a total blank. It was like I had never heard of this history junk before.

It was after school and I was the only one in the classroom. The teacher was working at his desk and I was staring off into space. "What's the matter?" he asked. And I said, "I can't do this. I don't know any of these answers." He got up and came over and looked at my paper and said, "You know the answer to that! We just talked about it in class yesterday. You answered a question I asked about that." I said, "I don't remember. I just can't remember." He gave me a few hints, but I still couldn't remember. I realized that I was on overload, and my straight A's in history were now a thing of the past. I looked at him and I said,

"Look. You're just gonna have to give me an F. I can't do it. I feel too bad." He reached down with his red pencil and I watched him, certain he was going to put an F on my paper—I mean, there was not one answer on this test! But he put an A on the top.

I said, "What are you doing?" And he said, "If you'd been here and you felt good and you'd had time to study, that's what you'd have gotten. So that's what you're gonna get." This guy really did recognize that I had been operating out of excellence all the time I had been in his class, and that I was telling the truth. My mind was a blank and I was willing to take the F, because that's what I deserved. But I didn't have to.

I then realized that there are people out there who will give you a break once in a while. It was empowering. It was like he was saying, "I know who you are, not just what you do." That's an amazing gift to give somebody. I will be grateful to that guy till the day I die. I thought, "That's the kind of teacher I want to be."[26]

What an excellent example of how God has given us, undeserving sinners, salvation and immediate acceptance by Him through what his Son did on the cross for us. We are saved through faith in Jesus. This faith involves knowledge of the gospel (Romans 10:14), acknowledgment of the truth of its message, and personal reception of the Savior (John 1:12). Paul states that works cannot save (Ephesians 2:9), but that good works should always accompany salvation (James 2:17).

Even though we cannot make a complete biblical comparison from a story such as today's, we do find a teacher who bestowed grace on his pupil.

By all rights the student deserved an F on his grade, but the teacher was willing to give him an A because of who he was. The teacher knew the pupil's heart and his efforts of the past.

This is where we are in life without Christ. We deserve an F grade because we, in ourselves, are sinners and do not deserve anything more. However, Jesus went to the cross for us and died for our sins, so that by faith we would accept His act for us personally. Through God's grace, and His grace alone, and His grace only, our grade went from an F to an A because of our faith in God's Son, Jesus. The cross of Christ divides every other religion from Christianity. That's why the events surrounding the cross are paramount to us as Christians.

> *Father God, I come to You humbly in prayer, thanking You for Your grace upon my life. I would not want to go around for the rest of my life with an F stamped on me. There would be no hope in this world. Maybe that's why I see so many sad people. They have never received Your grace and have never gone from darkness to light. Thank You, thank You for my salvation through Your undeserved grace to me! Amen.*

Taking Action

- ❦ Thank God for your salvation.
- ❦ If you haven't received the act of His grace, you might want to go through these verses of Scripture:

  Romans 3:23

  Romans 6:23

  Acts 16:30,31

  Ephesians 2:8,9

  Romans 10:9,10

  Luke 18:13

After reading these verses, you may want to invite Jesus Christ into your heart. If you do, you can pray this prayer:

Lord Jesus, I need You. Thank You for dying on the cross for my sins. I open the door of my life and receive You as my Savior and Lord. Thank You for forgiving my sins and giving me eternal life. Take control of the throne of my life. Make me the kind of person You want me to be.[27]

If you prayed this prayer, Christ will come into your life, as He promised.

Reading On

Revelation 3:20   Hebrews 13:5
1 John 5:11-13   Colossians 1:14

Grace is not sought, nor bought,
nor wrought. It is a free gift of
Almighty God to needy mankind.

— *Billy Graham*

Notes

1. Luci Swindoll, *Women's Devotional Bible* (Grand Rapids: Zondervan Corporation, 1960), p. 1375.
2. Erma Bombeck, further documentation unavailable.
3. Kay Arthur, taken from a newsletter dated March 1996, Precept Ministries, Chattanooga, TN.
4. Lee Roberts, *Praying God's Will for My Son* and *Praying God's Will for My Daughter* (Nashville: Thomas Nelson Publishers, 1993).
5. Donna Otto, *The Stay at Home Mom* (Eugene, OR: Harvest House Publishers, 1991), pp. 51-54.
6. Roberts, *Praying God's Will.*
7. Otto, *Stay at Home Mom,* pp. 51-54.
8. Rudyard Kipling, *Just So Stories.* This poem is the finale of "How the Camel Got Its Humps."
9. Elon Foster, ed., *Six Thousand Sermon Illustrations* (Grand Rapids: Baker Book House, 1992), p. 353.
10. Ann Landers, printed in the *Press Enterprise,* Riverside, CA, Saturday, May 11, 1996, p. B-10.
11. Steve Farrar, *Point Man* (Portland: Multnomah Books, a part of the Questar publishing family, 1990). Adapted from pp. 81-83.
12. Adapted from Temple Bailey. This story first appeared in a pamphlet that Clifton's Cafeteria distributed to its customers in 1945.
13. H. Norman Wright, *Communication: Key to Your Marriage* (Ventura, CA: Regal Books, 1974), p. 52.
14. Florence Littauer, *Silver Boxes, The Gift of Encouragement* (Waco, Texas: Word Publishing, 1989), pp. 1-4.
15. Harold L. Myra, *The Family Book of Christian Virtues,* edited by Stuart and Jill Briscoe (Colorado Springs: Alive Communications, Inc., 1995), p. 252.
16. Adapted from Foster, *Six Thousand Sermon Illustrations,* p. 627.
17. Dennis and Barbara Rainey, *Building Your Mate's Self-Esteem* (San Bernardino: Here's Life Publishers, 1986), p. 154.
18. *The Woman's Study Bible,* edited by Dorothy Kelley Patterson and Rhonda Harringon Kelley (Nashville: Thomas Nelson Publishers, 1995), p. 450.
19. Ibid., p. 2071.
20. Anne Ortlund, *Disciplines of the Beautiful Woman* (Waco, TX: Word, 1977), p. 29.

21. Dennis and Barbara Rainey, *Building Your Mate's Self-Esteem* (San Bernardino: Here's Life Publishers, 1986), pp. 56-57.

22. Michael Johnson, "If Talking the Talk, Walk the Walk," in *The Richmond Register*, June 21, 1996, Section B-1.

23. Steve Farrar, *Standing Tall* (Sisters, OR: Multnomah Books, 1994), pp. 51-52.

24. Charles R. Swindoll, *You and Your Child* (Nashville: Thomas Nelson Publishers, 1977), p. 64.

25. Paul Brandt and Philip Yancey, *In His Image* (Grand Rapids: Zondervan Publishing House, 1994), pp. 25-29.

26. Jane Bluestein, (Deerfield Beach, FL: Health Communications, Inc., 1995), pp. 12-13.

27. Bill Bright, *Four Spiritual Laws* (San Bernardino: Campus Crusade for Christ Inc., 1965), p. 10.